Level 2

PRACTICAL GRAMMAR

John Hughes and Ceri Jones

HEINLE
CENGAGE Learning

Australia • Brazil • Japan • Korea • Mexico • Singapore • Spain • United Kingdom • United States

Practical Grammar Level 2
John Hughes and Ceri Jones
Series devised by David Riley

Publisher: Jason Mann

Commissioning Editor: Carol Goodwright

Development Editor: Jemma Hillyer

Consultants: Roy Norris, Mary Rigby

Marketing and Product Manager:
Ruth McAleavey

Senior Content Project Editor: Natalie Griffith

ELT Production Controller: Denise Power

Art Editor: Victoria Chappell

Cover Designer: Adam Renvoize

Text Designer: Rouli Manias

Compositor: MPS Limited, A Macmillan
Company

Audio: James Richardson

Dedication

The original concept for the *Practical Grammar* series was David Riley's. David was a well-known and highly respected ELT author, teacher and publisher. He died before the Practical Grammar books were completed but the memory of David inspired everyone working on the project.

© 2011 Heinle, Cengage Learning

ALL RIGHTS RESERVED. No part of this work covered by the copyright herein may be reproduced, transmitted, stored or used in any form or by any means graphic, electronic or mechanical, including but not limited to photocopying, recording, scanning, digitising, taping, Web distribution, information networks, or information storage and retrieval systems, except as permitted under Section 107 or 108 of the 1976 United States Copyright Act, without the prior written permission of the publisher.

For permission to use material from this text or product, submit all requests online at **cengage.com/permissions**
Further permissions questions can be emailed to
permissionrequest@cengage.com

ISBN: 978-1-4240-1805-5 [with answers]
ISBN: 978-1-4240-1804-8 [without answers]

Heinle ELT, Cengage Learning EMEA
Cheriton House
North Way
Andover
Hampshire
SP10 5BE
United Kingdom

Cengage Learning is a leading provider of customised learning solutions with office locations around the globe, including Singapore, the United Kingdom, Australia, Mexico, Brazil and Japan. Locate our local office at:
international.cengage.com/region

Cengage Learning products are represented in Canada by Nelson Education, Ltd.

Visit Heinle online at **elt.heinle.com**
Visit our corporate website at **cengage.com**

Printed in China, by RR Donnelley
2 3 4 5 6 7 8 9 10 – 14 13 12 11 10

Contents

Contents

Contents

Introduction

Welcome to *Practical Grammar* Level 2. This is the second in a series of grammar books for students of English. Level 2 introduces grammar to students at low-intermediate to intermediate level. It aims to:

- teach all the key grammar at intermediate level.
- improve accuracy with grammar.
- help students use grammar in real-life situations, including conversations.

Organisation of the book

Practical Grammar Level 2 has 100 units and is organised into blocks of five units. Each block is made up of four main units focusing on one area of grammar and a review unit. After every ten units, there is a progress test at the back of the book to check understanding. You'll also find extra useful information in the appendices (pages 232–239) and an index (pages 240–247) for quick reference. A key feature of the book is the CDs which you can use to listen to the conversations in the book and improve your pronunciation of grammar items.

Using *Practical Grammar* Level 2

Practical Grammar Level 2 is ideal for use as self study or in the classroom with a teacher. Some students may want to begin at unit 1 and work through the units in order. Other students may prefer to choose specific areas of grammar from the contents pages and index, and focus on those areas first. (Use the contents or the index to do this.) If you want to use *Practical Grammar* Level 2 as a supplementary study book with your classroom course, you can also select particular units to match the lessons.

Grammar in real contexts

The rules of grammar are important but it's also important to see the grammar being used in a real-life situation. For this reason, each unit introduces the grammar through a short conversation or text. After the presentation of the grammar, there are exercises that practise the new language in authentic contexts with recordings on the CDs to hear the language in use.

Study at home (to the student)

This book helps you understand English grammar. Here are some ideas for using *Practical Grammar* Level 2:

- Study the grammar regularly. For example, complete one unit every day. Read the introductory conversation or text and study the presentation of the grammar. Then complete the exercises and listen to the CDs.

- Complete the review unit and check you understand the grammar by doing the progress tests (pages 212–231).

- Study with a friend. Do the units together and read some of the conversations aloud.

- If you find some of the grammar in a unit especially difficult, it's a good idea to repeat the unit.

- Remember that grammar isn't the only part of English. If you find new words in *Practical Grammar* Level 2, check them in your dictionary and write them down.

- Use the online component my*pg* at **myelt.heinle.com**. The activities allow you to continue working with all the grammar in new contexts. There is a gradebook where you can build up a picture of your progress.

In the classroom (to the teacher)

Students can use *Practical Grammar* Level 2 for self study but you can also use it in class. It is aimed at students at low-intermediate and intermediate levels.

If you are using a course book, *Practical Grammar* Level 2 will be a useful supplementary grammar book as it reflects the order of the grammar often taught on many courses.

Ask students to read the conversation or text at the beginning of the unit. If there is a conversation, you could ask two students to read it aloud to the class. Then read through the presentation of the grammar and deal with any questions the students might have.

As students work through the exercises, monitor their progress and help out with any questions they have. Students could also work in pairs or small groups for some exercises and compare their answers. In some units, the final exercise asks students to personalise the grammar and write their own sentences. Afterwards, ask some students to read theirs aloud or to compare with a partner.

If you have done the first four units of a section in class, you could set the review unit for homework. However, the review unit also includes help with pronunciation and listening linked to the grammar, so sometimes you might want to work on these as a class.

The progress tests (pages 212–231) check students' progress after every ten units. You can use these in class to monitor how much students have learnt. If students have particular difficulties with certain parts of the test, you will be able to see if they need to work on any of the units again.

Also note that for further practice you can use the online component my*pg*. This component has a Content Management System, which allows you to set specific exercises to be completed in a set time. When students 'submit' the exercises, their scores appear in the gradebook, allowing you to see how each student is progressing.

There are two CDs at the back of the book. They contain all the listening and pronunciation activities. Use them to help students hear the grammar in use and also for revision of the forms.

Overview of *Practical Grammar* Level 2

The units

Every unit is made up of two pages and has a similar format so it's easy to follow.

Title

The title tells you the main grammar area. Some units also have subtitles to give extra information.

Context

Practical Grammar teaches you how to use grammar in real situations. Each unit starts with a conversation or a short text to show the grammar in context. Read this first.

Presentation

The presentation explains the rules of the grammar and has information on the form, meaning and use of the grammar with example sentences. Use the presentation to help you complete the exercises.

Tip

This gives you extra information about the grammar in real situations.

Review units

At the end of every block of four units, there is a review unit.

Grammar

This section gives extra practice of all the grammar in the four units. It's also a good way to check progress.

Grammar in context

It's important to be able to recognise and use grammar in real situations, so this section provides practice with the grammar from all four units in an authentic context.

Pronunciation

It's important to know the rules of grammar but you also need to be able to say the grammatical forms correctly. *Practical Grammar* includes a pronunciation practice section with recordings.

Listen again

A key feature of *Practical Grammar* is the listening practice. Listening is a great way to learn a new language. Here you listen again to one of the recordings from the four units and become more confident with the grammar in context.

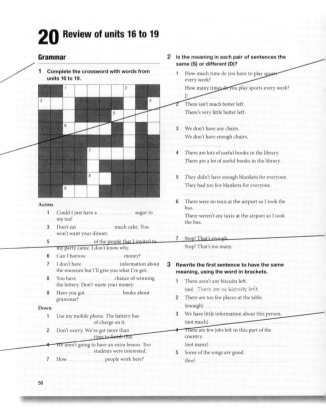

Exercises

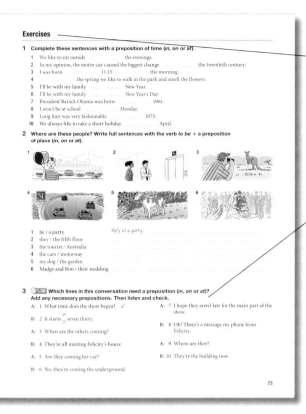

Exercises

1 Complete these sentences with a preposition of time (*in*, *on* or *at*).

1 We like to eat outside _____ the evenings.
2 In my opinion, the motor car caused the biggest change _____ the twentieth century.
3 I was born _____ 11.15 _____ the morning.
4 _____ the spring we like to walk in the park and smell the flowers.
5 I'll be with my family _____ New Year.
6 I'll be with my family _____ New Year's Day.
7 President Barack Obama was born _____ 1961.
8 I won't be at school _____ Monday.
9 Long hair was very fashionable _____ 1973.
10 We always like to take a short holiday _____ April.

2 Where are these people? Write full sentences with the verb *to be* + a preposition of place (*in*, *on* or *at*).

1 he / a party He's at a party.
2 they / the fifth floor
3 the tourist / Australia
4 the cars / motorway
5 my dog / the garden
6 Madge and Ron / their wedding

3 Which lines in this conversation need a preposition (*in*, *on* or *at*)? Add any necessary prepositions. Then listen and check.

A: 1 What time does the show begin? ✓
B: 2 It starts ^at seven thirty.
A: 3 When are the others coming?
B: 4 They're all meeting Felicity's house.
A: 5 Are they coming her car?
B: 6 No, they're coming the underground.
A: 7 I hope they aren't late for the main part of the show.
B: 8 Oh! There's a message my phone from Felicity.
A: 9 Where are they?
B: 10 They're the building now.

73

Grammar in context

4 Complete the questionnaire with the words in the box.

| any | enough | few | little | lot | many | much | none | some |

How can you help the environment at work?

Are you doing enough to help the environment? Find out with this quiz. Tick (✓) your answers to the four questions and add up your final score.

Are there any paper recycling bins in the building?
A Yes, there are lots of bins everywhere.
B Yes, there are a 1_____ bins in some of the offices, but not many.
C No, there aren't 2_____ bins at all.

How 3_____ people travel to your workplace by bicycle or public transport?
A A 4_____ of the people I work with travel by bike or public transport.
B A few people travel by bike or public transport.
C Zero people! 5_____ of the people in my office travel by bike or public transport.

How 6_____ equipment do you leave on overnight at your office?
A None. We switch everything off at the end of the day.
B We leave very 7_____ equipment on overnight – only essential equipment (e.g. security cameras).
C We leave everything on (e.g. computers).

How much time do you spend discussing ways to help the environment at work?
A We spend a lot of time discussing ways to help the environment at work.
B We don't spend 8_____ time.
C None. We never discuss the topic.

Mainly Cs: Oh dear! It's time for you to start making 9_____ changes around the office.
Mainly Bs: Not bad. Keep working on it.
Mainly As: Well done! You are working hard to help the environment at work.

Pronunciation: vowel sounds 2

5 Listen to each set of words. Cross out the word with a different vowel sound.

1 any many much
2 much some too
3 too few lots
4 some few none
5 any enough none
6 some not lots

Listen again

6 Listen to four short conversations. Are the statements true (T) or false (F)?

Conversation 1
1 One person doesn't have any change for the bus. T/F
2 The other person lends him some money. T/F

Conversation 2
3 There's a little petrol in the car but not enough. T/F
4 The other person thought there was some. T/F

Conversation 3
5 There are some letters on the table. T/F
6 There are a few letters on the chair. T/F

Conversation 4
7 Neither speaker has got any painkillers. T/F
8 Neither speaker has got any money. T/F

51

Exercises

Every unit gives lots of practice with the grammar. Always start with exercise 1 because it helps with learning the form of the grammar. Later exercises help you to understand its meaning.

Listening

A really useful feature in *Practical Grammar* is the recordings. Most units include a listening exercise so you can listen to the completed exercise and hear the grammar in a real situation.

Progress tests

After every ten units, there is a progress test (see pages 212–231).

Appendices

These have more useful information on spelling and punctuation. There are also summaries of the key grammar areas, including verb forms and phrasal verbs (see pages 232–239).

Index

Use the index to find items of grammar quickly and help with terminology (see pages 240–247).

my*pg*

This online component provides extra practice of all the language covered in the book through a wide range of exercise types.

11

1 Pronouns: subject, object, reflexive
I, me, myself, each other

A love story

1 He loves her. She's angry with him.
2 He phones her. She doesn't want to talk to him.
3 He sends her an email.
4 She doesn't answer it.
5 He asks himself what he's done wrong.
6 They see each other.
7 He smiles. She smiles.
8 He says, 'I'm sorry.' She says, 'Me, too.'
9 They love each other.

Presentation

You use pronouns to substitute for nouns.

*The **boy** loves the **girl**. **He** loves **her**. **They** love **each other**.*

Subject pronouns

You use subject pronouns (*I, you, he, she*, etc.) with verbs to show who or what the subject of the verb is:

***He** wrote an email. Did **she** reply? No, **she** didn't.*

Object pronouns

You use object pronouns (*me, you, him, her*, etc.) …

- after a verb to show who or what the object of the verb is:
  *He sent **her** an email. (object = the girl)*

- after a preposition:
  *She's angry with **him**. (object = the boy)*

- after *be*:
  *Hello, who's speaking? It's **me**.*
  *Who broke this window? It was **them**. / It wasn't **us**.*

- in short answers:
  *Who sent the email? **Me**.*
  *I'm sorry. **Me**, too.*

Reflexive pronouns

You use reflexive pronouns to show that both the subject and the object of the verb are the same thing or person:

*He asked **himself** what he'd done wrong.*

*He looked at **himself** in the mirror. = He looked at his reflection in the mirror.*

	Subject	Object	Reflexive
Singular	I	me	myself
	you	you	yourself
	he	him	himself
	she	her	herself
	it	it	itself
Plural	we	us	ourselves
	you	you	yourselves
	they	them	themselves

each other and *-self/-selves*

You use *each other* to say that each person or thing does the same to the other person/people or thing/things:

*They looked at **each other** = the boy looked at the girl and the girl looked at the boy.*

Exercises

1 Replace the nouns in bold with the pronouns in the box.

he (x4)   it (x2)   they (x5)   him   her (x2)   them   himself   each other

1 **The boy** looked at **the phone**. <u>He looked at it.</u>
2 **The boy** waited for **the girl** to call **the boy**.
3 **The phone** didn't ring.
4 So **the boy** called **the girl**.
5 **The boy and the girl** talked for a few minutes.
6 **The boy** smiled at **his reflection** in the mirror.
7 **The boy and the girl** met in their favourite café.
8 **The boy** looked **at the girl** and **the girl** looked at **the boy**.

9 The people in the café watched **the boy and the girl**.
10 **The people in the café** could see that **the boy and the girl** were in love.

2 Choose the correct pronouns.

1 It's the twins' birthday tomorrow. *We / Us* need to buy presents for *they / them*.
2 John's only three years old but he can dress *him / himself* and brush his teeth on his own.
3 Would *you / yourselves* like to come to the cinema with *us / we* this evening?
4 Jane can't come this evening. *Her / She* sent *I / me* a message on my mobile this morning.
5 Sue is really selfish. *She / Her* only thinks about *her / herself* and nobody else.
6 My boyfriend's working really hard at the moment so *us / we* only see *each other / ourselves* at weekends.
7 My brother's in hospital. *He / Him* hurt *him / himself* playing football.
8 Could you get my keys for *me / myself*, please? *It's / They're* in the office.

3 (⏱1.02) Complete the conversation with pronouns. Then listen and check.

A: Hi, Tom. Come in. Would [1] _____ like a coffee?

B: No, thanks. [2] _____ had one at home.

A: Did [3] _____ have a good weekend?

B: Yes, [4] _____ was great. Suzy and [5] _____ went camping with some friends. [6] _____ really enjoyed [7] _____.

A: Was Pete there?

B: Yes, [8] _____ was. [9] _____ came with [10] _____ in our car.

A: How is [11] _____?

B: He's fine. He asked [12] _____ to invite [13] _____ to come to a party at his house next weekend.

A: Great! I'd love to. Pete and I haven't seen [14] _____ for months.

2 *there*
to be + a/an/some/any

Presentation

You use *there is* and *there are* to talk about things that exist.

Affirmative

There's	a	class.
	an	instructor.
	some	water.
There are	some	classes.

Negative

There isn't	a	class.
	an	instructor.
	any	water.
There aren't	any	classes.

Questions and short answers

Is there	a	class?
	an	instructor?
	any	water?
Are there	any	towels?

Yes,	there is/are.	No,	there isn't/aren't.

Countable and uncountable nouns

- Countable nouns refer to things that we can count. They can have a singular form and a plural form: *a class, two classes.*

- Uncountable nouns refer to things that we cannot count. They do not have a plural form. We do not use them with *a/an*: *water, time, space.*

For more information about countable and uncountable nouns, see Unit 16.

a/an, some or *any*

Use *a/an* in affirmative statements, negative sentences and questions with singular countable nouns: *There's **a** class. There isn't **a** class. Is there **a** class?*

Use *some* in affirmative statements …

- with uncountable nouns: *There is **some** water.*

- with plural nouns: *There are **some** classes.*

Use *any* in negative statements and questions …

- with uncountable nouns: *There isn't **any** bread. Is there **any** water?*

- with plural nouns: *There aren't **any** classes. Are there **any** towels?*

Exercises

1 Choose the correct forms.

1 There 's / *are* water all over the floor!

2 A: *Is* / *Are* there a bus station near here?
    B: Yes, *there 's* / *is*. It's over there, next to the supermarket.

3 There *isn't* / *aren't* any taxis. I'll call one for you.

4 Waiter! There 's / *are* something in my soup.

5 There *isn't* / *aren't* any bread. Can you buy some when you go out?

6 Hi, it's John. *Is* / *Are* Katy there, please?

7 There 's / *are* some information about times and dates in the newspaper.

8 A: *Is* / *Are* there any of those chocolates left?
    B: No, there *isn't* / *aren't*. Someone ate them all.

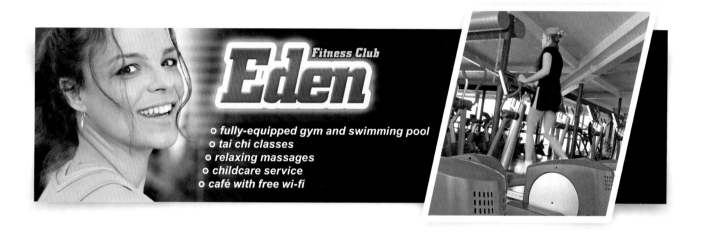

Eden **Fitness Club**

o **fully-equipped gym and swimming pool**
o **tai chi classes**
o **relaxing massages**
o **childcare service**
o **café with free wi-fi**

2 🔊 1.03 Complete the conversation about the advert with the correct form of *there is* or *there are*. Then listen and check.

A: ¹ Are there any fitness clubs near here?

B: Yes, ² _____. I go to the Eden Fitness Club.

A: Great. ³ _____ a swimming pool?

B: Yes, ⁴ _____. In fact,
    ⁵ _____ two. One for children.

A: ⁶ _____ any swimming classes for the kids?

B: Yes, ⁷ _____ – at the weekend,
    I think. And ⁸ _____ tai chi classes. They're very relaxing.

A: Sounds great. ⁹ _____ any yoga classes?

B: No, ¹⁰ _____, but ¹¹ _____
    massages and ¹² _____ free childcare.

A: That sounds good. ¹³ _____ a restaurant?

B: No, but ¹⁴ _____ a café with free wi-fi access.

3 Add *a, an, some* or *any* to the sentences.

1 There's ᵃ button missing on my shirt.

2 Is there alternative route to your house?

3 There aren't rooms at the hotel, I'm afraid.

4 There are messages on your voicemail.

5 Is there problem with the room?

6 There isn't information about the town in this book.

7 There isn't bridge over the river here.

8 There's interesting story about your teacher in the newspaper.

3 *this, that, these, those*

Presentation

You use *this, that, these* and *those* to show exactly which thing or person we are talking about.

this and *these*

Use *this* and *these* to talk about things that …

- are near you: ***This** is a good table. Let's sit here.*
- are happening now: ***This** has been a great holiday. I want to come back again!* (You are still on holiday.)

Use *this* with singular nouns and *these* with plural nouns: ***this** table,* ***these** olives.*

that and *those*

Use *that* and *those* to talk about things that …

- are not near you: ***That** table looks good. Let's go over there.*
- are near the person you're talking to: *Could you pass me **that** chair just behind you?*
- happened in the past: ***That** was a great holiday.* (The holiday has finished.)

Use *that* with singular nouns and *those* with plural nouns: ***that** table,* ***those** people.*

TIP You can also use *this, that, these* and *those* without nouns:
*Have you seen **this**?*
*Whose are **those**?*

Exercises

1 Choose the correct words.

1 Did you see *this / that* film on TV last night?

2 Whose shoes are *these / those* over there in the corner?

3 Mmm, I really like *this / that* cake. Did you make it yourself?

4 Hey, is *this / that* coat you're wearing new? It looks good on you.

5 Who were *these / those* people you were talking to at the party?

6 Are you hungry? Would you like to share *these / those* sandwiches with me?

7 Hey, come over here. Have you seen *this / that*?

8 A: What's *this / that* you've got in your hand?
  B: *This / That*? Oh, nothing.

2 🔊 1.04 Complete the conversations with *this, that, these* or *those*. Then listen and check.

Conversation 1

A: What's ¹_____ building over there?

B: Where?

A: ²_____ house in the distance, over there, behind ³_____ trees.

B: I don't know.

Conversation 2

C: Mmm, ⁴_____ tastes really good. Did you make it?

D: Yes. I used ⁵_____ new recipe Tim gave me last week …

C: Did you use ⁶_____ Indian spices he gave you as well?

D: No, I didn't. I used ⁷_____ Mexican spices instead. Here they are.

C: Let's see. Mmm, interesting. Where did you get them?

D: In ⁸_____ new shop on the High Street.

3 Correct the sentences. Four sentences are correct.

1 I'm sorry, I can't come to the meeting tomorrow. I'm really busy ~~that~~ week.
  this

2 Hi, John. This is my brother Steve. Steve, this is John. ✓

3 A: What does he do exactly?
  B: He works in this new shopping centre on the other side of town.

4 Wow! Are those shoes new? They look great!

5 Look, here. These are the photos I was telling you about on the phone.

6 Can you help me with this bags, please? They're really heavy!

7 In these days, there weren't any mobile phones or internet cafés.

8 A: How many cakes have you had?
  B: Only two. This is the second one.

4 Possessives

possessive adjectives, possessive pronouns, possessive *'s*, *of* and *whose*

| ≡ ▼ | **Subject:** | Surprise party! |

Hi Jemima

It's William's birthday on Friday so we're having a surprise party for him at my house. A friend of his is going to pick him up. She's going to tell him they're going to the cinema. Then, they'll stop at my house. We're going to surprise him when they come in. I can't wait to see his face! ☺

I hope you can come too!

Tiffany

Presentation

You can talk about possession in different ways.

Possessive adjectives

Use possessive adjectives before nouns:

*We're having a party at **my** house. It's **his** birthday.*

Possessive adjectives do not change for singular or plural nouns:

*We celebrated **his** birthday on Friday. He was really pleased with **his** presents.*

Possessive pronouns

Use possessive pronouns instead of nouns:

*We aren't having the party at his house. We're having it at **mine**. It isn't my birthday, it's **his**. (his birthday)*

Possessive pronouns do not change for singular or plural nouns:

*It's my bag. > It's **mine**.   They're my bags. > They're **mine**.*

Possessive *'s*

You generally use the possessive *'s* for people and animals:

- Add *'s* to a singular noun: *William's birthday.*
- Add *'* to a plural noun: *My parents' anniversary.*

You can add *'* or *'s* to a singular noun that finishes in *s*:
Charles' birthday or *Charles's birthday.*

See page 232: Punctuation rules

Subject pronouns	Possessive adjectives	Possessive pronouns
I	my	mine
you	your	yours
he	his	his
she	her	hers
it	its	its*
we	our	ours
they	their	theirs

* This form is not common in everyday English.

TIP *it's* = it is: ***It's** a nice day.*

TIP *its* = possessive adjective: *The dog shook **its** head.*

TIP There is no *'* before the *s* in *yours, hers, its, ours, theirs*.

of

You can also talk about possession with *of* + noun + *'s* or *of* + possessive pronoun:

*She's a friend **of Peter's**. = She's one of Peter's friends.*

*She's a friend **of his**. = She's one of his friends.*

*Did you borrow a **book of mine**? = Did you borrow one of my books?*

whose

With questions about possession, we often use *Whose …?*:

***Whose** birthday is it? It's William's.*

***Whose** presents are these? They're his.*

Exercises

1 🔊 **1.05** **Complete the conversation with the words in the box. Then listen and check.**

a   mine   my   of   Rita's   whose

A: I like your car.

B: Actually, it isn't [1]_____.

A: [2]_____ car is it?

B: It belongs to [3]_____ friend [4]_____ mine called Rita.

A: That's nice of her to lend it to you.

B: We're sharing it at the moment. She's staying at [5]_____ house for a month because [6]_____ new house isn't ready yet.

2 **Complete the sentences with a possessive adjective or a possessive pronoun.**

1 My coat is blue but this one is red so it isn't _mine_____.

2 This isn't _____ meal. I ordered the steak and chips.

3 The city of Florence in Italy is famous for _____ art and architecture.

4 He looks similar to my brother. _____ hair is dark, too.

5 Where are we going to meet, at your house or _____?

6 _____ taxi is waiting for us outside. Let's go!

7 Excuse me. Whose is this bag? Is it _____, sir?

8 Happy birthday! Here's _____ present. I hope you like it.

9 Waiter. I don't think this soup is _____. I ordered a salad.

10 That isn't Mr and Mrs Hanson's house. _____ is the one with the blue door.

11 Don't forget to put _____ coat on! It's really cold outside.

12 Sandra agreed but Jane shook _____ head and said, 'No.'

3 **Complete the second sentence so that it has the same meaning as the first sentence.**

1 He's a friend of Gillian's.   He's one of _Gillian's friends_____.

2 She's one of my cousins.   She's a cousin _____.

3 It's their idea.   The idea _____.

4 The paintings of Renoir are beautiful.   Renoir's _____.

5 Are these bags ours?   Are _____ bags?

6 Amsterdam is a city with amazing bridges.   Amsterdam's _____.

7 Who does this pen belong to?   Whose pen _____?

8 My bags are the big red bags over there.   The big red bags _____ are _____.

9 Is he a student of yours?   Is that _____ students?

10 Buckingham Palace is one of the most famous buildings in London.   One of London's _____.

5 Review of units 1 to 4

Grammar

1 Choose the correct responses.

1 Did your dad help you do that?
   a No, I did it me.
   b No, I did it myself.

2 Is this book yours?
   a No, it's Fred.
   b No, it's Fred's.

3 Is there any water left?
   a No, sorry, there isn't. I drank it all.
   b Yes, there is. It's in this bottle over there on the table.

4 I found this book on the floor.
   a Who book is it?
   b Whose is it?

5 Where are the kids?
   a My mum has taken they to the cinema.
   b They're in the park with my mum.

6 Who's that girl over there?
   a She's one of my sister's friends.
   b That's my sister, Jane. He's staying with me at the moment.

7 Are there any tomatoes? I want to make a salad.
   a Yes, there are any in the fridge I think.
   b No, I don't think there are. Have a look in the fridge.

8 There's a strange man at the door. Do you know him?
   a Is there woman with him, too?
   b Yes, that's the plumber. He's come to fix the shower.

2 Correct the mistake in each sentence.

1 Would you like to come to the cinema with ~~we~~ tomorrow? us

2 Thanks for last night. We really enjoyed us.

3 John, this is Pat. Have you two met yourselves before?

4 Is there any new students in your class?

5 There aren't some email messages for you. I've just looked.

6 What's this down there on the street? Is it a bird or is it a piece of paper?

7 Did you bring these shoes you bought yesterday?

8 A: Whose bag is this? B: It's my.

9 And that over there is Martin office. He's the head of the department.

10 A: Are these yours books? B: No, they're Jill's.

11 That's one of Dad paintings. It's good, isn't it?

12 Does anyone know who mobile phone this is?

3 Complete the texts with the words in the boxes.

each other	he	her (x3)	herself
him	his	she	there

The woman stopped and looked at
¹_____ in the window.
²_____ put ³_____ hair
behind ⁴_____ ear and walked into
the café. ⁵_____ was a man sitting
in the corner. ⁶_____ was reading a
newspaper. When he saw ⁷_____ he
stood up. She walked over to ⁸_____
table and smiled at ⁹_____. They
looked at ¹⁰_____ for a moment in
silence, then they both sat down.

my	that	there	these	this	those	your

Hi, come in. ¹¹_____ is my flat.
It isn't very modern, but it's comfortable.
¹²_____ are three bedrooms and a
living room. ¹³_____ are the bedrooms,
here. One for me and one for ¹⁴_____
brother. ¹⁵_____'s his computer over
there in the corner and ¹⁶_____
are his drawings next to it. He's studying
architecture. And this is ¹⁷_____
bedroom for the next month. Please, go in,
make yourself at home!

Grammar in context

4 Complete the text with the correct answer a, b or c.

Welcome to the Blogosphere!
A new website where you can post your blog for all to see!

There ¹ _____a_____ a new world where everyone is writing about ² _____ or her life, thoughts and weekly activities. The Blogosphere is a place where you can introduce ³ _____ to the world and let ⁴ _____ friends know what ⁵ _____ are doing. People also use blogs to publish ⁶ _____ own writing. So what makes a good blog? ⁷ _____ original and attracts visitors. As a result there are ⁸ _____ blogs which also make money.

This is how you do it:

- The writers don't write for ⁹ _____. They write for ¹⁰ _____ readers.
- Make sure your blog has ¹¹ _____ own unique style.
- Are there ¹² _____ blogs on similar topics? How is ¹³ _____ different?

1	a 's	b 're	c 'm		8	a a	b any	c some
2	a he	b his	c himself		9	a there	b their	c themselves
3	a you	b your	c yourself		10	a there	b their	c theirs
4	a you	b your	c yourself		11	a it	b it's	c its
5	a you	b your	c yourself		12	a a	b any	c some
6	a them	b their	c themselves		13	a your	b yours	c you
7	a It	b It's	c Its					

Pronunciation: vowel sounds 1

5 🔊 **1.06** Listen to the sounds in the table and the words.

/ɪ/	/iː/	/aɪ/
it	we	my

6 🔊 **1.07** Write these words in the table. Then listen and check.

mine	his	this	I	he's
she	these	him	its	me

Listen again

7 🔊 **1.08** Listen and choose the correct answers.

1 Whose car is it?
   a the man's
   b the woman's
   c Rita's

2 Who is Rita?
   a one of the speakers
   b one of the woman's friends
   c one of the man's friends

3 Where is Rita staying at the moment?
   a at her new house
   b at the man's house
   c at the woman's house

6 Present simple

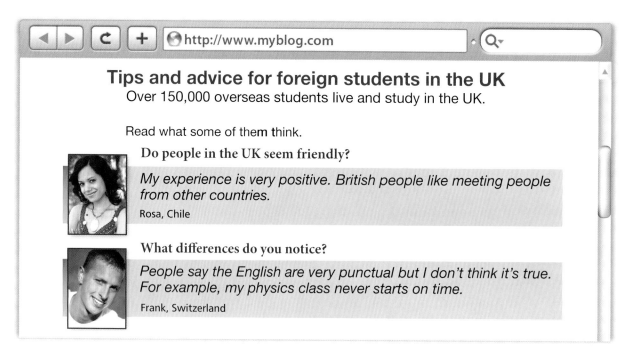

Tips and advice for foreign students in the UK
Over 150,000 overseas students live and study in the UK.

Read what some of them think.

Do people in the UK seem friendly?

My experience is very positive. British people like meeting people from other countries.

Rosa, Chile

What differences do you notice?

People say the English are very punctual but I don't think it's true. For example, my physics class never starts on time.

Frank, Switzerland

Presentation

Use the present simple tense to talk about …

- facts (things that are always or currently true):
  *Over 150,000 overseas students **live** and **study** in the UK.*
- repeated events and routines:
  *I **have** a Physics classes every Monday at 9 a.m. It never **starts** on time!*
- likes/dislikes and opinions:
  *British people **like** meeting people from other countries.*
  *I **don't think** it's true.*

Third person (*he/she/it*) -s: key spelling rules

You usually add -*s*: *live → lives*

However, there are exceptions:

1. Add -*es* to verbs ending in -*ch*, -*o*, -*s*, -*ss*, -*sh*, and -*x*: *watch → watches, go → goes*
2. Change verbs ending in consonant + *y* to -*i*: *study → studies*
3. Do NOT change the ending -*y* after a vowel: *buy → buys* NOT ~~buies~~
4. Note also *have → has*

See page 233: Spelling rules

Affirmative

I / You / We / They	live	
He / She / It	lives	in the UK.

Negative

I / You / We / They	don't (do not)		
He / She / It	does not (doesn't)	think	it's true.

You usually use the contracted forms *don't/doesn't* when speaking and writing informally.

Questions and short answers

Do	I / you / we / they		
Does	he / she / it	seem	friendly?

Yes,	I am.	No,	I'm not.
	you / we / they are.		you / we / they aren't.
	he / she / it is.		he / she / it isn't.

Where	do	I / you / we / they	
	does	he / she / it	come from?

Exercises

1 **Complete the sentences with the present simple form of the verbs in the box.**

catch cost enjoy feel ~~go~~ have live study travel understand

1 Ricki *goes* to English lessons twice a week.
2 The US President _____ in the White House.
3 We always _____ the bus to work at eight in the morning.
4 This bicycle _____ over €500.
5 He _____ playing computer games with his friends.
6 Most people in France _____ their summer holiday in July and August.
7 Nigel and Bruce _____ for their exams in the evenings.
8 The moon _____ round the Earth at 3,683 kilometres per hour.
9 How do you _____ today? Are you better?
10 I don't _____ this question. Can you help me?

2 ⊙ **1.09** **Complete the interview for a school magazine. Use the present simple form of the verbs in brackets. Then listen and check.**

Gabi Teschner, a German exchange student, is spending three months in the USA.

Interviewer: What [1] *do you notice* (notice) about students in the USA?

Gabi: They [2] *get up* (get up) very early for school.

Interviewer: What time [3] _____ (school/start) in Germany?

Gabi: We also [4] _____ (begin) at eight o'clock but in the USA the school day [5] _____ (last) longer. Also the timetable [6] _____ (not give) much time for breaks and lunch.

Interviewer: What [7] _____ (you think) of American food, Gabi?

Gabi: I [8] _____ (like) the breakfasts because they are similar to Germany but the school lunch [9] _____ (not taste) very good. It's always burgers or pizza and fries.

Interviewer: And what [10] _____ (students do) in their free time?

Gabi: Sport is very important in the USA so they [11] _____ (play) baseball or football after school.

Interviewer: [12] _____ (you play) these sports in Germany?

Gabi: Yes, I'm in a women's football team but we [13] _____ (not use) an oval ball. Our footballs, or soccer balls, are round!

Gabi Teschner

3 **Correct the sentences. Three sentences are correct.**

1 Everyone has a mobile phone these days. ✓
2 What time ~~does~~ you get up? *do*
3 I doesn't believe everything in newspapers. _____
4 Do they like meeting people? _____
5 The postman bring the letters in the morning. _____
6 The children like the cake. _____
7 How often does he goes to the gym? _____
8 It not feel very comfortable. _____
9 My sister studys modern languages at university. _____
10 What similarities you see between the two nationalities? _____

7 Adverbs and expressions of frequency
Present simple

The Culture Quiz

Are these true or false?

1 You don't need to arrive for dinner on time in the UK. Guests are often late.

2 The Queen celebrates her birthday twice a year.

3 The Chinese New Year is always on the same day of the year.

4 On her fifteenth birthday, a girl often receives gold in Colombia.

5 The Irish always celebrate St Patrick's Day on 27th March.

6 In Russia, people don't often give presents on 25th December. Christmas Day for them is on 7th January.

Answers: 1F 2T (She has an official birthday and her normal birthday.) 3F (The date changes from year to year.) 4T 5F (St Patrick's Day is on 17th March.) 6T

Presentation

Use adverbs and expressions of frequency to say how often something happens. You often use these adverbs and expressions with the present simple tense.

Adverbs of frequency

These are some of the most common adverbs of frequency:

0%	never
↑	hardly ever/rarely
	not often
	occasionally/sometimes
	often
↓	normally/usually
100%	always

*The Irish **always** celebrate St Patrick's Day on 17th March.*

Position of adverbs of frequency

Adverbs of frequency normally come …
• before the main verb

*The Irish **always wear** green on St Patrick's Day.*

*Russian people **don't often give** presents on 25th December.*

*Do Russian people **often give** presents on 25th December?*
• after the verb *to be*

*Guests **are often** late.*

*Guests **aren't often** late.*

*Are guests **often late**?*

Expressions of frequency

once a(n) twice a(n) three times a(n)	hour / day / week / month / year
every	hour / day / week / month / year / Monday / Tuesday / Wednesday / six months / five years

The Queen celebrates her birthday **twice a year.**

*The Irish celebrate St Patrick's Day **every year.***

*We play football **once a week.***

Position of expressions of frequency

Expressions of frequency can come at the beginning or the end of the sentence:

Every year they celebrate St Patrick's Day.

*They celebrate St Patrick's Day **every year.***

(don't say *They every year celebrate St Patrick's Day.*)

24

Exercises

1 A hotel interviewed the guests about meals. Look at the results and then choose the correct words in the summary.

1 How often do you use the hotel room service for your meals?

Every meal _5%_ Once a day _45%_ Not often _50%_

2 Which do you normally prefer for breakfast?

Continental breakfast _85%_ Full English breakfast _12%_ Don't eat breakfast _3%_

3 Do you ever eat at the restaurant in the evening?

Yes, every night _6%_ Sometimes _25%_ No, I usually eat out _69%_

Five percent of the guests [1] *always / often* use room service for meals and 45% eat in their rooms [2] *every / all* day. The rest [3] *hardly ever / sometimes* use room service. Only 3% [4] *rarely / never* eat breakfast and most people [5] *occasionally / usually* have the Continental breakfast instead of the Full English breakfast. Most people [6] *always / normally* eat out in the evening. Only 6% [7] *always / sometimes* eat there.

2 Complete the second sentence so that it has the same meaning as the first sentence. Use the phrases in the box.

always	don't normally	don't often
hardly ever	once a year	twice a week

1   My brother is never on time.

My brother is _____ late.

2   Spanish people rarely eat before nine in the evening.

Spanish people _____ eat before nine in the evening.

3   We have English lessons on Mondays and Thursdays.

We have English lessons _____

4   My family live apart but we always meet on the first of January.

My family live apart but we meet _____

5   People in my country usually offer tea to a visitor.

People in my country _____ offer coffee to a visitor.

6   My schedule is busy so I often work at weekends.

My schedule is busy so I _____ have a free weekend.

3 Add the adverbs and expressions of frequency in brackets to the sentences.

Cultural Habits

Breakfast habits around the world

1   What we eat for breakfast is the same every day. (usually)
    usually ∧

2   In Madagascar, people eat dried beef. (a few times a week)

3   Canadians put maple syrup on their morning pancakes. (always)

4   Many of us start the day without either tea or coffee. (rarely)

5   Italians drink a cup of coffee before they do anything else. (normally)

6   Most breakfast tables around the world include bread. (every day)

8 Present continuous

Presentation

Use the present continuous to describe …

- temporary events and actions at the moment of speaking:

  I'm calling about my computer.

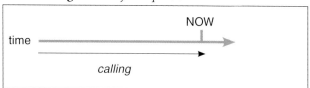

- events around now (but not always at the moment of speaking). These events are often repeated events over a period of time:

  I'm having a lot of problems with it.

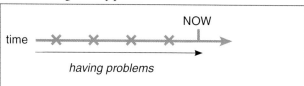

- a changing trend or situation:
  It's getting worse.

Affirmative and negative

I	'm (am) / 'm not (am not)	
He / She / It	's (is) / isn't (is not)	calling about a computer.
You / We / They	're (are) / aren't (are not)	

TIP You usually use the contracted forms *'m, 's, isn't, 're, aren't* when speaking and writing informally.

Yes/No questions

Is	he / she / it	having a lot of problems?
Are	you / we / they	

Short answers

Yes, he / she / it is.	No, he / she / it isn't.
Yes, you / we / they are	No, you / we / they aren't.

Key spelling rules

- With most verbs, add *-ing* to the verb: *call → calling*
- When a verb ends with *-e*, delete it: *have → having, live → living*
- When a verb with one syllable ends in consonant, vowel, consonant, double the final consonant: *get → getting, stop → stopping, run → running, swim → swimming, jog → jogging*

Note also: *die → dying, travel → travelling*

See page 233 for more examples.

Exercises

1 **Complete the sentences with the present participle (*-ing* form) of the verbs in brackets.**

1 Please turn off the television. I'm _____ (try) to study for an exam.
2 We're _____ (go) to bed early every day this week.
3 Sorry, I can't hear you. Someone's _____ (make) a lot of noise.
4 David's in the kitchen. He's _____ (get) dinner ready, so come into the garden and have a drink.
5 They aren't here at the moment. They're _____ (have) lunch I think.
6 He's _____ (do) a lot of training for the marathon.
7 Is someone _____ (live) in that house?
8 That ice cream looks delicious. I'm _____ (die) to try some!

2 **Look at the present continuous verbs in exercise 1. Do they describe an action now or around now?**

1 now / around now   2 now / around now   3 now / around now   4 now / around now
5 now / around now   6 now / around now   7 now / around now   8 now / around now

3 **📀1.10 Complete the telephone conversation with the present continuous of the verbs in brackets. Then listen and check.**

A: Hello, can I speak to the manager of your shop, please?

B: I'm afraid she ¹ 's talking (talk) to another customer at the moment. Can I help?

A: Well, I ² _____ (call) about a TV I bought from your website.
It ³ _____ (not work). For example, I ⁴ _____ (try) to change the channels now and it ⁵ _____ (not do) anything.

B: ⁶ _____ you _____ (look) at the television now?

A: Yes, I am.

B: OK. Press the 'on' button. ⁷ _____ anything _____ (happen)?

A: No, it isn't.

B: Can you check it's plugged in?

A: One moment. I ⁸ _____ just _____ (plug) it in now …. Sorry!

4 **Complete the texts about changing situations and trends. Use the present continuous form of the verbs in the box.**

fall	~~get~~	get	increase

As you can see the weather ¹ is getting worse with terrible wind and rain. Temperatures
² _____ across the country . . .

This graph shows that profits
³ _____ and that the situation
⁴ _____ much better for us.

9 Present simple and present continuous

Presentation

Present simple	Present continuous
Use the present simple to talk about …	Use the present continuous to talk about …
• facts and things that are always true: *The moon **orbits** the Earth once a day.* (= this is always true)	• actions happening now: *I'm currently **orbiting** the Earth.* (= this is happening now)
• things that are generally true: *I often **have** problems with my computer.* (= this is generally true)	• something that is happening now or around now: *I'm **having** lots of problems with my computer.* (= at the moment)
• general tendencies and repeated situations: *It **gets** cold at this time of year.* (= every year)	• changing situations: *It's **getting** colder.* (= at the moment)
• permanent situations: *Where **does** he **live**? He **lives** with his mum.* (= there's no plan to change this situation)	• temporary or new situations: *Where **is** he **living** now? He's **staying** with friends* (= for the moment, but this situation will change)

Stative verbs

You usually use the present simple with verbs such as *be, like, believe, look, understand* and *know*. These verbs describe states. You rarely use them in the present continuous form:

I understand what you mean. ✓

I'm understanding what you mean. ✗

Time expressions and adverbs

You often use these adverbs and expressions with the present simple tense: *always, sometimes, every day, all the time.*

You often use these time expressions with the present continuous: *at the moment, currently, now, today.*

Exercises

1 Choose the correct forms.

1 The Earth *has / is having* a population of 6.7 billion people.
2 The climate of the Earth *becomes / is becoming* warmer at the moment.
3 As you move towards the equator, the temperature *becomes / is becoming* warmer.
4 You live in France now but where *do you come / are you coming* from originally?
5 My family *lives / is living* in Nigeria for two years. After that we'll move to Alaska.
6 Sorry, I can't hear you because I *stand / 'm standing* on the platform at the train station.
7 The train *comes / is coming* into the station now. I'll be home in ten minutes.
8 This car *never starts / is never starting* in the winter.
9 How often *do you take / are you taking* a holiday?
10 *Do you understand / Are you understanding* what I'm saying?

2 Complete the article about an internet businessman. Use the present simple or present continuous forms of the verbs in brackets.

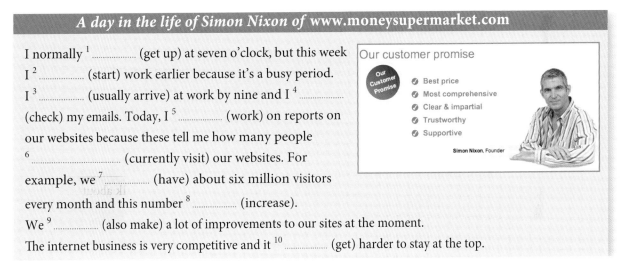

A day in the life of Simon Nixon of www.moneysupermarket.com

I normally ¹ .... (get up) at seven o'clock, but this week
I ² .... (start) work earlier because it's a busy period.
I ³ .... (usually arrive) at work by nine and I ⁴ ....
(check) my emails. Today, I ⁵ .... (work) on reports on
our websites because these tell me how many people
⁶ .... (currently visit) our websites. For
example, we ⁷ .... (have) about six million visitors
every month and this number ⁸ .... (increase).
We ⁹ .... (also make) a lot of improvements to our sites at the moment.
The internet business is very competitive and it ¹⁰ .... (get) harder to stay at the top.

Our customer promise

Our Customer Promise

✔ Best price
✔ Most comprehensive
✔ Clear & impartial
✔ Trustworthy
✔ Supportive

Simon Nixon, Founder

3 Complete these questions for Simon. Use the present simple or present continuous forms.

1 What time do you get up?
   At seven o'clock.
2 Why .... earlier this week?
   Because it's a busy period.
3 When .... at work?
   Around nine.
4 What .... today?
   The reports on our websites.
5 How many people .... every month?
   About 6 million.
6 .... the number of people who visit your sites .... ?
   Yes, it is.
7 .... easier to stay at the top?
   No it isn't.

10 Review of units 6 to 9

Grammar

1 Put the words in order.

1 on arrive time always does she?

2 I a twice girlfriend my see week.

3 watch time we never to TV have.

4 start nine work usually do at you?

5 are dinner early always they for.

6 normally do celebrate you when Christmas?

7 is hardly my brother trouble ever in.

8 a once the company year closes.

9 we to don't the go cinema often.

10 the bus you how do often catch?

2 Correct the mistakes.

1 The train ~~leave~~ at five o'clock every day.
   The train leaves at five o'clock every day.

2 Don't believe everything he is saying.

3 What are you making?

4 I'm afraid my colleague are visiting a client.

5 What do you wait for? Let's go.

6 You look very similar to someone else I'm knowing.

7 How much do that cost?

8 What time does usually he arrive?

3 Choose the correct options.

1 I'm leaving the office *now / often* so I'll be home in twenty minutes.

2 *Currently / Once a year* we celebrate Independence Day.

3 What are you doing *today / often*?

4 Where does Rowena come from *now / originally*?

5 They aren't answering the phone *right now / always*.

6 We visit the gardens in the park *always / every weekend*.

7 You need to get a new passport *every / once* five years.

8 We visit my grandparents *always / once a week*.

4 Write questions 1–6 using the words given. Use the present simple or present continuous. Match 1–6 to a–f.

1 How often / you / eat out?

2 Why / you / leave / now?

3 What time / the match / normally / start?

4 Which sister / talk / to Harry?

5 Where / Nigel / wait for us?

6 What / you do / in your free time?

a I think it's the youngest but I'm not sure.

b Because it's late.

c At the bus stop.

d About twice a week.

e I read and sometimes go to the cinema. And you?

f At three.

Grammar in context

5 Read the letter. Correct the mistake in each line.

Dear Sir or Madam,

       writing
1 I am ~~write~~ to request a copy of your brochure.
2 Currently, my wife and I plan a cruise round the
3 Mediterranean and we is very interested in your tours.
4 Your advert in the newspaper show a picture of a
5 traditional fishing village. It is looking fascinating.
6 We also wants to know about trips to the USA.
7 Do you offering any tours to California this year?

Yours sincerely,

George & Bertha Wright

Pronunciation: linking sounds 1

6 🔊 **1.11** Listen to these sentences. Notice how the speaker links the word ending with the consonant /s/ or /z/ to the word beginning with a vowel.

     /s/
She gets ‿ up before nine.
     /z/
He goes ‿ out to work.

7 🔊 **1.12** Listen to these sentences. Draw the link and decide if the consonant is /s/ or /z/.

             /z/
1 The Chinese New Year is ‿ always different.
2 The US President lives in the White House.
3 Nicola likes any kind of music.
4 My boss drives a red Porsche.
5 Simon works at the supermarket.
6 This meat tastes awful.
7 She's often late.

Then listen again and repeat the sentences.

Listen again

8 🔊 **1.13** Read the article in a student magazine about a visiting student from Germany. Then listen and correct the four mistakes.

                 girl
You might see a new ~~boy~~ at our school. She's Gabi Teschner and she's visiting our school for three months so we interviewed her about life in her home country of Germany and the USA. One difference is students in the USA get up late for school. It's similar in Germany but the school day here is longer with more time for breaks. As for the food, she likes breakfast but loves school lunches! German students also like to play sport after school but the shape of their ball is square not oval!

11 *a/an* and *the*

Receptionist: Come in. Take a seat. Would you like a coffee? Or an orange juice?

Visitor: No, thanks. I'm fine.

Receptionist: OK, I'll tell the director you're here … Mr White, there's a gentleman to see you.

Receptionist: Ah, Mr White, this is the gentleman.

Mr White: Thank you. Please come this way.

Mr White: So, how can I help you?

Visitor: I've come about the job.

Mr White: The job? Which job?

Visitor: The job you advertised in the paper. I understand you're looking for a new director.

Presentation

You use indefinite articles (*a/an*) and the definite article (*the*) in the following ways …

a/an	*the*
Use *a/an*	Use *the*
• to talk about a person or a thing in a general way: *I'm looking for **a** job.* (I don't have a specific job in mind.)	• to talk about a specific person or thing: ***The** job advertised in the paper.*
• to talk about something or someone for the first time: *There's **a** gentleman to see you.*	• to refer back to the same thing or person for a second time: *It's **the** man I told you about earlier.*
• to say that a person or thing is one of many: *He's **a** director.* (There are lots of directors, he's one of them.) *Mars is **a** planet in the solar system.* (There are lots of planets in the solar system.)	• to say that a person or thing is the only one in that context: *He's **the** director.* (There's only one director in this company.) ***The** earth goes around **the** sun.* (There is only one earth and only one sun.)
• to talk about what job someone does: *I'm **a** teacher. He's **an** architect.*	• when it is clear in the context which person or thing you are talking about: *I've come about **the** job.* (It's a particular job.)
Use *a/an* with singular, countable nouns (see Units 2 and 16): We use *a* before a consonant sound and *an* before a vowel sound: ***a** cup of coffee, **an** orange juice, **a** university, **an** umbrella*	Use *the* with all nouns (singular, plural and uncountable): ***the** gentleman, **the** men, **the** coffee*

Exercises

1 Choose the correct words.

1 Mum! There's *a / an / the* woman on *a / an / the* phone for you.

2 A: Hello, can I speak to *a / an / the* manager, please?
   B: I'm afraid he isn't in *a / an / the* office at the moment.

3 I'd like to make *a / an / the* appointment, please.

4 John just phoned to cancel *a / an / the* meeting for this afternoon.

5 Excuse me, have you got *a / an / the* pen I can use?

6 Sorry to disturb you. Can I ask you *a / an / the* question?

7 Is that *a / an / the* computer you bought last week?

8 I've got *a / an / the* problem with my computer.

9 A: Can I have *a / an / the* apple, please?
   B: Sure. Help yourself.

10 A: Excuse me. What's *a / an / the* time?
   B: It's half past ten.

2 Find and correct ten mistakes in the story.

A man took ~~the~~ a pair of trousers to a shop for cleaning.

The shop assistant gave a man a receipt. He put receipt

in his wallet. Two days later a police officer arrested

him and he went to prison for ten years.

When he finally got out of prison, he got in the taxi and

went to a centre of town. He opened his wallet to pay a

taxi driver and he found the receipt for his trousers. He

decided to see if a shop still had his trousers. He walked

into the shop. There was a old woman behind the counter.

He gave her the receipt. An old woman looked at a receipt

and said, 'They're not ready yet. Come back in a week.'

3 📀 1.14 Add articles to the conversations where necessary.

1 A: Shall we go to see a film?
   B: Yes, OK. What do you want to see?

2 A: Did you enjoy show?
   B: Yes, it was great. Music was fantastic.

3 A: Is there bus stop near here?
   B: Yes, nearest bus stop is on corner, opposite police station.

4 A: Is that new mobile phone? Where did you get it?
   B: In shop in town centre. It's new shop. It opened last week.

5 A: This is first time I've been to this restaurant. Is it new?
   B: No, it's been here for years. Friend brought me here once after work.

6 A: Look! There's man waving at you over there, on other side of street.
   B: Who? Man with black dog?

12 Zero article

Home **About Me** **My friends** **Messages**   **Settings** **Logout**

Name: Natasha, but everyone calls me Tash!

Occupation: Illustrator. I love it! I don't go out to work. I work from home!

Favourite food: I love pasta. I hate peas and green beans.

Likes and dislikes: I love cats but I hate dogs, especially really small dogs – and the two big black dogs that live next door.

Free time activities: I spend hours listening to the radio on my computer and watching TV. I love playing football and I'm learning to play the guitar.

What you admire in a friend: A good sense of humour, honesty, intelligence – and a great music collection!

Presentation

The zero article means you do not use *a/an* or *the*.

You do not use an article with plural or uncountable nouns to talk about people, animals or things in a general way.

- plural nouns
  I hate dogs = You hate all dogs. (don't say ~~I hate the dogs.~~)
  Compare with: *The two big black dogs that live next door.* (= two specific dogs)

- uncountable nouns
  I love pasta. = You love all types of pasta. (don't say ~~I love the pasta.~~)
  Compare with: *I love the pasta your mum makes.* (= a specific type of pasta)

- abstract nouns and concepts
  I love silence. (don't say ~~I love the silence.~~)
  Compare with: *I love the silence in the early morning when everyone is sleeping.* (= a specific example of silence)

Some special cases

- *play* + sports
  You say *play tennis* (and other sports) with **no article**, but you say *play **the** piano* (and other instruments).
  I play football. I'm learning to play the guitar.

- *home, work* and *school*
  You do not use an article when talking about *home, work* or *school* as part of your day to day life.
  I'm staying at home tonight.
  I'm not going in to work tomorrow.
  Where are the children? They're at school.

  Compare with:

  Her grandmother lives in an old people's home.
  (= a specific kind of home)

  I've finished all the work I had to do this weekend.
  (= a specific amount of work)

  The children go to the school at the end of the road.
  (= explaining which school)

- *by* + transport
  by car, by taxi, by train

Exercises

1 Complete the text with *the* or Ø (zero article).

Name: Fred

Favourite food: I love [1]_____ homemade food. I particularly love [2]_____ food my grandmother makes. I hate [3]_____ burgers and [4]_____ chips and [5]_____ coffee from [6]_____ machine at work.

Likes and dislikes: I love [7]_____ dancing and spending time with my friends. I especially love going to [8]_____ park and listening to [9]_____ music on my mp3 player.

Free time activities: I like to keep fit. I play [10]_____ basketball twice a week and go swimming in [11]_____ local pool every morning. I spend [12]_____ hours playing [13]_____ games on my computer and I love watching [14]_____ DVDs of old black and white films. I'm learning to play [15]_____ saxophone. I'm not very good but it's [16]_____ great fun.

2 Cross out the definite articles which are not necessary.

1 I admire ~~the~~ people who know what they want to do in ~~the~~ life.

2 Those are the people who live in the house next door to us.

3 I loved the apple pie your mum made for us last night.

4 The bus is always late in the morning and I'm always late for the work!

5 The money cannot buy the happiness.

6 Jim is the happiest person I know.

7 A: How did you get here?
  B: I came by the bus.
  A: The number 1?
  B: No, the number 3.

8 A: Where are you working at the moment?
  B: At the new school near the stadium.

9 A: Does Tom do any sport at the school?
  B: Yes, he plays the football twice a week.

3 (1.15) Add *the* to the conversation where necessary. Then listen and check.

A: Would you and ^the^ kids like to have lunch with us on Sunday?

B: Yes, we'd love to. Kids love food you cook!

A: Is there anything they don't like? I'm thinking of making chicken and rice. And ice cream for dessert.

B: Great! They both love chicken – especially with special homemade tomato sauce you always make.

A: And maybe we can go and see a film later? New Disney film is on at Odeon Cinema near us.

B: I can take them if you want and you can stay at home and enjoy some peace and quiet.

A: That sounds great!

B: No problem. See you on Sunday then.

A: Yeah, bye.

13 *the* or no article with names

How much do you know about geography?
Try our quick quiz and see!

1 Which ocean is the smallest?
a) the Pacific
b) the Atlantic
c) the Arctic

2 Which desert is the biggest?
a) the Sahara
b) the Gobi
c) the Kalahari

3 Which country was the first to give women the vote?
a) the USA
b) Australia
c) New Zealand

4 Which is the world's second longest river?
a) the Amazon
b) the Nile
c) the Yangtze

5 Which town is the home of the White House?
a) New York
b) Washington
c) Chicago

6 In which country is English not an official language?
a) the USA
b) South Africa
c) the Philippines

7 Who was the first European to sail around the world?
a) Christopher Columbus
b) Ferdinand Magellan
c) Juan Sebastian Elcano

8 When is the best time to see the Aurora Borealis (the Northern Lights)?
a) September and October
b) December and January
c) June and July

Quiz answers
1 the Arctic 2 the Sahara 3 New Zealand 4 the Amazon 5 Washington 6 the USA: there is no official language in the USA
7 Juan Sebastian Elcano – he was a member of Magellan's crew. Magellan died in a battle before his ships got home.
8 September and October (or March and April)

Presentation

Names without *the*

You do **not** normally use *the* with the names of ...

- people: *Ferdinand Magellan, Christopher Columbus*
- towns: *Washington, New York*
- countries: *New Zealand, Australia, South Africa*
- continents: *Asia, Africa, Europe, Antarctica*
- lakes and mountains: *Lake Geneva, Lake Titicaca, Mount Everest, Mount Whitney*
- months and days of the week: *January, February, Monday, Tuesday*
- languages: *English, French, Japanese*
- school subjects: *geography, history, art*

Names with *the*

You use *the* with the names of ...

- deserts: *the Gobi, the Kalahari*
- rivers: *the Amazon, the Nile*
- mountain ranges: *the Alps, the Himalayas, the Andes*
- oceans and seas: *the Pacific, the Mediterranean*
- groups of countries or states: *the USA, the European Union*
- countries whose names are plural: *the Philippines, the Maldives*
- countries whose names include a political label: *the Republic of Ireland, the United Kingdom*
- some buildings: *the White House, the Eiffel Tower, the Sheraton Hotel*
- periods of time: *the nineties, the 21st century, the holidays, the weekend*
- geographical regions: *the Middle East, the north, the coast, the mountains, the countryside, the Antarctic*

Exercises

1 Complete sentences 1–10 with *the* or Ø (no article).

1   Ø   Roald Amundsen was the first man to reach _the_ South Pole.

2   More than 370 million people speak _____ English at home.

3   The population of _____ China is four times bigger than the population of _____ United States.

4   _____ Nile is the longest river in the world.

5   _____ Kilimanjaro is the highest mountain in _____ Africa.

6   _____ Sahara desert is expanding to _____ south at a rate of 30 miles a year.

7   Most children study _____ history and _____ geography at school.

8   The coldest month of the year in _____ Antarctica is _____ July.

9   _____ Middle East is the region of the world east of _____ Mediterranean Sea and west of _____ India.

10 Global warming is one of the biggest problems facing the world in _____ 21st century.

2 🔊 **1.16** **Cross out any unnecessary articles. Then listen and check.**

1   A: Where are you from?

    B: A small town called ~~the~~ Amasra. It's in the Turkey on the Black Sea.

2   A: Who's your teacher for the Maths this year?

    B: It's the Mr Smith I think.

3   A: What are you reading?

    B: It's a book about the British explorer, the Scott of the Antarctic.

4   A: What did you do at the weekend?

    B: We went to the country. We stayed at a hotel near the Lake Balaton.

5   A: Excuse me, do you speak the German?

    B: No, I'm sorry. I don't. Do you speak the Portuguese?

6   A: What are you doing in the holidays?

    B: We're going to the beach, in the south of the France.

3 **Add the ten missing definite articles (*the*) to the text.**

Chile

Chile, officially known as Republic of Chile, is the longest country in world. This long, thin country is situated between Pacific Ocean in west and Andes to east. It is more than 4,300 km long and is a land of extremes, from Atacama desert in north to the frozen lakes in south. The official language is Spanish and the capital city is Santiago, although the main government buildings are in the city of Valparaiso, on coast.

14 one/ones

Julie: Look, that's the one I told you about. The red one with the black sleeves. Do you like it?

Karen: Yes, I do. But I liked the pink one too. And there was a lovely green one in that other shop too.

Julie: I know but I can only afford to get one dress. The problem is: which one?

Julie: Which shoes should I get?

Karen: There are some nice black ones over there.

Julie: Do you mean these ones?

Karen: No, the ones with the red dots.

Presentation

one or a/an

Use *a/an* when you are talking about a single person or thing without saying which person or thing (see Unit 11): *I want to buy a new dress.* (You don't know which dress yet.)

Use *one* when you want to emphasise that you are talking about a single thing and not two or more things: *I can only afford one dress, not both.*

one/ones

You can use *one/ones* as pronouns:

Look that's the dress. Look that's the one.

There are some nice shoes over there. There are some nice ones over there.

Is there a shoe shop near here? Yes, there's one on the next street.

You can use *one/ones* with *the, this, that, these* and *those*:

This one? Not that one, the one behind you.

These ones here? No, those ones over there.

You can also use *one/ones* with adjectives:

the pink one, a red one, those pretty ones, some nice black ones

You cannot use *a/an + one* without an adjective.

Say *I saw a nice one in the window* or *I saw one in the window.* (don't say *I saw a one in the window.*)

Which one?

Use *Which one?* when you want to identify which thing or person from two or more things or people:

A: I like this one.

B: Which one?

A: The one with the black sleeves.

Time expressions with one

Use *one* in time expressions to talk about …

- a particular time in the past (often in stories):
  One day a man was walking down the road.

- some time in the future without specifying when:
  We must go out for lunch one day.

Exercises

1 **Complete the conversations with *one* or *ones*.**

1   A: Can you pass me my keys, please?

   B: Which _____?

   A: The _____ next to your cup of coffee.

2   A: I got _____ of those remote control cars for Tim's birthday.

   B: Which _____? The _____ with the big wheels?

   A: Yes, that's right.

3   A: I'm having problems with my computer. I think I'm going to have to buy a new _____.

   B: I saw some cheap _____ in an advert in the newspaper yesterday.

4   A: Are there any pens around? I can't find _____ anywhere!

   B: I think there's _____ in the kitchen.

5   A: Which sunglasses do you like?

   B: I like the red _____. They're really cool.

2 **Choose the correct words.**

1   *A / One* day we visited the mosque in Cordoba.

2   Do you fancy *a / one* game of tennis *an / one* afternoon next week?

3   She's *a / one* really good friend of my brother's.

4   Would you like *a / one* cup of coffee?

5   Sorry, I asked for *a / one* cheese sandwich, not two.

6   Excuse me, I've got *a / one* problem with my computer.

7   I'm sorry, but there's only *a / one* ticket left.

8   I think *a / one* car is enough for any family.

3 **🔊 1.17 Complete the conversation with the words in the box. Then listen and check.**

> one (x2)   one of (x2)   the one   the ones   this one   these ones   which one

A: Excuse me, I'm looking for a new computer. I was looking at some over there –
   ¹_____ in the corner. ²_____ would you recommend?

B: Well, ³_____'s very popular at the moment. It's ⁴_____ the best on the market.

A: Yes, but it's the most expensive ⁵_____ in the shop! I don't want to pay that much.

B: How about ⁶_____ here? They're light and easy to carry. This is ⁷_____
   all the students want. And there's a 10% discount at the moment.

A: OK. I'll take ⁸_____ those. Could you get me ⁹_____ with a green bag, please?

B: Sure. I'll bring it to you at the cash desk.

A: Thanks.

4 **Complete the sentences so that they are true for you.**

1   My favourite films are the ones that _____.

2   One of my favourite books is _____.

3   The one thing I hate is _____.

4   One day I want to _____.

15 Review of units 11 to 14

Grammar

1 Correct the mistake in each sentence.

1 Excuse me, did you ask for ~~a~~ ^{one} coffee or two?

2 This is a book I was telling you about last night.

3 I love the dancing. I go to class every Friday.

4 I play the golf once or twice a week.

5 Tim and Helen are going to Maldives on their honeymoon.

6 It's a most beautiful present I've ever received. Thank you!

7 This is last time I'm coming to this restaurant. The service is terrible!

8 We really must play tennis again a day next week.

9 My daughter is studying French and the Film Studies at university.

10 My husband usually takes the kids to school in morning.

2 Complete the conversations with *a, an, one, the* or Ø (no article).

A: We need to buy ¹_____ new car. Ours is very old. But ²_____ cars are so expensive these days.

B: Why don't you buy ³_____ second-hand ⁴_____?

A: Yes, that's ⁵_____ good idea.

C: There's ⁶_____ man to see you. He says he has ⁷_____ appointment.

D: Ask him to wait in ⁸_____ meeting room, please.

C: Which ⁹_____?

D: The ¹⁰_____ next to reception.

E: Can you speak ¹¹_____ Japanese?

F: Yes, I took ¹²_____ classes when I was at ¹³_____ school. I really enjoyed it.

E: Do you ever speak it these days?

F: No, not often. Only when I go to ¹⁴_____ local sushi bar!

3 Cross out the unnecessary articles.

1 We visited the Eiffel Tower when we were in ~~the~~ Paris.

2 My uncle teaches the Philosophy at an American university.

3 We always take the bus to go to the work.

4 I'm looking for a job. I'd like an one in a local bar or restaurant.

5 I love watching the old movies, especially the silent ones from the 1920s.

6 What time do the children get back home from the school in the afternoon?

7 My favourite food is a pasta with a rich tomato sauce.

8 Which the ones do you mean? The new ones on the kitchen table?

4 Add *a, an, the, one* or *ones* where necessary.

1 A: Who's that man over there, one with long hair? He's got guitar.

B: He's my cousin. He's singer. He's really good.

2 A: Did you see Bond film last night?

B: Yes, we did. It was great. Action scenes were fantastic.

3 A: You look tired.

B: I am. I really need holiday!

4 A: Where are you going for your holidays this year?

B: We don't know. We're thinking of going to south of France, or maybe north coast of Africa.

Grammar in context

5 Complete the text with the correct answer a, b or c.

¹........... Mount Everest is ²........... highest mountain in the world. ³........... first men to reach the top were ⁴........... climber from New Zealand, Edmund Hillary, and Tenzing Norgay, his Nepalese guide. They reached the summit at 11.30 a.m. on 29th May 1953. They placed ⁵........... cross in the snow, took a few photos and then climbed back down.

In 1978 ⁶........... Italian climber, Rheinhold Messner became the first climber to reach the summit without using ⁷........... oxygen. And in 2005 Frenchman Didier Desalle landed ⁸........... helicopter on the summit. In 2008 ⁹........... Olympic torch was carried up the mountain. ¹⁰........... Chinese government put up ¹¹........... mobile phone tower so that people can now use ¹²........... mobile phones on the summit.

1	a Ø	b The	c A	7	a the	b Ø	c one
2	a one	b a	c the	8	a one	b a	c an
3	a A	b Ø	c The	9	a the	b one	c a
4	a an	b a	c one	10	a Ø	b The	c One
5	a Ø	b one	c a	11	a a	b one	c an
6	a one	b a	c the	12	a Ø	b a	c one

Pronunciation: *the*

6 (🎧 1.18) **Listen to the sentence and notice the difference in the pronunciation of *the*.**

The Amazon is the widest river in the world.

We pronounce *the* as /ði:/ before a vowel sound: *the Amazon*.

We pronounce *the* as /ðə/ before a consonant sound: *the widest*.

7 (🎧 1.19) **How is *the* pronounced in the sentences? Write /ðə/ or /ði:/. Listen and check.**

1 **The** Eiffel Tower was built in 1889. /ði:/
2 Sir Edmund Hilary was **the** first man to climb Everest.
3 **The** Danube is **the** longest river in Europe.
4 **The** Andes are **the** longest mountain range on Earth.
5 **The** largest desert in **the** world is **the** Antarctic.
6 **The** Panama canal links **the** Atlantic with **the** Pacific.

Listen again

8 (🎧 1.20) **Listen and correct the sentences.**

1 The family are going to have lunch with their friends on Saturday.
2 They're going to have steak and chips.
3 The children don't like chicken.
4 Later they're going to see an old, classic film.
5 The cinema is far away.

16 Countable and uncountable nouns
Plural nouns

Presentation

Countable nouns are words for things that you can count. They have both a singular and a plural form. You can use them with *a/an* and numbers:

one phone, two phones, an announcement, two announcements.

Uncountable nouns are words for things that you cannot count, e.g. *music, liquid*. They are singular. You cannot use them with *a/an* or numbers. They have no plurals forms.

Countable nouns	Uncountable nouns
an apple	music / news
two apples	a piece of music
some apples	some music / news

When you want to measure uncountable nouns, or talk about a specific quantity you can use an expression with *a/an* or a number and *of: a cup of coffee, three bottles of water, a bowl of salad, two tins of soup, a packet of sugar.*

TIP Some nouns which are uncountable in English are often countable in other languages: *luggage, money, news, information, advice.*

Say *some information, a piece of luggage* (don't say *some informations, some luggages*)

Some nouns can be both countable and uncountable with different meanings:

*Keep your luggage with you at all **times**. (= on all occasions)*

*Quick, we haven't got much **time**! (= the general concept of time)*

*I love Italian **coffee**. (= uncountable)*

*Can I have **three coffees**, please? (= three cups of coffee)*

*Can I have **some cake**? (= part of a cake)*

*Can I have **some cakes**? (= a number of whole cakes)*

You use *some* with uncountable nouns and plural countable nouns: *some music, some cups*

Plural nouns

You usually form plural nouns by adding *-s, -es* or *-ies*: *belt/belts, key/keys, watch/watches, family/families*
See page 233: Spelling rules

Some nouns have an irregular plural form: *child/children, man/men*
See page 233: Plural nouns

Exercises

1 Add *a/an* to the countable nouns and *some* to the uncountable nouns.

1	an	apple	6		child	11		song
2	some	orange juice	7		family	12		tooth
3		box	8		foot	13		toothpaste
4		bus	9		music	14		toy
5		meat	10		snow	15		watch

2 Write the plural form of the countable nouns in exercise 1.

1	apples	3		5		7		9	
2		4		6		8		10	

3 Complete the labels with the words in the box.

| bread | cheese | pasta | rice | sugar | toothpaste | water | wine |

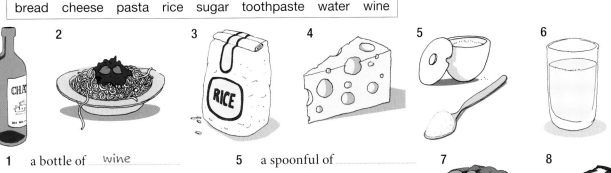

1   a bottle of   wine
2   a plate of
3   a kilo of
4   a piece of

5   a spoonful of
6   a glass of
7   a slice of
8   a tube of

4 Correct the sentences. One sentence is correct.

1   I'd like some informations about the new English course.

2   Excuse me, can I ask you for an advice?

3   Quiet, please. I have one important news to give you.

4   She let the sand run slowly between her fingers.

5   Have you got any moneys I can borrow?

6   I'm sorry, I haven't got a time to talk. I'm late for work.

5 Complete the sentences a) and b) with the pairs of words in the box.

| glasses / glass   light / lights   paper / papers   room / rooms   time / times   cake / cakes |

1   **a**   How many .... a week do you go to the gym?
     b   How much .... have we got before the train arrives?

2   **a**   The Christmas .... look wonderful.
     b   Can you open the curtains, please. We need some .... in here.

3   **a**   Is there enough .... in your car for one more person?
     b   It's a big house. It's got ten ....

4   **a**   Be careful where you put your feet. There's some broken .... on the floor.
     b   Can I have two .... of water, please?

5   **a**   There's no .... in the photocopier.
     b   Have you seen the .... today? They've all got the same story on the front page.

6   **a**   I loved those .... your mum made for the party. Can I have the recipe?
     b   Are you hungry? Would you like a sandwich or some ....

17 some, any, no, none
some of, any of, none of

A: Is there any coffee? There isn't any in the machine.
B: No, you'll have to make some.
A: OK. Do you want one?
B: No thanks. I had some earlier. But I'll have a slice of cake.
A: There's no cake left.
B: What, none at all?
A: No, it's all gone. I had the last piece for breakfast.

A: What are these?
B: Oh, those are some CDs Kevin gave me last week.
A: What are they like?
B: Some of them are great. Some of them aren't very good. Have a look.
A: I haven't heard of any of them! Can I borrow some?
B: Yes. Sure, take them all if you want.

Presentation

You use *some, any* and *no* with plural and uncountable nouns to show the number or quantity of things or people you are talking about.

some

You generally use *some* in …

- affirmative sentences: *There are **some** CDs on the table.*

- in requests and offers when you are referring to something specific: *Can I have **some** cake? / Would you like **some** cake?* (= A piece of the cake I have here on the plate and I am offering to you.)

any

You generally use *any* in …

- negative sentences and questions: *There isn't **any** coffee in the machine. Is there **any** coffee?*

some and any

You can use *some* and *any* without a noun when the meaning is clear in the context:

*Can I borrow some money? Sorry, I haven't got **any**.* (= any money)

*Have you got any coins? Yes, there are **some** over there.* (= some coins)

no and none

You use *no* with an affirmative verb in both questions and statements. The meaning is similar to '*not any*':
*Is there **no** coffee? There's **no** coffee.*

Don't use *no* with negative verbs: ~~There isn't no coffee~~.

You cannot use *no* without a noun. You have to use *none*:
*Is there no coffee left? No, there's **none**.* (= no coffee)

No / None is more emphatic than *any / not any.*

Isn't there any coffee? Is there no coffee?
There isn't any. There's none.

some of, any of, none of

You can use *some, any* and *none* with *of* + plural or uncountable nouns:

***Some of** the songs are great.*
***None of** the songs is/are very good. Are **any of** the songs new?*

You can also use *some of* in negative sentences:

*I don't like **some of** their new songs.* (= certain songs but not all)

You can also use *any of* and *none of* with object pronouns (*it, them, us, you*):

*I don't like **any of** them. **None of** us is very good at tennis.*

- **TIP** *None of* means 'not one of' so is usually followed by a singular verb but a plural verb is also common in speech.

Exercises

1 Choose the correct words.

1 Would you like *some / no* coffee?

2 Have you got *no / any* old magazines you don't need?

3 I've just made *any / some* biscuits. Would you like to try them?

4 There isn't *any / no* milk left. I finished it all last night.

5 I'm really thirsty but there's *some / no* water left!

6 I'd like *some / any* apples. Two or three of those red ones, please.

7 I've got so much work at the moment I have *any / no* time to relax!

8 I met *some / any* really interesting people on holiday.

2 🔊 **1.21** **Complete the conversations with *some, any, no* or *none*. Then listen and check.**

Conversation 1

A: Can I borrow [1] _____some_____ money? I need [2] _____ change for the bus.

B: Just a second. I think I've got [3] _____ in the pocket of my coat. Here you are.

Conversation 2

C: There's [4] _____ petrol in the car. It won't start!

D: What? [5] _____? Are you sure? I put [6] _____ in last night.

C: Well, there isn't [7] _____ there now.

Conversation 3

E: I was sure I left [8] _____ letters here on the table. Have you seen them?

F: No, I haven't seen [9] _____ letters, sorry. Oh, wait a minute, there are [10] _____ over there. Look! On the chair.

Conversation 4

G: Have you got any painkillers? I've got a terrible headache.

H: Let's see. No, I'm sorry, there's [11] _____ left. Shall I get [12] _____ from the chemist for you?

G: Thanks. Here's [13] _____ money.

3 Correct the mistakes. Four sentences are correct.

1 Any of my friends came to my house on Friday evening and we watched a DVD.

2 We rented three films from the DVD club but none of them was any good!

3 Do you keep in touch with any of the people you went to school with?

4 Don't listen to none of the stories he tells you.

5 You won't believe some of the things we saw on holiday!

6 A: Can I borrow some sugar?
   B: Sorry, I haven't got some.

7 I really didn't enjoy the course. Some of the people on it wasn't very friendly.

8 She's my favourite author at the moment. Have you read any of her books?

4 Complete the sentences so that they are true for you.

1 Some of my friends like _____.

2 None of my family ever _____.

3 I don't like any of the _____.

4 I really like some of the _____.

18 *much/many, lots/a lot of, a little/a few*

Presentation

Use *much, many, lots, a lot of, a little* and *a few* to talk about quantity.

much / many

You usually use *much / many* in questions and negative statements. Use *much* with uncountable nouns and *many* with plural countable nouns:

*I haven't got **much** time. I don't have **many** friends. How **much** money do you earn? How **many** different sports do you play?*

Don't use *much* in speech in affirmative statements. You normally use *a lot / lots*:

Say *I've got **a lot of** free time this weekend.* (don't say *I've got ~~much~~ free time this weekend.*)

You can use *many* in affirmative statements, but it can seem very formal:

*I've got **many** things to do today.* (formal)
*I've got **a lot of** things to do today.* (more common)

not much / not many

Use *not much* and *not many* to talk about small quantities.

Use *not much* with uncountable nouns:
*I haven't got **much** work to do this weekend.*

Use *not many* with plural countable nouns:
*I don't exercise **many** hours a week.*

You can also use *not much* and *not many* in short answers:
How many hours a week do you exercise? **Not many.**

a lot of / lots of

Use *lots of* or *a lot of* to talk about large quantities with uncountable nouns and plural countable nouns:

*I spend **a lot of** money on food. I have **lots of** meetings.*

There is no difference in meaning or use between *lots of* and *a lot of*:

*I spend **a lot of** money on food. = I spend **lots of** money on food.*

Do not use *of* when there is no noun:

How much exercise do you do?

Say *A lot.* (don't say *A lot ~~of.~~*)

a little / a few

Use *a little* and *a few* to talk about small quantities.

Use *a little* with uncountable nouns: *I have **a little** free time.*

Use *a few* with plural countable nouns: *I play **a few** sports.*

You can also use *little* and *few* without *a* but there is a difference in meaning.

A little or *a few* has a positive meaning. *Little* or *few* has a negative meaning:

*I have **a little** free time today so let's play golf.* ☺
*I have **little** free time so I can't play golf.* ☹

TIP *not much / not many* have a similar meaning to *very little / few*:

*I don't have **much** free time = I have **very little** time.*
*I don't have **many** friends at work = I have **very few** friends.*

Exercises

1 (🔊 **1.22**) **Choose the correct words. Then listen and check.**

A: Are you spending [1] *lot / lots* of time at the gym these days?

B: No, not [2] *much / many*. What about you?

A: No, I have very [3] *little / few* spare time at the moment.

B: Me too. A [4] *little / few* of my friends find time to go out after work but I find there aren't any hours left for anything else.

A: How [5] *much / many* hours do you work a week?

B: A [6] *lot / lots*! Last week I worked over one hundred hours.

A: Don't you get any holiday?

B: I have a [7] *little / few* days off next week, actually.

2 **Correct the mistake in lines 1–7. Underline the mistake and write the correction.**

1   A survey of gyms and fitness centres suggests that people spend <u>a lots</u> of   *a lot / lots of*

2   their spare time at the gym, but very little people are actually losing any weight.

3   In answer to the question 'How many weight have you lost since joining the

4   gym?' only 23% of the members said they were fitter. A little people (4%) even

5   said they had gained a few weight. But gyms needn't worry about these results.

6   When asked the question 'Will you pay your membership next year?' only few

7   people answered 'no' (9%). It's clear that much members are more interested in

the extra benefit, e.g. the sauna.

3 **Choose the correct words. In two sentences both answers are possible.**

1   A: How *much / many* milk do you like in your tea?
    B: A *lot / lot of,* please.

2   *Lot / Lots* of students study online nowadays.

3   *Few / A few* people write letters anymore. Everyone uses email.

4   Can I have *much / a little* ice cream, please? It looks delicious!

5   Would you like *a little / few* milk?

6   Sorry, but we don't have *much / many* information about train times.

7   You don't earn *much / little* money as a teacher!

8   There *isn't much / 's very little* bread left. Can you buy some?

9   The post office is only *a little / a few* metres from the cinema.

10 In my opinion, *not many / few* children learn to be polite anymore.

19 *enough, too many/much, too few/little*

Too many patients, not enough doctors

TOO LITTLE SLEEP MAY MAKE YOU FAT

Too few women in senior jobs

Too much information, too little time

Presentation

enough

Use *enough* to say you have the correct or sufficient quantity. Use *enough* with uncountable nouns and plural countable nouns:

*We've got **enough** hospital beds for all our patients.*
(= all our patients have beds)
*Have you had **enough** sleep? You look tired.*
(= a sufficient amount of sleep)

Use *not enough* to say you have less than you want or need:

*We haven't got **enough** doctors.*

too many / too much

Use *too many* or *too much* to say you have more than you want or need.

You use *too much* with uncountable nouns:
*There's **too much** information.*
(There's more information on the internet than we have time to read.)

You use *too many* with plural countable nouns:
*There are **too many** patients. We can't treat them all.*

too few / too little

Use *too few* or *too little* to say you have **less** than you want or need.

You use *too little* with uncountable nouns:
***Too little** sleep can be very bad for you.*

You use *too few* with plural countable nouns:
***Too few** senior jobs in the world of finance go to women.*

Too few and *too little* mean the same as *not enough*:

***Too few** women take senior posts in the world of finance.*
***Not enough** women take senior posts in the world of finance.*

Too few and *too little* are more formal in style. You usually see them in writing. When you speak, you tend to use *not enough*.

Less than you want or need	The correct amount ✓	More than you want or need
not enough doctors	*enough doctors*	*too much information*
too little sleep	*enough sleep*	*too many patients*
too few women		

Exercises

1 **Choose the correct options.**

1 A: Would you like any more to eat?
   B: No, thanks. I've had *enough /
   too little*. That was delicious.

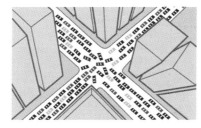

2 There are *too many / too much*
   cars on the road.

3 A: Is that OK?
   B: No, that's *enough / too much*,
   actually.

4 The match was cancelled
   as there were *too few / little*
   players.

5 A: Why are you stopping at
      the garage?
   B: We don't have *enough / too
      little* petrol.

6 There's *too much / isn't enough*
   time in the day.

2 **Rewrite the sentences with the word in bold.**

1 We have the right amount of money to pay for this. **enough**
   We .... to pay for this.

2 There's too little space in the house for more furniture. **enough**
   There .... for more furniture.

3 There aren't enough male teachers in primary schools. **too**
   There are .... in primary schools.

4 The police don't have enough evidence to be able to arrest them. **little**
   The police .... to be able to arrest them.

5 Was that the right amount of food for everyone? **enough**
   Has everyone had .... ?

6 There isn't enough time in the day to do all the things I need to do. **little**
   There's .... to do everything.

7 That's more luggage than you need. We're only going for one night. **much**
   That's .... We're only going for one night.

8 You've had lots of sweets. Don't eat any more. It'll soon be lunch. **enough**
   You've had more than .... It'll soon be lunch.

3 **Complete this description of your home.**

In my home, I have plenty of ....

but there *isn't / aren't* enough ....

My home has too many ....

and there are too few ....

20 Review of units 16 to 19

Grammar

1 Complete the crossword with words from units 16 to 19.

Across

1 Could I just have a _____ sugar in my tea?

3 Don't eat _____ much cake. You won't want your dinner.

5 _____ of the people that I invited to my party came. I don't know why.

6 Can I borrow _____ money?

7 I don't have _____ information about the museum but I'll give you what I've got.

8 You have _____ chance of winning the lottery. Don't waste your money.

9 Have you got _____ books about grammar?

Down

1 Use my mobile phone. The battery has _____ of charge on it.

2 Don't worry. We've got more than _____ time to finish this.

4 We aren't going to have an extra lesson. Too _____ students were interested.

7 How _____ people work here?

2 Is the meaning in each pair of sentences the same (S) or different (D)?

1 How much time do you have to play sports every week?

How many times do you play sports every week?
D

2 There isn't much butter left.

There's very little butter left.

3 We don't have any chairs.

We don't have enough chairs.

4 There are lots of useful books in the library.

There are a lot of useful books in the library.

5 They didn't have enough blankets for everyone.

They had too few blankets for everyone.

6 There were no taxis at the airport so I took the bus.

There weren't any taxis at the airport so I took the bus.

7 Stop! That's enough.

Stop! That's too many.

3 Rewrite the first sentence to have the same meaning, using the word in brackets.

1 There aren't any biscuits left.

(no) There are no biscuits left.

2 There are too few places at the table.

(enough) _____

3 We have little information about this person.

(not much) _____

4 There are few jobs left in this part of the country.

(not many) _____

5 Some of the songs are good.

(few) _____

Grammar in context

4 Complete the questionnaire with the words in the box.

any	enough	few	little	lot	many	much	none	some

How can you help the environment at work?

Are you doing enough at work to help the environment? Find out with this quiz.
Tick (✔) your answers to the four questions and add up your final score.

Are there any paper recycling bins in the building?

A Yes, there are lots of bins everywhere.

B Yes, there are a ¹ _____ bins in some of the offices, but not many.

C No, there aren't ² _____ bins at all.

How ³ _____ people travel to your workplace by bicycle or public transport?

A A ⁴ _____ of the people I work with travel by bike or public transport.

B A few people travel by bike or public transport.

C Zero people! ⁵ _____ of the people in my office travel by bike or public transport.

How ⁶ _____ equipment do you leave on overnight at your office?

A None. We switch everything off at the end of the day.

B We leave very ⁷ _____ equipment on overnight – only essential equipment (e.g. security cameras).

C We leave everything on (e.g. computers).

How much time do you spend discussing ways to help the environment at work?

A We spend a lot of time discussing ways to help the environment at work.

B We don't spend ⁸ _____ time.

C None. We never discuss the topic.

Mainly Cs: Oh dear! It's time for you to start making ⁹ _____ changes around the office.

Mainly Bs: Not bad. Keep working on it.

Mainly As: Well done! You are working hard to help the environment at work.

Pronunciation: vowel sounds 2

5 🎧**1.23** Listen to each set of words. Cross out the word with a different vowel sound.

1 any   many   much

2 much   some   too

3 too   few   lots

4 some   few   none

5 any   e<u>n</u>ough   none

6 some   not   lots

Listen again

6 🎧**1.24** Listen to four short conversations. Are the statements true (T) or false (F)?

Conversation 1

1 One person doesn't have any change for the bus. T/F

2 The other person lends him some money. T/F

Conversation 2

3 There's a little petrol in the car but not enough. T/F

4 The other person thought there was some. T/F

Conversation 3

5 There are some letters on the table. T/F

6 There are a few letters on the chair. T/F

Conversation 4

7 Neither speaker has got any painkillers. T/F

8 Neither speaker has got any money. T/F

21 Past simple
Time expressions

http://www.mytoptwentyfilms.com

MY TOP TWENTY FILMS

15 In A Lonely Place

For Dix and Laura it was love at first sight. But then a girl died. The police were sure that it was Dix who murdered her. Laura defended him. She didn't believe the stories about his violent past. But Dix became more and more possessive and she wasn't so sure. Did Dix kill the girl? Was their love strong enough to survive?

Presentation

Use the past simple to talk about actions and situations in the past.

to be

The past simple forms of *to be* are *was* and *were*:

*It **was** love at first sight. The police **were** sure Dix was the murderer.*

Regular Verbs

With most other verbs add *-ed* to form affirmative verbs:

kill → killed, defend → defended

Use *did/didn't* + infinitive to form questions and negatives.
***Did** Dix **kill** the girl?* (not *Did Dix killed the girl?*)
*Laura **didn't believe** the stories.* (not *Laura didn't believed the stories*)

Use *did/didn't* to form short answers.
*Did Laura believe the police? No, she **didn't**.*

Irregular Verbs

Some verbs have an irregular affirmative form in the past simple:

become → became, leave → left, tell → told

See page 235: Irregular verb list

Time expressions

Here are some common time expressions often used with the past simple: *yesterday, last week, last year, two years ago, five minutes ago*

to be

I / He / She / It	was wasn't (was not)	
You / We / They	were weren't (were not)	sure.

Was	I / he / she / it	right?	Yes, I / he / she / it was. No, I / he / she / it wasn't.
Were	you / we / they		Yes, you / we / they were. No, you / we / they weren't.

Other verbs

I / You / He / She / It / We / They	believed didn't believe	the stories.

What	did	I / you / he / she / it / we / they	ask	Laura?
Did		I / you / he / she / it / we / they	believe	the stories?

Yes, I / you / he / she / it / we / they	did.	No, I / you / he / she / it / we / they	didn't.

Key spelling rules

You may need to make small changes to the spelling of the verb at times:

1. live → lived (not ~~liveed~~)

2. cry → cried (not ~~cryed~~)

See page 233: Spelling rules

Exercises

1 Complete the text with the past simple form of the verb in brackets or short answers.

Dix [1]_____ (be) a writer and Laura [2]_____ (be) a young actress. They
[3]_____ (live) in the same apartment block, but they [4]_____ (not know)
each other. One night Dix [5]_____ (bring) a young girl back to his flat. As they arrived,
they [6]_____ (meet) Laura. She and Dix [7]_____ (look) at each other.
They [8]_____ (not speak), but they were instantly attracted to each other.

The next morning the police [9]_____ (ask) Laura to go to the police station.
The girl [10]_____ (be) dead. The police [11]_____ (think) that Dix was the murderer.

'[12]_____ (you see) Dix leave with the girl?' they [13]_____ (ask).

'No, I [14]_____,' she replied, 'I [15]_____ (see) him standing at his bedroom
window – alone.'

Dix and Laura's eyes met across the room. Everyone could see they [16]_____ (be) in love.

2 Complete the questions with the past simple form of the verbs in the box.

ask   be (× 2)   do   meet   talk   tell

1 What job _____ Dix _____? He was a writer.
2 When _____ Dix and Laura first _____? One night, when Dix brought a girl home
   to his flat.
3 _____ they _____ to each other? No, they didn't. They just looked at each other.
4 Why _____ the police _____ Laura to go to the police station? They wanted to ask
   her some questions.
5 _____ Dix worried? No, he was sure Laura could prove his innocence.
6 What _____ she _____ the police? That she saw him standing alone at his
   bedroom window.
7 _____ they in love? Yes, it was obvious to everybody.

3 Put the words in the correct order to make questions.

1 night what you last do did? _____
2 see you what film did? _____
3 actors were who the? _____
4 about was what it? _____
5 it you enjoy did? _____

4 🔊1.25 Match the responses a–e to the questions in exercise 3. Then listen and check.

a Yes, it was great.   ☐
b A writer and an actress who fell in love.   ☐
c An old black and white film called *In A Lonely Place*.   ☐
d We went to the cinema.   ☐
e Humphrey Bogart and Gloria Grahame.   ☐

22 Past continuous and past simple

Actions in progress, temporary actions and situations, the background to a story

It was winter. I was staying with my grandparents at the time. One day I needed to go to London. My grandparents offered to drive me to the station. It was snowing and the traffic was moving really slowly so I decided to get out and walk. As I arrived at the station the last passengers were getting on the train. I ran to the platform, but it was too late. The train was leaving the station.

Presentation

Use the past continuous to talk about actions and situations in progress at a particular moment in the past:

*It **was snowing** and the traffic **was moving** really slowly.*

Past continuous

Affirmative and negative

I / He / She / It	was	running.
	wasn't (was not)	
We / You / They	were	
	weren't (were not)	

Questions and short answers

| Where | was | I / he / she / it | going? |
| | were | we / you / they | |

| Yes, I / he / she / it was. | No, I / he / she / it wasn't. |
| Yes, you / we / they were. | No, you / we / they weren't. |

You also often use the past continuous to describe the background to a story:

*It was winter. I **was staying** with my grandparents at the time.*

Do not use the past continuous with stative verbs:

I needed … (not I ~~was needing~~.)

See Unit 9 for information about stative verbs.

Past continuous and past simple

You can use the past continuous with the past simple to talk about two actions that happened at the same time. Use the past continuous to talk about the action which was already in progress. Use the past simple to talk about a second, shorter action:

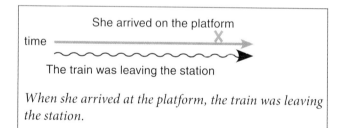

When she arrived at the platform, the train was leaving the station.

The second, shorter action sometimes interrupts the action already in progress:

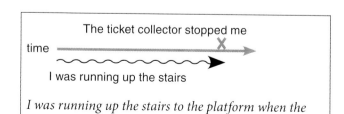

I was running up the stairs to the platform when the ticket collector stopped me.

Exercises

1 Complete the sentences with *was, were, wasn't* or *weren't*.

1 What _____ you doing at ten o'clock last night?

2 Why _____ he running away so fast?

3 He _____ doing his homework. He _____ watching TV instead!

4 They _____ disturbing the neighbours with their loud music.

5 I'm sorry. I _____ working late at the office and I forgot to call.

6 Sorry, we _____ listening. What did you say?

7 She _____ living there for very long, only a few weeks, I think.

8 They _____ having problems with their car, so they took a taxi.

2 ⊙ **1.26** **Choose the correct form of the verb. Then listen and check.**

Conversation 1

A: What ¹ *did you do / were you doing* at 2 a.m. this morning? ² *Did you have / Were you having* a party?

B: No, not a party. We ³ *invited / were inviting* some friends round for dinner. Why?

A: The music was really loud! I ⁴ *tried / was trying* to get to sleep.

B: Sorry! I ⁵ *didn't know / wasn't knowing* it was so loud.

Conversation 2

C: Oh! Hello! I didn't know you ⁶ *waited / were waiting* for me. I ⁷ *spoke / was speaking* to Mark on the phone.

D: It's OK. I ⁸ *finished / was finishing* work about half an hour ago. Would you like to go for a quick coffee? Have you got time?

C: Yes, I have. I ⁹ *just looked / was just looking* at a report, but I can finish it later.

3 Complete the text with the past continuous or past simple of the verbs in brackets.

A man ¹ _____ (walk) down the street. It ² _____ (be) a beautiful day – the sun ³ _____ (shine) and the birds ⁴ _____ (sing). The man ⁵ _____ (walk) past a park bench when he ⁶ _____ (see) a piece of paper on the floor. He ⁷ _____ (pick) it up. It ⁸ _____ (be) a lottery ticket. He ⁹ _____ (cross) the street to a shop where a woman ¹⁰ _____ (write) the winning lottery numbers on a board. He ¹¹ _____ (read) the numbers on the board and ¹² _____ (look) at the numbers on his ticket. He couldn't believe his eyes! As he ¹³ _____ (walk) out of the shop, he ¹⁴ _____ (dream) about how he would spend his three-million-pound prize!

23 Present perfect and past simple 1
ever, never

Presentation

Use the present perfect to talk about your experiences – the things you've done, and haven't done, in your life.

Form the present perfect with *have / has* + past participle.

Past participle

With regular verbs, add *-ed: ski → skied*

Some verbs are irregular: *see → seen, fly → flown*

See page 235: irregular verb list

Affirmative and negative

I / You / We / They	've (have) haven't (have not)		
He / She / It	's (has) hasn't (has not)	visited	Paris.

Questions

How many countries	have	I / you / we / they	visited?	
	has	he / she / it		
	Have	I / you / we / they	visited	Paris?
	Has	he / she / it		

Short answers

Yes, I / you / we / they	have.	No, I / you / we / they	haven't.
Yes, he / she / it	has.	No, he / she / it	hasn't.

ever / never

You often use the present perfect with *ever* and *never*:

*Have you **ever** driven a jeep?* (ever = in your life)

*I've **never** been to India.* (never = not in my whole life)

You also use the present perfect with *not / never … before*:

*I **haven't been** here **before**. I've **never skied before**.*

You use the present perfect and not the present simple with *the first / second / third time.*

Say *This is the first time I've ridden a bike.* (don't say *This is the first time I ~~ride~~ a bike.*)

Present perfect and past simple

Use the present perfect to talk about experiences in general. You do not say when it happened.

Have you been to Paris? (= at any time in your life)

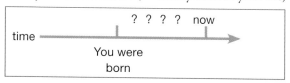

You often use the past simple after present perfect questions to give information about specific events and times in the past.

Yes, I have. I went last year, with my friend Maddy.

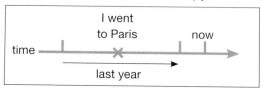

been

When you are talking about experiences, you often use *been* as the past participle for *go*.

Say *I've been to Paris three times.* (don't say *I've ~~gone~~ to Paris three times.*)

See Unit 24 for more information about *been* and *gone*.

Exercises

1 Complete the sentences with the present perfect of the verb in brackets.

1 This is the first time I _____ (eat) here. The food is really good.

2 Dave _____ never _____ (win) a prize before. He's so pleased!

3 _____ Jamie _____ (meet) Klara? I think he'd like her.

4 I _____ (not do) anything like this before. It's great fun!

5 _____ you ever _____ (go) to a football match?

6 My parents _____ (not be) here before. It's their first time.

7 _____ you _____ (study) this before? You're very good at it.

8 _____ Abby _____ (see) the new photo exhibition? She'd love it.

2 Write questions using *you* and the present perfect.

1 travel / abroad? *Have you ever travelled abroad?*

2 be / a live concert? _____

3 take part / sports competition? _____

4 be / on TV ? _____

3 Answer the questions in exercise 2. If the answer is yes, give more details. Use the present perfect or simple past as appropriate.

1 *Yes, I have. I've been to France, Morocco and Thailand. I went to Thailand last year for a month.*
It was great!

4 🔊 1.27 Choose the correct form of the verb. Then listen and check.

Conversation 1

A: [1] *Have you tried / Did you try* the new Korean restaurant in town?

B: Yes, I [2] *have / did*. We [3] *'ve been / went* there a couple of times. We [4] *'ve been / went* last weekend.

A: What [5] *have you thought / did you think* of it?

B: It was good, really good.

Conversation 2

C: I hate my job!

D: [6] *Have you ever thought / Did you ever think* about changing it?

C: Yes, I [7] *have / did*, lots of times! In fact I [8] *'ve spoken / spoke* to my boss about it yesterday.

D: Really? What [9] *has he said / did he say*?

5 Underline the mistake in each sentence and write the correct version.

1 <u>Have you eaten</u> well when you were in London? *Did you eat*

2 This is only the second time I sleep in a tent. _____

3 I never went here before. It's really beautiful. _____

4 Have you ever gone to Australia? I'd love to go. _____

5 He visited so many interesting places in these last three months. _____

6 Have you enjoyed the film last night? Yes, we did. It was great. _____

7 Is this the first time your kids visited Disneyland? _____

8 I've seen Paul at the swimming pool yesterday. _____

24 Present perfect and past simple 2
Unfinished time, present result, recent actions, *just*, *yet* and *already*

Tom	Hi Kay, Have you seen Jack this morning? The boss is looking for him. It's about the report. Has he finished it yet?
Kay	Hi Tom, Jack's just gone out to the post office. He says he's already handed the report in. It's on the boss's desk,
Tom	Thanks! I've just found it. Panic over!

Presentation

Unfinished time and finished time

Use the present perfect to talk about past actions within a period of time that is unfinished (*this week, this year, ever, never, yet*):

Have you seen Jack this morning? (It's still morning; the morning has not finished.)

I've seen Jack a couple of times this morning.

Use the past simple to talk about actions in a period of time which is finished (*last week, yesterday, five minutes ago*):

Did you see Jack this morning? (It's now evening, the morning has finished.)

I saw Jack about five minutes ago.

Present result

Use the present perfect to talk about a past action which has a result in the present. You do not say when the action happened: *He's handed in the report.* (The present result is it's on the boss's desk now.)

If you want to say when the action happened, use the past simple: *He handed in the report last night.*

just, yet, already

You often use the present perfect with *just, yet* and *already* to talk about actions that happened recently, or actions that we are expecting to happen soon.

*I've **just** found it. He's **already** handed it in. The boss hasn't seen it **yet**.*

- Use *just* to show that an action happened in the recent past:

*He's **just** gone out.* (It happened a few minutes ago.)
*They've **just** got married.* (It happened a few weeks ago.)

- Use *yet* in *yes/no* questions and in negative sentences with *not*.

*Has he finished it **yet**?*

- Use *yet* in negative sentences to say that something we are expecting to happen hasn't happened:

*He hasn't finished it **yet**.*

- Use *already* to emphasise that something has happened *before now*:

*I've **already** finished the report.* (We don't know exactly when this happened. The important thing is that it happened before now.)

been and gone

In the present perfect there are two possible past participles forms for the verb *go*.

- Use *been* to say that someone went somewhere and came back:

*I've **been** to Paris three times.* (I'm not in Paris now.) See Unit 23.

- Use *gone* to say that someone went somewhere and is still there.

*Suzi's **gone** to Paris for the weekend.* (She's still there.)

Exercises

1 **Match the sentences in column A to the responses in column B.**

A

1   Has anyone seen my phone? [c]
2   Have you washed my shirt? [ ]
3   I haven't had a shower yet. [ ]
4   Have you had lunch? [ ]
5   Can I get you a coffee? [ ]
6   Do you want me to make dinner? [ ]
7   You look really sleepy. [ ]
8   Does Lynne know about the party? [ ]

B

a   Yes, I've already told her.
b   Well, hurry up! We're late.
c   ~~It was here two minutes ago.~~
d   No, thanks. I've just had one.
e   No, I've already done it, thanks.
f   Yes, it's on the back of the chair in your room.
g   Yes, I've just got up.
h   No, I haven't. Would you like to go to that new café?

2 **Add the words in brackets to the sentences.**

1   Don't throw that away! I haven't finished it ∧ yet . (yet)

2   I've spoken to Polly. She's coming at two o'clock. (just)

3   There's no need to clean the kitchen. I've done it. (already)

4   Have you spoken to Simon? He's called you a couple of times. (yet)

5   Jo and Matt are so happy. They've had their first baby. (just)

6   Don't make any lunch. I've eaten. (already)

7   Careful! I've painted the front door. It hasn't dried. (just / yet)

3 **(🔊 1.28) Choose the correct forms. Then listen and check.**

Conversation 1

A: What's happening about Mum's birthday present? [1] *Have you phoned / Did you phone* Dad yet?

B: No, but [2] *he has sent / sent* me an email earlier. It's OK. He [3] *'s already bought / already bought* the flowers. He [4] *has been / went* to the market first thing this morning to pick them up.

Conversation 2

C: Oh no, I've just remembered something! Last night I [5] *'ve promised / promised* Jane that I'd pick her up after class today.

D: It's OK, don't worry. Tom's just [6] *been / gone* to get her. He's on his way now.

Conversation 3

E: I think everything's almost ready. I [7] *'ve packed / packed* the bags, I've got the tickets and the passports. I [8] *haven't called / didn't call* the taxi yet.

F: Don't worry. I [9] *'ve already booked / just booked* one. I phoned them last night.

4 **Complete these sentences so that they are true for you.**

1   I've just ....
2   I haven't .... yet.
3   I've already ....
4   I haven't done any .... this week.
5   I've done a lot of .... over the past month.
6   I've never been ....

25 Review of units 21 to 24

Grammar

1 Correct the mistakes. There is one mistake in each item.

1   One day I was walking down the road when I
     saw
     ~~was seeing~~ a very strange thing.

2   A: Have you ever been to India?

     B: Yes, I went three times.

3   Have you spoken to Jim yesterday?

4   A: Can I have the newspaper?

     B: No, sorry, I haven't read it already.

5   A: Where's Hugh?

     B: He's just been to the shop. He left two
          minutes ago.

6   A: Have you finished yet?

     B: Yes, I have. I've finished half an hour ago.

7   He was breaking his leg when he was playing
     football.

8   I never rode a motorbike in my life. Have you?

2 Put the words in order.

1   you me for looking were yesterday?

2   get time what there you did?

3   this morning seen have Beth you?

4   exam you about worried were the?

5   learn play did you tennis where to?

6   were working you last late night?

7   you what doing were?

8   worked have children before with you?

3 Match the questions in exercise 2 to the answers below.

a   I don't know, but it was really late. ☐

b   No, I don't think she's come in yet. ☐

c   Yes, I sometimes babysit for Beth at the
     weekends. ☐

d   I was busy. I was studying for an exam. ☐

e   Yes, I wanted to ask you about the new
     timetable. ☐

f   Yes, I was working on that report. ☐

g   My dad taught me. He was a professional. ☐

h   Yes, I was. I really wanted to pass it. ☐

4 Underline the correct form of the verb.

Conversation 1

A: What ¹ *did you do / were you doing* in the library
     at 10 p.m. last night?

B: I ² *studied / was studying* for my driving test.

A: I ³ *thought / was thinking* you ⁴ *have taken / took*
     it last week.

B: I ⁵ *have / did*! But I ⁶ *failed / was failing*.

Conversation 2

C: ⁷ *Have you been / Have you gone* to the photo
     exhibition in the town hall?

D: No, I haven't. But Paula ⁸ *has been / went* last
     week.

C: ⁹ *Has she liked / Did she like* it?

D: Yes, she said it was great. She ¹⁰ *bought / was
     buying* me a poster. I ¹¹ *'ve put / was putting* it on
     the wall in the office.

C: Oh, was that you? I ¹² *'ve noticed / noticed* it
     yesterday when I was coming in to work.

Grammar in context

5 **Complete the text with the correct answer, a, b, or c.**

I ¹ _a_ a lot of strange things in my life, but this ² _____ definitely the strangest. A few years ago I ³ _____ as a travelling librarian for the summer. Once a week we ⁴ _____ to visit a small village in the middle of the country. One day a hen ⁵ _____ into the library and asked for three books. I don't know about you, but I ⁶ _____ a talking hen before. I was so surprised I gave her the books. The next week, when we came back, the hen ⁷ _____ for us when we arrived. She gave me her books back and ⁸ _____ for some more. This went on for a few weeks. I got curious. ⁹ _____ really read all those books? I ¹⁰ _____ to follow her. The hen walked out of the village and into a field. In the middle of the field, there was a pond where a frog ¹¹ _____ for the hen. The hen ¹² _____ up to the frog and put the books down at his feet, one by one. As she put each book down at his feet, the frog looked up and said '¹³ _____.'

1	**a** 've seen	**b** was seeing	**c** saw
2	**a** has been	**b** was being	**c** was
3	**a** have worked	**b** was working	**c** worked
4	**a** went	**b** been	**c** gone
5	**a** was coming	**b** has come	**c** came
6	**a** never saw	**b** never see	**c** have never seen
7	**a** waited	**b** have waited	**c** was waiting

8	**a** asked	**b** didn't ask	**c** was asking
9	**a** Did the hen	**b** Was the hen	**c** The hen did
10	**a** was deciding	**b** decided	**c** decide
11	**a** waited	**b** were waiting	**c** was waiting
12	**a** was walking	**b** walks	**c** walked
13	**a** I've read it	**b** I was reading it	**c** I read it

Pronunciation: past simple *-ed* endings

6 🔊 **1.29** **When you add an *-ed* to verbs, you can pronounce the final sound of the verb in three ways: /t/, /d/ or /ɪd/.**

Listen and repeat these examples:
1 help - help**ed** /t/
2 want - want**ed** /ɪd/
3 listen - listen**ed** /d/

7 🔊 **1.30** **Listen to these verbs with *-ed* endings and write the phoneme /t/, /d/ or /ɪd/ over the *-ed* ending:**

/ɪd/   /t/   /d/
deci**ded** as**ked** arri**ved** looked needed started
lived played visited promised dreamed waited

Listen again

8 🔊 **1.31** **Listen to two short conversations. Answer the questions for each one.**

Conversation 1

1 How many times have they been to the new restaurant?

2 When did they last go there?

Conversation 2

3 What did she talk to her boss about?

4 When did she talk to him?

26 Present perfect 3
for and *since*

Presentation

You use the present perfect with *how long, for* and *since* to talk about an action or a situation that started in the past and continues in the present.

*He's worked here **for** over fifty-five years.* (He started working here fifty-five years ago – he still works here.)

*I haven't played tennis **since** I left school.*

***How long** have you known Steve?*

You do not use the present simple. (don't say *He ~~works~~ here for over fifty-five years.*)

for and *since*

You use *for* to talk about **a period of time**:

*He's worked here **for** fifty-five years / a long time.*

You use *since* with **the point in time when the action started**:

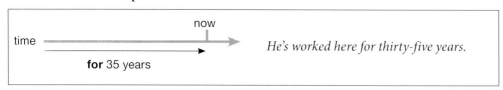

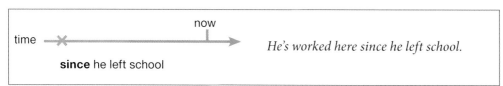

TIP You use the past simple in time expressions with *since*:

*He's worked for his father since he **left** school.*

*I've made a lot of friends since I **moved** here.*

*I've known Jim since I **was** a child.*

Exercises

1 Look at the pictures and write sentences using the present perfect of the verbs in brackets and time expressions with *for* or *since*.

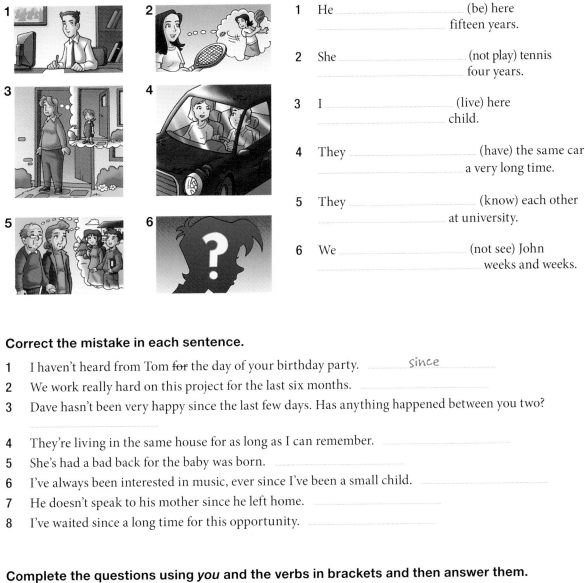

1 He _____ (be) here _____ fifteen years.

2 She _____ (not play) tennis _____ four years.

3 I _____ (live) here _____ child.

4 They _____ (have) the same car _____ a very long time.

5 They _____ (know) each other _____ at university.

6 We _____ (not see) John _____ weeks and weeks.

2 Correct the mistake in each sentence.

1 I haven't heard from Tom ~~for~~ the day of your birthday party. _____*since*_____

2 We work really hard on this project for the last six months. _____

3 Dave hasn't been very happy since the last few days. Has anything happened between you two?
_____

4 They're living in the same house for as long as I can remember. _____

5 She's had a bad back for the baby was born. _____

6 I've always been interested in music, ever since I've been a small child. _____

7 He doesn't speak to his mother since he left home. _____

8 I've waited since a long time for this opportunity. _____

3 Complete the questions using *you* and the verbs in brackets and then answer them. Give two answers each time, one with *for* and one with *since*.

1 How long _have you lived_ (live) in your present home?
   For _____   Since _____

2 How long _____ (know) your best friend?
   For _____   Since _____

3 How long _____ (study) English?
   For _____   Since _____

4 How long _____ (have) this grammar book?
   For _____   Since _____

27 Present perfect continuous

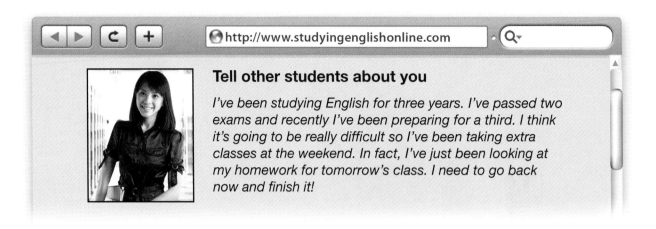

Tell other students about you

I've been studying English for three years. I've passed two exams and recently I've been preparing for a third. I think it's going to be really difficult so I've been taking extra classes at the weekend. In fact, I've just been looking at my homework for tomorrow's class. I need to go back now and finish it!

Presentation

Use the present perfect continuous to talk about recent continuous or repeated actions:

I've just been looking at my homework. (continuous)

I've been going to extra classes at the weekend. (repeated)

To form the present perfect continuous, use
have / has + *been* + verb + *-ing*

Affirmative and negative

I / You / We / They	've (have)			
	haven't (have not)	been	preparing	for an exam.
He / She / It	's (has)			
	hasn't (has not)			

Questions

How long	have	I / you / we / they	been	studying English?
	has	he / she / it		
	Have	I / you / we / they	been	studying English?
	Has	he / she / it		

Short answers

| Yes, I / you / we / they | have. | No, I / you / we / they | haven't. |
| Yes, he / she / it | has. | No, he / she / it | hasn't. |

Present perfect simple or present perfect continuous?

Use the present perfect continuous to talk about **how long** an action has lasted. The action may or may not be complete. *I've been studying grammar all morning!* You use the present perfect simple to emphasise the **completion** of an action.

I've studied the section on the past simple and the one on the present perfect.

You do not use the present perfect continuous to say **how many things** you have done or **how many times** an action has happened. Use the present perfect simple.

Say *I've passed two exams.* (don't say *I've ~~been passing~~ two exams.*)

Say *I've changed schools three times.* (don't say *I've ~~been changing~~ schools three times.*)

Note you do not usually use stative verbs in the present perfect continuous. Say *I've known him for years.* (don't say *I've ~~been knowing~~ him for years.*)

See Unit 9 for more on stative verbs.

You can use either the present perfect continuous or the present perfect simple to talk about the present results of a past action (see also Unit 24):

I've been working really hard this morning and I'm really tired.

I've worked really hard this morning and I'm really tired.

Exercises

1 **Look at the pictures. Complete the sentences with the present perfect continuous of the verbs in the box.**

> build   dance   eat   paint   run   swim

1 They _____ a marathon.
2 She _____ all day.
3 He _____ the living room.
4 They _____ in the pool.
5 They _____ ice cream.
6 He _____ a wall all morning.

2 **Match the two halves of the sentences.**

1	I've been writing	b	a money for a holiday.
2	I've written	☐	b ~~emails all morning~~.
3	I've been saving	☐	c three times this week.
4	I've saved	☐	d 300 euros in the last three months.
5	I've been playing tennis	☐	e with Sarah and now we're going for a drink.
6	I've played tennis	☐	f five emails this morning.

3 **1.32 Look at the verbs in bold. Four of the verbs should be in the present perfect simple. Correct the sentences. Then listen and check.**

A: How long [1] **have you been being** interested in science fiction?

B: Since I was a child. I used to read science fiction books all the time.

A: And how long [2] **have you been writing** science fiction stories yourself?

B: For about five years. I wrote my first short story when I was at university.

A: How many books [3] **have you been publishing**?

B: Well, not many. I mainly write short stories for magazines. [4] **I've been writing** more than 200 stories.

A: 200 stories? But that's 40 stories a year! How do you find the time?

B: Well, I used to write at night. But last year I gave up my job and since then [5] **I've been writing** full time.

A: What [6] **have you been working on** recently?

B: Well, for the last six weeks, [7] **I've been working on** a film version of one of my first stories. It's really exciting. It's the first time [8] **someone's been asking** me to do anything for film.

65

28 Past perfect
Time expressions

This month's winning photo:

The Iceberg

Before I went to Tierra del Fuego, I'd travelled all over the world and I'd seen all kinds of incredible sights. But this was definitely more impressive than anything else I'd ever seen. I'd never been so close to an iceberg before. I took this photo just as it started to turn. I hadn't realized how big it was until then. The side that had previously been underwater came to the top. It was a beautiful deep blue.

Roberto F. (Buenos Aires)

Presentation

Use the past perfect to talk about an action that happened before a certain time in the past:

Before I went to Tierra del Fuego, I'd travelled all around the world. I'd been to Japan, Mexico and Kenya.

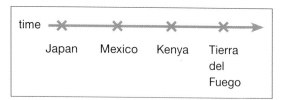

You can also use the past perfect to talk about an action that did not happen before the given time in the past:

I'd never been so close to an iceberg before.

Affirmative and negative

I / You / He / She / It / They	'd (had) hadn't (had not)	seen an iceberg before.

Yes/No questions

Had	I / you / he / she / it / they	seen an iceberg before?

Short answers

Yes	I / you / he / she / it / they	had.
No	I / you / he / she / it / they	hadn't (had not).

TIP Don't confuse the contracted forms of *had* ('d) and *would* ('d):

I'd seen an iceberg. (I had seen an iceberg.)
I'd like to see an iceberg. (I would like to see an iceberg.)

Past perfect and past simple

You often use the past perfect and the past simple together. Use the past simple to talk about the most recent past action. Use the past perfect to talk about actions and situations that happened before a certain time in the past:

I hadn't realised how big it was until it turned over.

The side that had previously been underwater came to the top.

Time expressions

The past perfect is often used with the following adverbs to emphasise the fact that the action happened earlier: *already, just, recently, before, previously, earlier.*

- *Already, just* and *recently* come between *had* and the past participle.

  He had just come back from Laos. I had recently sold my car.

- *Before* comes at the end of the sentence. In negative sentences it is often used with *never.*

  I'd been to Argentina many times before. I had never seen anything like it before.

Exercises

1 Complete the text with the past perfect of the verbs.

When I first met Mark, he was working for an advertising agency in London. He [1] _____ (recently finish) his MBA and he was very happy because his company [2] _____ (just offer) him a post in Tokyo. He [3] _____ (never work) abroad before and he [4] _____ (always want) to go to Japan. Then two weeks before he planned to leave, the company told him that they [5] _____ (close) their office in Tokyo. He was so disappointed. He [6] _____ (already book) his flight. He [7] _____ (even start) learning Japanese. I [8] _____ (just come back) from Tokyo. My company still (not find) [9] _____ anyone to take my job. I told Mark to call them. Ten days later Mark's dreams [10] _____ (come) true: he was finally in Japan!

2 Look at the text in exercise 1. Write questions using the verbs in the brackets. Use the past perfect or past simple.

1 Where _____ (you meet) Mark for the first time?
   At a party in London.

2 What _____ (his company offer) him a few weeks before?
   A job in Tokyo.

3 _____ (he ever work) abroad before?
   No, never.

4 When _____ (his company tell) him the Tokyo office had closed?
   Only two weeks before he was leaving.

5 How _____ (Mark feel)?
   Very disappointed.

6 _____ (he already book) his flight?
   Yes, he had and he'd paid for it too!

7 How _____ (you help) him?
   I told him to call my company.

8 So, _____ (he go) to Japan in the end?
   Yes, he did. Ten days later he was living in my old flat in Tokyo.

3 ⏵**1.33** **Complete the conversations with the past perfect or the past simple of the verbs. Then listen and check.**

Conversation 1

A: [1] _____ you [2] _____ (meet) Kris before the party last week?
B: No, not really. I [3] _____ (see) her around, but I [4] _____ (not / speak) to her. She's really nice, isn't she?

Conversation 2

C: I didn't know that Rae [5] _____ (leave) her job! When [6] _____ that [7] _____ (happen)?
D: Last week. She [8] _____ (have) an argument with her boss the day before.

Conversation 3

E: Have you heard? John and Beth [9] _____ (get) divorced last month.
F: But they'd only just got married!
E: Yes, three months ago! They [10] _____ (only just / come back) from their honeymoon when John [11] _____ (decide) that he wanted a divorce.

29 *used to*

Woman:	I didn't use to like spiders until I met Kevin. I used to be really scared of them. I used to scream and run away if I saw one.
Reporter:	Kevin, did you use to be scared of spiders too?
Man:	No, I've always loved them. I used to keep them in a box under my bed when I was a kid.

Presentation

Use *used to* to talk about …

- past habitual actions (things that happened regularly in the past): *I **used to** scream and run away.*

The past habitual action may or may not still be true in the present.

No longer true: *I used to run away from spiders, now I keep them as pets.*

Still true: *I used to scream when I saw a spider when I was a child, and I still do.*

- situations and states that are no longer true: *I **used to** hate spiders but I don't mind them now.*

You only use *used to* to talk about the past. You cannot use it to talk about the present.

Say *I don't **usually do** any work at the weekend.* (don't say *I don't ~~use to~~ do any work at the weekend.*)

You can also use the past simple to talk about past habits and situations:

*I **kept** spiders as pets.* (I used to keep spiders as pets.)

You do not use *used to* to talk about …

- a specific time or action in the past:

Say *I got up at six this morning.* (don't say *I ~~used to get up~~ at six this morning.*)

- the number of times something happened in total:

Say *We **went** to the zoo three times last year.* (don't say *We ~~used to go~~ to the zoo three times last year.*)

- when you say how long a single action or situation lasted:

Say *We **lived** in France for three years.* (don't say *We ~~used to live~~ in France for three years.*)

Affirmative and negative

I / You / He / She / It / We / They	used to didn't use to	keep spiders. like spiders.

Questions

Where	did	I / you / he / she / it / we / they	use to	keep the spiders?
	Did	I / you/ he / she / it / we / they	use to	be scared of spiders?

Short answers

Yes,	I / you / he / she / it / we / they	did.	No,	I / you / he / she / it / we / they	didn't.

TIP Be careful with the question and negative forms: there is no *-d* in *use to*:

*Did you **use to** have pets when you were in school?* (not *Did you ~~used~~ to …?*)

*I didn't **use to** like dogs when I was younger.* (not *I didn't ~~used~~ to …*)

Exercises

1 Choose the correct form.

 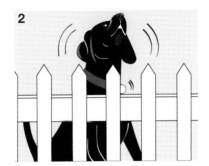 

1. When I was a kid, I [1] *used to / didn't use to* think there were monsters under my bed. I never [2] *used to / didn't use to* go to sleep until my mum had looked under the bed.

2. I [3] *used to / didn't use to* like dogs. Our neighbours had a big black dog that always [4] *used to / didn't use to* bark at me whenever I went near it. I [5] *used to / didn't use to* cross the road to get away from it.

3. I [6] *used to / didn't use to* like visiting my great aunt. She [7] *used to / didn't use to* have any toys for us to play with and she never [8] *used to / didn't use to* let us watch TV.

2 🔊 1.34 Complete the conversation using the correct form of *used to* and short answers. Then listen and check.

A: [1] _____ (you have) any pets when you were young?

B: Yes, we [2] _____ . We always [3] _____ (have) animals in the house: cats and dogs, and sometimes birds and fish too.

A: [4] _____ (you help) to look after them?

B: Yes, my dad said that we could only have pets if we promised to look after them. We [5] _____ (take) it in turns. My sister [6] _____ (not like) looking after the birds very much. She [7] _____ (be) scared they'd peck her.

3 Rewrite the sentences using *used to* where possible.

1. My brother kept snakes when he was younger. _My brother used to keep snakes._
2. He got his first snake when he was eight. _____
3. He kept them in a box in the garage. _____
4. He looked after them very well. _____
5. They lived there for almost six years. _____
6. Then he lost interest and he took them all to the local zoo. _____
7. He visited them there once a week. _____
8. I think he went about nine or ten times before he forgot about them. _____

4 Write about three things that used to be true for you when you were younger.

1. I used to _____ .
2. I didn't use to _____ .
3. I always used to _____ .

30 Review of units 26 to 29

Grammar

1 Choose the correct responses.

1 Did you go to university?
   a No, but I used to go to the local technical college.
   b Yes, I used to study Law at the university in Manchester for three years.

2 How long have you been studying English?
   a For a long time.
   b Since about five years.

3 Was it the first time you'd seen the sea?
   a No, my grandparents used to take me to the sea on holiday one summer.
   b No, my grandparents used to take me to the sea on holiday every summer.

4 Chris and Sue are getting married.
   a Really? How long have they been knowing each other?
   b Really? They haven't been dating for very long.

5 Pete won the tennis tournament again last week.
   a Great! How many times has he won it?
   b Great! How many championships has he been winning?

6 Did you see what happened?
   a No, the car was leaving before I got here.
   b No, the car had left before I got there.

7 I haven't seen you for ages. What have you been doing?
   a I've studied really hard. I've got exams next month.
   b I've been travelling a lot with work.

8 Did you enjoy the trip?
   a Yes, it was the most exciting thing I'd ever done.
   b Yes, I haven't done anything like that since a long time.

2 Complete the sentences with the present perfect simple, present perfect continuous or past perfect of the verbs. Sometimes more than one form is possible.

1 We _____ (know) each other since university.

2 They _____ (stay) at our house for the last three weeks.

3 He _____ (write) more than 40 books before his death two years ago.

4 They _____ (work) really hard all morning and they still haven't finished.

5 He _____ (write) two best-selling novels in the last twelve months.

6 He _____ (never eat) curry before he went to London.

7 They _____ (play) chess all morning.

8 He's really good. He _____ (play) against some of the best players in the world.

9 She _____ (never visit) Paris before and she instantly fell in love with the city.

3 Complete the second sentence so that it means the same as the first section.

1 He started studying five hours ago and is still studying.
   He's _____ for five hours.

2 He went to India and then he went to Japan.
   Before he went to Japan, _____ to India.

3 John went to the post office and he hasn't come back.
   John _____ to the post office.

4 I washed the car. The car is clean.
   I _____ the car.

5 I did an exam yesterday. I did another exam the day before. I had another exam today.
   I _____ three exams this week.

6 Every Sunday we visited my grandparents.
   We used _____ my grandparents every Sunday.

Grammar in context

4 **Complete the text with the correct answer a, b, or c.**

Here we are. We've almost reached the top of the volcano. ¹............... for six hours over ice and snow and we're really tired. The locals in the last village we visited ²............... it was going to be difficult. I had no idea how difficult! The air is thick with the smell of the smoke from the volcano. It's getting difficult to breathe. The volcano ³............... out small rocks at us ⁴............... the last hour or so. The last one came very close, but luckily the guide ⁵............... it coming and pulled me out of the way just in time. I ⁶............... volcanoes were magical and romantic. Now I just think they're dangerous! ⁷............... for this moment for ⁸............... and I certainly don't want to turn back now. But I can't help remembering that very few climbers have ever succeeded in getting to the top. A few years ago, two climbers had almost managed to reach the top when the volcano ⁹............... and covered them in lava. I know I've done some crazy things in my life, but I think this might just be one of the craziest!

1	**a** We walk	**b** We're walking	**c** We've been walking
2	**a** have told us	**b** used to tell us	**c** told us
3	**a** threw	**b** has been throwing	**c** is throwing
4	**a** for	**b** since	**c** during
5	**a** has seen	**b** used to see	**c** had seen
6	**a** 've thought	**b** 've been thinking	**c** used to think
7	**a** We'd waited	**b** We've been waiting	**c** We used to wait
8	**a** a long time	**b** last year	**c** many years ago
9	**a** has erupted	**b** had erupted	**c** erupted

Pronunciation: irregular past participles

5 🔊**1.35** **Write the past participles. Then listen and check.**

1	buy...............	7	teach...............
2	fly...............	8	throw...............
3	show...............	9	do...............
4	think...............	10	swim...............
5	bring...............	11	grow...............
6	run...............	12	win...............

6 🔊**1.36** **Listen again and write the past participles in the correct column.**

/ɔː/	/əʊ/	/ʌ/
bought	flown	done

Listen again

7 🔊**1.37** **Listen to the conversation. What do the numbers refer to?**

1 5 *He's been writing science fiction for 5 years.*

2 200 ....

3 40 ....

4 6 ....

31 Prepositions of time and place
in, on, at

Presentation

Use the prepositions *in, on* and *at* to talk about time and place.

	time	place
in	• parts of the day: *in the morning/afternoon/evening* • weeks: *in two weeks, in the second week of August* • months: *in August* • years: *in 2012* • seasons: *in the summer / in summer* • centuries: *in the 20th century*	• when we mean *inside* something: *in the house, in the car* • with towns, regions, countries, continents: *in London, in Texas, in France, in Africa* • common expressions: *in school, in a book, in the front/middle/back, in prison, in hospital*
on	• days: *on Saturday* • dates: *on 1st January* • special days: *on her birthday, on Christmas Day*	• surfaces of objects: *on the table, on the wall* • floors of a building: *on the fifth floor* • roads and water: *on the motorway* • types of scheduled or public transport: *on the bus, on the midday train* • attached objects: *the note is on the fridge, a leaf on a tree* • common expressions: *on a farm, on a train, on the plane, on the phone, on the TV*
at	• times of the day: *at 10 a.m., at midday* • these expressions: *at the weekend, at Christmas, at New Year, at night*	• a point in a journey: *We stopped at a pub for lunch.* • events with groups of people: *at a party, at a meeting* • addresses: *at 1600 Pennsylvania Avenue, Washington DC* • common expressions: *at home, at school, at work, at the front/back/side*

in or *at*?

With locations such as buildings, we use *in* to emphasise the location: *He's **in** the library.* (He's inside the library.)

You use *at* to emphasise the activity that takes place there: *He's doing some research **at** the library.*

TIP In everyday English you don't normally include prepositions of time and place in the question form:

Say *What year was she born?* (don't say *What year was she born ~~in~~?*)

Say *What day is your birthday?* (don't say *What day is your birthday ~~on~~?*)

Say *What time does it open?* (don't say *What time does it open ~~at~~?*)

Exercises

1 **Complete these sentences with a preposition of time (*in, on* or *at*).**

1 We like to eat outside _____ the evenings.
2 In my opinion, the motor car caused the biggest change _____ the twentieth century.
3 I was born _____ 11.15 _____ the morning.
4 _____ the spring we like to walk in the park and smell the flowers.
5 I'll be with my family _____ New Year.
6 I'll be with my family _____ New Year's Day.
7 President Barack Obama was born _____ 1961.
8 I won't be at school _____ Monday.
9 Long hair was very fashionable _____ 1973.
10 We always like to take a short holiday _____ April.

2 **Where are these people? Write full sentences with the verb *to be* + a preposition of place (*in, on* or *at*).**

1

2

3

4

5

6

1 he / a party   He's at a party.
2 they / the fifth floor
3 the tourist / Australia
4 the cars / motorway
5 my dog / the garden
6 Madge and Ron / their wedding

3 **🎧 1.38 Which lines in this conversation need a preposition (*in, on* or *at*)? Add any necessary prepositions. Then listen and check.**

A: 1 What time does the show begin? ✓

B: 2 It starts ∧^{at} seven thirty.

A: 3 When are the others coming?

B: 4 They're all meeting Felicity's house.

A: 5 Are they coming her car?

B: 6 No, they're coming the underground.

A: 7 I hope they aren't late for the main part of the show.

B: 8 Oh! There's a message my phone from Felicity.

A: 9 Where are they?

B: 10 They're the building now.

32 Prepositions of time
before, after, until, by, from … to … , for

Hours of Admission
We are open every day from 10 a.m. to 8 p.m. except on Sundays when we open at midday. No admissions after 7.30 p.m.

Extended hours for three months!
In the summer (June, July, August), the museum will be open until 10 p.m. on Saturday nights with live music in the museum park. Buy tickets for these concerts before 20th April and receive 20% off the ticket price. Some tickets are available on the day but you need to buy these by 2 p.m. Call the box office for further details.

Presentation

before, after

Use *before* to talk about actions or events leading to a point in time: *Buy tickets for these concerts **before** 20th April for a 20% discount.* (= You won't get a discount on or after 20th April.)

Use *after* to talk about actions or events following a point in time: *No admissions **after** 7.30 p.m.* (= You cannot enter later than 7.30 p.m.)

until (till)

Use *until* to talk about the period of time for an action or situation up to a point in time: *The museum will be open **until** 10 p.m.* (= the museum closes at 10 p.m.)

Till is an informal way to say *until*: *The museum will be open **till** 10 p.m.*

by

Use *by* to talk about a single event or situation happening *at* or *before* a point in time: *We need to open the museum **by** 10 a.m.* (= Because visitors expect to enter at 10 a.m.)

from … to …

Use *from … to …* to talk about when something begins and ends: *We are open every day **from** 10 a.m. **to** 8 p.m.*

You can also use *from … until/till …*:

*We are open every day **from** 10 a.m. **until** 8 p.m.*

*We are open every day **from** 10 a.m. **till** 8 p.m.*

for

Use *for* to talk about periods of time: *There will be longer opening hours **for** three months.*

Exercises

1 Match 1–6 to a–f.

A

1 The film this afternoon doesn't start   [d]
2 If we want a good seat, we need to be there   [ ]
3 I work really late. I never get home   [ ]
4 The shop is open every day from nine to   [ ]
5 We don't go out much   [ ]
6 Can you take messages for the rest of the day? I'm going out   [ ]

B

a five.
b by a quarter to seven.
c for the whole afternoon.
d ~~until five.~~
e during the winter.
f till ten or even later sometimes.

2 Read the information about an art gallery. Choose the correct preposition.

Art Gallery

OPENING HOURS

The gallery is open every day ¹ *until / from* 9 a.m. ² *before / to* 8 p.m. On Saturdays, exhibitions continue ³ *by / until* 11 p.m. The ticket office closes at 7.15 p.m. There are no admissions ⁴ *before / after* this time.

BOOK TICKETS ONLINE

Buy your tickets from this website ⁵ *before / after* your visit and you will receive a 10% discount.

SPECIAL FAMILY DAY!

Why not try being an artist ⁶ *for / before* a day? On 23rd July, parents and children can join in our summer family art experience. ⁷ *Before / For* the whole day (11 a.m. – 5 p.m.) there will be art classes and the chance to create your own masterpieces! Places are limited so be sure to reserve tickets ⁸ *until / by* 20th July at the latest.

3 🔊 1.39 Two organisers are discussing the schedule for opening a new exhibition. Complete their conversation with the prepositions in the box. Then listen and check.

after before by during for from to

Opening event

7.30–8.00   Guests arrive

8.00   Speech by artists

8.15–10.00   Exhibition of paintings and buffet

A: OK. So here's the schedule. As you can see the guests need to arrive ¹_____ 8 p.m. at the latest.

B: Why at eight?

A: Because they have to be here ²_____ the artists give their speeches.

B: Of course. So then the artists speak ³_____ everyone has arrived and then the main exhibition is ⁴_____ eight fifteen ⁵_____ ten o'clock.

A: That's right.

B: What about food? When does everyone eat?

A: The guests can eat ⁶_____ the exhibition.

B: Good idea. So the whole event lasts ⁷_____ two and a half hours.

A: Yes. Do you think that's too long?

33 Prepositions of place

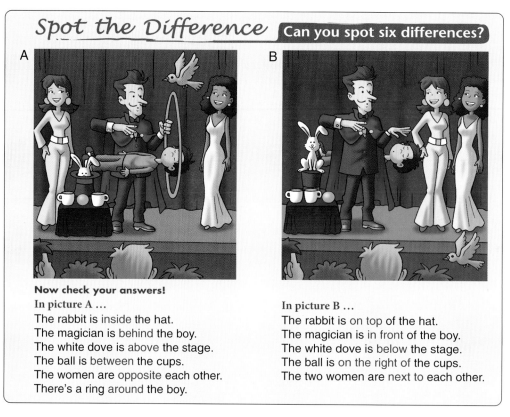

Spot the Difference — Can you spot six differences?

A

B

Now check your answers!

In picture A ...
The rabbit is inside the hat.
The magician is behind the boy.
The white dove is above the stage.
The ball is between the cups.
The women are opposite each other.
There's a ring around the boy.

In picture B ...
The rabbit is on top of the hat.
The magician is in front of the boy.
The white dove is below the stage.
The ball is on the right of the cups.
The two women are next to each other.

Presentation

We use prepositions of place to answer the question *Where is it?*

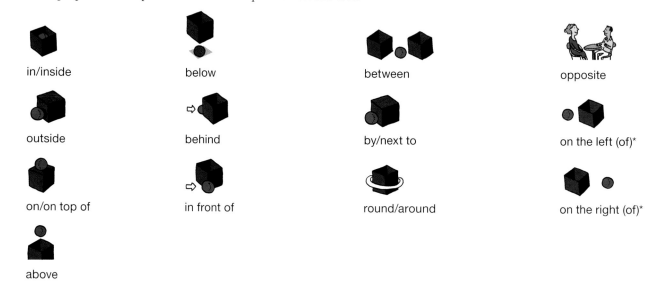

in/inside	below	between	opposite
outside	behind	by/next to	on the left (of)*
on/on top of	in front of	round/around	on the right (of)*
above			

TIP

- * In answer to the question: *Where's the ball?* Say *It's on the left of the cup. It's on the left.* (don't say *It's on the left of.*)
- You often say *in*, *on* and *round* instead of *inside*, *on top of* and *around* when you are speaking.

Exercises

1 **Complete the sentences with a preposition of place.**

1 The man is _above_ the people.

2 The lion is _____ a ball.

3 The shop is _____ the circus tent.

4 The clown is _____ the strong man.

5 They're _____ each other.

6 His head is _____ the lion's mouth.

7 He's _____ the elephants.

8 He's _____ the car.

2 **Choose the correct answer a, b, or c.**

1 The cat's still _____. Let it in.
   a outside   b inside   c above

2 I think that car _____ you wants to get past.
   a in front of   b behind   c between

3 We're putting a fence _____ our house.
   a at   b above   c around

4 I'm feeling _____ of the world today. I've never felt better!
   a on the right   b on top   c on the left

5 The bank is _____ so let's cross the road here.
   a next to   b by   c opposite

6 In the photograph you can see Ralph when he was six. He's _____ his two sisters.
   a between   b around   c round

7 Don't let them sit _____ each other. They'll cause trouble.
   a in front of   b between   c next to

8 In the majority of countries the driver sits _____.
   a on the right   b on the left   c on the top

3 **Where are you reading this? Describe the location with these sentences and a preposition.**

1 I'm reading this *in / on / by* _____.

2 I'm sitting *next to / between / in front of* _____.

34 Prepositions of movement

There's a great new ride at the theme park. It's called Niagara. At the beginning you get into a car and it moves along really slowly. Then you go up a hill and suddenly you're travelling down at an incredible speed. Next you're coming towards a mountain. You go around a huge rock and you think you're going to crash, but at the last minute the mountain opens and you drive through a dark tunnel. When you come out of the mountain the car falls off the end of the track and you drop into a huge lake. You get so wet. Then, amazingly, the car floats across the lake and sails away.

Presentation

Use prepositions of movement to talk about the direction of the movement:

*It moves **along**. You go **up** the hill. You're travelling **down**.*

Prepositions of movement usually follow a verb of movement, for example: *go, travel, get, put, walk, run, dive, fall, come, move, sail, float, drive.*

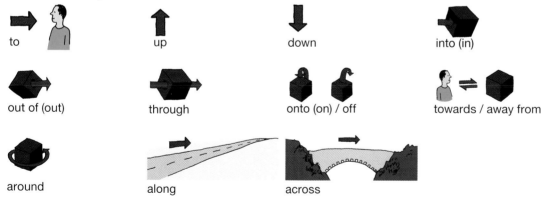

You sometimes use *in/out* for *into/out of* and *on* for *onto* when speaking informally:

*We got into the car = We got **in** the car.*

Note that *into* and *out of* must be followed by a noun.

Say *We got in the car. We got into the car. We got in.* (don't say *We got ~~into~~.*)

Exercises

1 🔊**1.40** **Choose the correct prepositions. Then listen and check.**

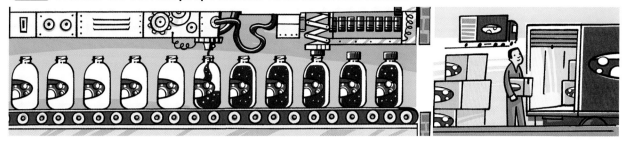

Good morning and thank you for coming. Welcome to our factory. First of all the bottles move ¹ *along / across* this conveyor belt and the cola comes ² *out of / towards* this tap and ³ *onto / into* the bottles. Next, we put caps ⁴ *onto / to* the bottles. After that, the bottles go ⁵ *up / through* this hole in the wall to the warehouse. We load them ⁶ *off / onto* the lorries and the driver takes them ⁷ *along / away*.

2 **Complete the sentences with the present continuous form of the verbs and the prepositions in the box.**

| climb dive drive fall ~~float~~ get put run |
| swim take travel walk |

| across ~~along~~ around away down into |
| off onto out of through towards up |

1 The boat is *floating along* the river.

2 The comet _____ the planet.

3 He _____ the statue _____ this plinth.

4 He _____ .

5 He _____ his car.

6 She _____ a tunnel.

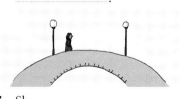

7 She _____ the bridge.

8 The criminal _____ from the police officer.

9 They _____ the mountain.

10 The girl _____ the board.

11 He _____ the statue _____ the box.

12 The sharks _____ the boat.

35 Review of units 31 to 34

Grammar

1 Complete the pairs of sentences with the same preposition.

1 a The meeting starts __at__ 2 p.m.

  b She lives __at__ 99 Crescent Road.

2 a We're open seven days a week from seven _____ eleven.

  b How do you get _____ the train station from here?

3 a Your keys are _____ the table.

  b My favourite TV show is _____ Thursday.

4 a See you again _____ two weeks.

  b The keys are _____ your coat pocket.

5 a Your umbrella is _____ the door.

  b You need to let them know _____ the end of today.

6 a The bus leaves _____ the station.

  b He works _____ 10 a.m. until 6 p.m. every day.

2 Is the meaning in each pair of sentences the same (S) or different (D)?

1 a She goes to St Medes School for girls.

  b She's at St Medes School for girls. _____

2 a Tickets are available until midnight.

  b Tickets are not available after midnight. _____

3 a We'll be there from two till five.

  b We'll be there for three hours. _____

4 a Sorry the traffic's bad. We won't get there by five.

  b Sorry the traffic's bad. We won't get there until five. _____

5 a John's in hospital. But he's coming home later today.

  b John's at the hospital. But he'll be home later. _____

6 a I'm working nights for the whole of this week.

  b I'm working nights until the beginning of next week. _____

3 Complete this message for a friend using this map. Use the prepositions in the box.

| across   along   in front of   on the left |
| out of   over   towards |

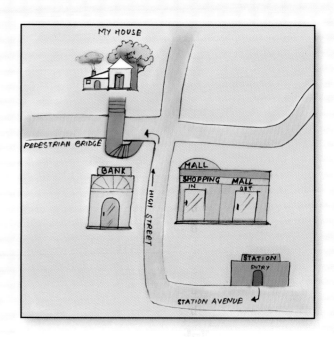

Come ¹ .... the station and

walk ² .... Station Avenue.

Go ³ .... the High Street

⁴ .... the shopping mall.

The bank is ⁵ .... Go

⁶ .... the pedestrian bridge

and my house is ⁷ .... you.

Grammar in context

4 Complete the text with the correct answer a, b or c.

UFO over town centre

[1] __c__ ten-thirty [2]_____ Saturday night, the whole population of Over-by-Marsh was standing [3]_____ the town square. Police officers stopped and got [4]_____ their cars but not to arrest anyone. Everyone was looking [5]_____ into the night sky at five bright lights which seemed to be travelling slowly [6]_____ the earth. Tom Lawless was one of the people. 'We were [7]_____ the restaurant but ran [8]_____ when we heard what was happening. There were four lights and then another one flew [9]_____ the sky to the others. After an hour or so they started moving [10]_____ from us so [11]_____ midnight we couldn't see them anymore.'
The following morning, local people got [12]_____ to find that their town was busy again – this time with journalists and TV news reporters!

1	a In	b On	c At	7	a out	b in	c on
2	a in	b on	c at	8	a outside	b inside	c out of
3	a in	b on	c at	9	a onto	b off	c across
4	a away	b into	c out of	10	a towards	b away	c down
5	a up	b down	c across	11	a until	b by	c to
6	a along	b across	c towards	12	a down	b into	c up

Pronunciation: linking sounds 2

5 English speakers often link two words together. If one word ends with a consonant sound and the next word begins with a vowel sound they often sound like one word.

🔊1.41 Listen and notice the linking in sentences 1 and 2. Then listen and draw the linking in sentences 3 to 9.

1 Put‿it‿in this box.
2 Drive‿along this road.
3 It's in five minutes.
4 I'm on top of the world.
5 The lifeguard dived into the water.
6 Don't run away!
7 Walk up Rupert Street.
8 We're at home until ten.
9 It came across the sky.

Then listen again and repeat the sentences.

Listen again

6 🔊1.42 Listen. Are these statements about the schedule true (T) or false (F)?

1 The guests cannot arrive before 8 p.m. _____
2 The speeches are after everyone arrives. _____
3 The speeches last fifteen minutes. _____
4 Everyone eats at 8.15 p.m. _____
5 The exhibition ends at 2.30 p.m. _____

36 Imperatives

Police officer:	Stop! This is a one way street!
Man:	Sorry, but I'm lost. I need Welbeck Street.
Police officer:	OK. Turn the car around. Go up this street and turn right.
Man:	Thank you very much.
Police officer:	You're welcome. But be more careful next time.

Man:	Hi, sorry I'm late.
Woman:	Don't worry. Did you have problems finding us?
Man:	Yes!
Woman:	Relax! Have a seat and tell me about it.

Presentation

No subject is used with the imperative. *You* (singular or plural) is the missing subject.

Affirmative

Stop
——————— here.
Turn

Negative

Don't
  stop
  —————— here.
  turn

Use the imperative form for …

- Giving orders: *Stop!*
- Giving instructions and directions: *Go up this street and turn right.*
- Requesting: *Please help me.*
- Warning: *Be more careful.*
- Giving advice or making suggestions: *Relax.*
- Inviting: *Come to the cinema with us. Come for a drink.*
- Requests and offers (informal): *Come in! Have a seat.*

Exercises

1 **Match the imperatives 1–7 to the situations a–g.**

1	Look out!	`c`	a	You are angry with your children for breaking something.
2	Slow down.		b	You have just read something interesting in the newspaper.
3	Hold on a moment.		c	A brick is falling from a building.
4	Be more careful!		d	A teacher can't hear a student very well.
5	Speak up, please.		e	You ask someone to wait on the phone.
6	Listen to this!		f	A librarian speaks to some noisy children.
7	Be quiet, please.		g	You are breaking the speed limit in your car.

2 **Make these sentences into the shortest possible imperative expressions.**

1   You need to stop the car now! *Stop!*
2   Can you pass me the salt, please? *Pass the salt, please.*
3   Would you mind holding this, please? ....
4   You don't need to say anything to them. ....
5   You ought to take more exercise. ....
6   You press this button when you want to switch the computer on. ....
7   I want you all to help me with this. ....
8   You're running across the road. Don't do it. It's dangerous. ....

3 **① 1.43** **Complete the advice with the affirmative or negative form of the verbs in the box. Then listen and check.**

do   drink   eat   get up   go   have   relax   switch   take

How to get a good night's sleep

1 ....*Take*........ a long walk before you go to bed.
2 .... some relaxing exercises or yoga.
3 .... too much before bedtime. A full stomach stops you sleeping.
If you have a TV in the bedroom, 4 .... it on!
5 .... to bed and 6 .... at regular times.
If you can't sleep, 7 .... in a warm bath or 8 .... a hot drink
but 9 .... anything with caffeine.

4 **Write a similar 'How to . . .' text. Give advice on something you know about. For example: *How to get healthy.***

37 Phrasal verbs 1
Transitive and intransitive verbs

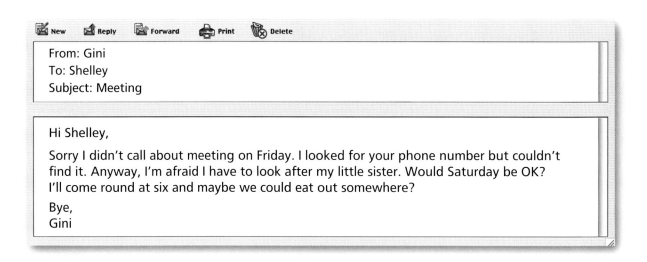

New   Reply   Forward   Print   Delete

From: Gini
To: Shelley
Subject: Meeting

Hi Shelley,

Sorry I didn't call about meeting on Friday. I looked for your phone number but couldn't find it. Anyway, I'm afraid I have to look after my little sister. Would Saturday be OK? I'll come round at six and maybe we could eat out somewhere?

Bye,
Gini

Presentation

A phrasal verb is a verb + a particle:

*I've been **looking for** your phone number.*

*I have to **look after** my younger sister.*

When you combine the verb with a particle, it creates a new meaning:

***Look** at this picture.* (= direct your eyes towards something)

*I've been **looking for** your phone number.* (= try to find something in different places)

*I have to **look after** my younger sister.* (= take care of someone)

TIP It can be difficult to guess the meaning of a phrasal verb by trying to understand the meaning of the verb and particle separately. Learn them as one word.

Common verbs in phrasal verbs include: *bring, call, come, get, give, go, keep, look, make, pick, put, run, set, take, turn*

Common particles in phrasal verbs include: *about, round, at, away, back, down, for, in, into, off, on, out through, to up*

See page 239: Common phrasal verbs.

Transitive or intransitive?

Many phrasal verbs need a <u>direct object</u>. They are **transitive verbs**:

*I've been **looking for** <u>your phone number</u>.*

*I have to **look after** <u>my younger sister</u>.*

Some phrasal verbs do not take a direct object. They are **intransitive verbs**:

*I'll **come round** at six.*

*Maybe we could **eat out** somewhere.*

Common intransitive verbs: *call round, come back, come round, eat out, get away, get on, get up, go down, go up, grow up, log in, look out, look up, take off*

TIP A good dictionary will tell you if a phrasal verb is transitive or intransitive. For example, the *Collins Cobuild Advanced Dictionary* provides this information with the symbols v (verb), p (particle), n (noun):

look after [v p n] = look after is transitive because the verb and particle must be followed by a noun.

go out [v p] = go out is intransitive because there is no noun after the verb and particle.

See page 239: Common transitive and intransitive phrasal verbs.

Exercises

1 **Complete the sentences with the phrasal verbs in the box.**

pick up   come back   call round   wake up   look after   put on   take off

1 _____! It's time for school.

2 Don't forget to _____ a coat. It's cold outside.

3 _____ your clothes.

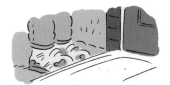

4 _____ those dirty shoes!

5 Can you _____ your sister while I go to the shops?

6 I don't want any of your friends to _____ until you've done all your homework.

7 _____ here this minute!

2 **Choose the correct particles.**

1 When can I come *at / round / to* for tea?
2 I'm looking *for / after / at* your house. Where is it?
3 The temperature goes *up / away / down* in the summer.
4 Turn *up / out / down* the TV. It's too loud.
5 Look *to / off / out*! It's going to fall on your head.
6 Don't give *up / out / off*. Keep trying.
7 Have you picked *on / off / out* the one you want yet?
8 The plane is about to take *away / off / up*.

3 **Categorise all the phrasal verbs in exercises 1 and 2 as transitive or intransitive.**

Transitive (verb + particle + direct object): _____

Intransitive (verb + particle): _____

4 **Answer these questions so that they are true for you. Write complete sentences.**

1 What time do you wake up? _____.
2 How often do you eat out? _____.
3 Do you look after anyone or anything? (e.g. a younger brother or sister, a pet) _____.
4 How well do you get on with your neighbours? _____.

38 Phrasal verbs 2
Separable and inseparable phrasal verbs

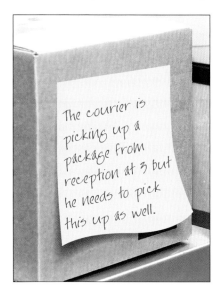

Presentation

Many phrasal verbs are transitive and they need a direct object (see unit 37). Transitive phrasal verbs can be separable or inseparable.

Separable phrasal verbs

With separable phrasal verbs the direct object can go before or after the particle:

The courier is picking up a package.

The courier is picking a package up.

Common separable verbs: *bring up, give away, give out, give up, pay out, pick out, put in, put on, set up, turn down, turn off, take over, turn up*

If the direct object is a pronoun, it must go before the particle:

Say *The courier is picking it up.* (don't say *The courier is picking up it.*)

A few transitive verbs are only separable. The direct object must always go before the particle:

Say *Can you ring Shannon back?* (don't say *Can you ring back Shannon?*)

Other verbs like this include: *ask (someone) over, get (someone) up, see (someone) around.*

Inseparable phrasal verbs

Some phrasal verbs are inseparable. The direct object must go after the participle. It cannot go between the verb and the particle:

Say *Please look after Mr Wu for a few minutes.* (don't say *Please look Mr Wu after for a few minutes.*)

Say *Please look after him for a few minutes.* (don't say *Please look him after for a few minutes.*)

Common inseparable verbs: *come across, go through, look after, look for*

TIP A good dictionary will tell you if a phrasal verb is separable or inseparable. For example, the *Collins Cobuild Advanced Dictionary* provides this information with the symbols v (verb), p (particle), n (noun):

pick up [v n p] and [v p n] = the phrasal verb *pick up*, the noun can follow the verb and particle [v n p] or it can also separate the verb and the particle [v p n]

ring up [v n p] = *ring up* is only separable because the noun [n] is between the verb [v] and the particle [p].

look after [v p n] = *look after* is inseparable because the noun [n] comes after the verb [v] and the particle [p].

See page 239: Common separable and inseparable phrasal verbs.

Exercises

1 Choose the correct options. Both answers are possible in some questions.

¹Log onto my computer / Log my computer onto and ²look the file for / look for the file marked EXPO.

Alex might call. ³Take down his number / Take his number down and I'll ⁴call him back / call back him.

If Donald Sterling arrives, please ⁵look after him / look him after until I get back from lunch. Perhaps you could ⁶take out him / take him out for a coffee.

Julia's leaving on Friday. Can you ⁷pick a nice present out / pick out a nice present for her.

Can we ⁸set up a meeting / set a meeting up about the conference? Is tomorrow OK?

2 Put the words in order. Sometimes there are two possible answers.

1 pick I'll up Melanie
   I'll pick up Melanie.
   I'll pick Melanie up.

2 mother after baby is looking the my
   My mother is looking after the baby.

3 new looking for apartment we're a
   ....

4 me these let sunglasses on put
   ....

5 across he old came an photograph
   ....

6 stupid off that hat take
   ....

7 the up her number in look phone book
   ....

3 🔊 **1.44 Write the missing pronouns *it* and *them* in the conversation. Then listen and check.**

A: ¹Can you call Mandy and Paul back?

B: ²Why do I have to call ˄them back?

A: ³They want to go through your offer again.

B: ⁴But we've already gone through.

A: ⁵But I think they want to bring up the cost. There's a problem.

B: ⁶Not again. They brought up last time.

39 Verbs with two objects

Are you a good friend?

Do this quiz and find out. Read each situation and circle your answer.

1 You take a very embarrassing photograph of your friend.

   A You give the only copy to your friend.

   B You show the photograph to your friend and promise not to show it to anyone else.

   C You email it to everyone you know!

2 You're having a romantic evening with a new boyfriend / girlfriend. Suddenly your best friend calls. His / Her car has broken down ten kilometres away.

   A Drive to your friend and give him / her a lift home.

   B You order your friend a taxi.

   C You give your best friend the number of a local mechanic.

3 Your best friend was at parties all weekend and didn't study for the geography test on Monday morning.

   A You show him / her your answers during the test.

   B You lend him / her your notes.

   C Don't help but wish him / her good luck!

Mainly As = I'd like to be your best friend! Mainly Bs = You are a good friend. Mainly Cs = I wouldn't want to meet your enemies!

Presentation

You can use two objects, a direct object and an indirect object with some verbs:

You show the photograph to your friend .

You give your friend a lift home.

Add the prepositions *to* or *for* to the indirect object if it comes after the direct object:

You give the only copy to him.

You make a copy for him.

You can also put the indirect object before the direct object but don't add the preposition *to* or *for*:

You give your best friend the number. (don't say *You give to your best friend the number.*)

You show her your answers during the test.

If the direct and indirect objects are pronouns, you can put them in either order (but don't forget to include *to* or *for*):

*You show him it and promise not to show it **to** anyone else.*

*You show it **to** him and promise not to show anyone else it .*

These verbs often have two objects: *bring, play, lend, pay, give, show, wish, email, write, promise, buy, get, leave, make, pass, teach, tell*

Exercises

1 Complete the sentences with the pairs of words.

get + another one   tell + your answer   show + me   play + tune   a letter + my mother

wish + a Happy Birthday

1 We _____ you _____ .

2 I'm writing _____ to _____ .

3 Can you _____ me _____ , please?

4 _____ me for number two.

5 _____ your driving licence, please.

6 _____ me a little _____ .

2 Rewrite these sentences. Put the direct object before the indirect object. Use the preposition *to* or *for*.

1 I bought you these flowers.
   I bought these flowers for you .

2 Lend me your car, please.
   Lend _____ , please.

3 I think you should pay the salesman the full price.
   I think you should pay _____ .

4 Play the children a song by The Beatles.
   Play _____ .

5 We're making you dinner.
   We're making _____ .

6 Julia can get everyone a drink.
   Julia can get _____ .

7 Today I'm teaching my students some grammar.
   Today I'm teaching _____ .

8 Leave Martin the report.
   Leave _____ .

40 Review of units 36 to 39

Grammar

1 Match the two halves of the sentences.

A

1 Press the small green button   `e`
2 Take a photo ☐
3 Don't forget to ☐
4 Dial the number ☐
5 Push ☐

B

a by pressing the large button.
b for customer services and then ask to speak to the assistant.
c this button to record a message.
d recharge the phone every 48 hours.
e ~~to switch it on.~~

Help!
Use the list of phrasal verbs in appendix 5 on page 239 to complete exercises 2, 3, 4 and 5.

2 Write the word in brackets in the correct position in sentences 1–12. Where there are two possible positions, show both.

1 Can you email ʌ back to me? (it) *(it above ʌ)*
2 When are you going to write a letter? (me)
3 Please look after for a moment. (this)
4 Can you give these keys him? (to)
5 Turn off and go outside and play! (that)
6 Don't tell my number. (anyone)
7 Have you picked a book? (out)
8 Tell me. (your news)
9 I made this sweater you. (for)
10 Look it on the internet. (up)
11 Put on. It's cold. (a coat)
12 Let me take all your details. (down)

3 For each sentence (1–8), match a verb with a particle to make the phrasal verb. Use the definition in brackets to help you. Change the form or tense where necessary.

come   pick   take   go   turn   set   give   get

out   through   off   out   up   away   across   up

1 I was putting some books away when I _____ (find by accident) the first book I ever read!
2 The criminals never _____ (escape) in these old detective films.
3 Can you _____ (distribute to people) these leaflets to people walking by?
4 Make sure you _____ (choose) something you really like.
5 Bill Gates _____ (start a business) Microsoft in 1975.
6 Let me _____ (study or examine) your application and I'll make a decision.
7 I want to listen to the news. _____ (increase volume) the radio!
8 _____ (remove) your glasses and I'll check your eyes.

4 In each sentence there is one word which should not be there. Delete it.

1 Come in! ~~You~~ take a seat.
2 This is interesting. I came this across it in the newspaper.
3 Take it off your coat.
4 Pass to me the salt.
5 That child is running across the road. Look out him!
6 Make for your grandmother a cup of tea.
7 Can you give to the bag to John?
8 I've prepared your favourite meal for to you.

Grammar in context

5 **Complete the text with the correct form of the verbs in the box.**

~~take~~	grew	come	eat	set	log	look

How social networking grew up

NOWADAYS it seems as if social networking sites have [1] _taken_ **over** the internet AND our social lives. Everyone is on the web these days – even the rich and famous. [2] _____ **up** the name of your favourite celebrity on MySpace.com and you'll [3] _____ **across** information such as where Madonna likes to [4] _____ **out** or a download of U2's latest song.

Chris DeWolfe and Tom Anderson were some of the social networking pioneers when they [5] _____ **up** MySpace in 2002. Within months, millions of visitors were [6] _____ **on** every day. In 2006 the News Corporation paid 580 million dollars for the site. From being a meeting place for friends, social networking sites had finally [7] _____ **up** and become big business.

Pronunciation: intrusive /w/

6 🔊**1.45** **If one word ends with a vowel sound and the next word begins with a vowel sound, some speakers link them with a /w/ sound:**

/w/

Go_in through the front door.

Listen to these sentences. Where is the /w/ sound?

1   We wish you a Happy Birthday.
2   We always go out on Tuesdays.
3   Don't go away!
4   You ask him to help you.
5   Go up this hill and turn left.
6   Give the books to Arthur.

Listen again

7 🔊**1.46** **Listen and answer the questions.**

1   What should you do outside before you go to bed?

2   What can you do as well as doing some exercise?

3   What can stop you sleeping?

4   What do you need to switch off?

5   When should you go to bed or get up?

6   Where can you relax if you can't sleep?

7   What should you drink?

41 Position and order of adjectives

Presentation

There are two common positions for adjectives in sentences: after copula verbs and before nouns.

Adjectives after copula verbs

Copula verbs are also called linking verbs. They link the subject of the sentence with a description of the subject. The most common copula verbs include *be, appear, look, feel, sound, smell, taste, become, seem, get.* Adjectives come after these verbs to describe the subject.

Your dress looks ***awful!***

*I feel **great**.*

The design is *Italian*.

Some adjectives can only come after the verb. Many of these begin with *a-*, e.g., *asleep, afraid, alone, awake, alive*:

*Are the children **awake** yet?*

Order of adjectives after copula verbs

When you use more than one adjective after a verb, you usually add *and* between the last two adjectives:

*They look cold, tired **and** hungry.*

There is no rule for word order with adjectives joined by *and*. However, some adjectives are placed according to convention: *tall, dark and handsome* (not ~~handsome, dark and tall~~.)

Adjectives before nouns

When you use adjectives with a noun, the adjective comes before the noun:

Say *I like your **new** dress.* (don't say *I like your ~~dress new~~.*)

When the noun is plural, the adjective doesn't change:

Say *I love your **black** boots.* (don't say *I love your ~~blacks boots~~.*)

Order of adjectives before nouns

You can use more than one adjective before the noun:

*Dorothy put on her **red, Italian** dress.*

When you use more than one adjective before the noun, you usually place them in this order:

opinion	size/shape	age	colour	origin/nationality	material	noun
			red	Italian		dress
awful			blue			shoes
		old			wooden	wardrobe
beautiful	tall					woman

When you use more than one adjective, you normally use two or three at the most. If you want to use four, you use two sentences.

Say *That's a **beautiful, old, wooden** wardrobe. It's **English**.* (don't say *That's a **beautiful, old, ~~English~~, wooden** wardrobe.*)

Use commas in sentences with more than one adjective: *It's a beautiful, old, wooden wardrobe.*

When you have two adjectives before the noun referring to the same feature (e.g. colour, origin), use *and*:

Say *My grandfather still watches a black and white TV.* (don't say *My grandfather still watches a ~~black, white~~ TV.*)

TIP The choice of word order is often based on convention: *a black and white TV* (not *a ~~white and black~~ TV*)

Exercises

1 Put the words in order.

1 here your is new assistant ....

2 cars these look new ....

3 dress that's nice a ....

4 him is for chocolate hot the ....

5 sale is the house big for ....

6 sounds idea good your ....

2 Correct the mistakes.

beautiful, blue, silk

1 This is Monika and she's wearing a ~~beautiful, silk, blue~~ shirt.

2 Item number 112 is a metal, stylish, French table and chairs. Let's start the bidding at £100.

3 It's an old, brick, attractive house in the centre of the city.

4 That's her over there. She's with that dark, tall, Russian-looking man.

3 Combine the sentences to make one sentence.

1 I left an old hat here. It's black and very large.
   I left *a very large, old, black hat here.*

2 Their new dog is a puppy. It's really cute and little.
   Their new dog is ....

3 Would you like to try on this stylish suit? It's woollen.
   Would you like to try on .... ?

4 Spend your next holiday on an island. It's exotic.
   Spend your next holiday on ....

5 We're looking for a tall filing cabinet. We need it in metal and we'd like a black one.
   We're looking for ....

6 You have a large apartment. It's modern.
   You have a ....

93

42 Participles as adjectives
Dependent prepositions

Are you bored of reading film reviews by so-called experts and critics? Then let the world know what you think. Review the latest films.

MANHUNT 10
'The main actor looks tired in this and the film was so boring!!!'
Nigel, UK

BOLLYWOOD ROMEO
'I was surprised how much I liked this. Loads of great music and dancing and even the script is amusing.'
Raj, Delhi

NIGHT OF THE GHOSTS
'It was very frightening and I was shocked at the violence. Don't take your mother!'
Melanie, Melbourne

Presentation

The present participle (verb + -ing) and past participle (verb + -ed) forms of some verbs can be used as adjectives:

to bore – boring – bored

to frighten – frightening – frightened

Present participles as adjectives

Use **present participles** as adjectives to describe **the person or thing** that makes you feel a certain way:

*The film was **boring**.*

*Dracula is a very **frightening** book.*

> **Common present participles as adjectives:**
>
> *amusing, annoying, boring, confusing, convincing, depressing, disappointing, embarrassing, exciting, frustrating, interesting, pleasing, relaxing, satisfying, shocking, surprising, terrifying, tiring, worrying*

Past participles as adjectives

Use **past participles** as adjectives to describe **how you feel** about someone or something:

*He was **bored** of work.*

*I was **surprised** how much I liked this.*

Say *I'm **bored** (of this film).* (don't say *I'm ~~boring~~ (of this film)*.

Say *This film is **boring**.* (don't say *This film is ~~bored~~*.)

> **Common past participles as adjectives:**
>
> *amused, annoyed, bored, confused, convinced, depressed, disappointed, embarrassed, excited, frustrated, interested, pleased, relaxed, satisfied, scared, shocked, surprised, terrified, tired, worried*

Dependent prepositions

-ed adjectives are often followed by dependent prepositions:

*Are you excited about **the show** tonight?*

Dependent prepositions are followed by either nouns or gerunds:

*I'm tired of **working** on this.*

> **Common past -ed adjectives and their dependent prepositions:**
>
> *annoyed with, bored with, excited about, fascinated by, frightened of, interested in, irritated by, pleased with, satisfied with, scared of, tired of, terrified of, worried about*

Exercises

1 Choose the correct adjectives in the film reviews.

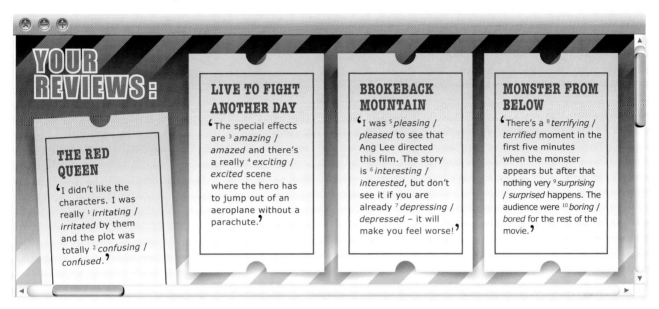

YOUR REVIEWS:

THE RED QUEEN
'I didn't like the characters. I was really ¹ *irritating / irritated* by them and the plot was totally ² *confusing / confused*.'

LIVE TO FIGHT ANOTHER DAY
'The special effects are ³ *amazing / amazed* and there's a really ⁴ *exciting / excited* scene where the hero has to jump out of an aeroplane without a parachute.'

BROKEBACK MOUNTAIN
'I was ⁵ *pleasing / pleased* to see that Ang Lee directed this film. The story is ⁶ *interesting / interested*, but don't see it if you are already ⁷ *depressing / depressed* – it will make you feel worse!'

MONSTER FROM BELOW
'There's a ⁸ *terrifying / terrified* moment in the first five minutes when the monster appears but after that nothing very ⁹ *surprising / surprised* happens. The audience were ¹⁰ *boring / bored* for the rest of the movie.'

2 🔊 **1.47** Two people are discussing a holiday. Complete their conversations with the present or past participle form of the verbs in the box. Then listen and check.

amuse   annoy   depress   embarrass   interest   please   ~~relax~~

A: So, how was your holiday?

B: Great. It was so ¹ <u>relaxing</u>. I didn't think about work once. And I was really
² _____ with the hotel. The service was five star.

A: And what were the other people like in your group?

B: Everyone was really nice except for one person. She was really
³ _____ because she wouldn't stop talking. But apart from her
it was fine.

A: And did you meet anyone ⁴ _____?

B: Well, there was one man I enjoyed talking to. He was a friendly waiter
at the hotel.

A: Really?

B: He also told jokes and was very ⁵ _____. He made everyone laugh. And on the last
night he asked me to dance and everyone was watching us.

A: Were you ⁶ _____?

B: Yes, I was! I went bright red but it was wonderful! Then I flew home the next day and it was raining.
I'm so ⁷ _____ to be home.

3 Add a preposition to make complete sentences.

1 elephants / frighten / mice
   <u>Elephants are frightened of mice.</u>

2 my children / excite / the holidays
   _____

3 my best friend / interest / the books of JRR Tolkien
   _____

4 are you / worry / leave / home?
   _____

43 Adjectives and adverbs
Adverbs of manner

friendbook — What are you doing right now?

Richard: The weather isn't very good and I'm a bit ill. I'm going back to bed.

Julia: My exams went well yesterday so I'm having a quiet day today!

Sandy: I had a late night so I got up late and I'm drinking my morning coffee slowly.

Presentation

Adjectives and adverbs

Use adjectives to describe nouns:

*The **weather** isn't very **good**.*

*I'm having a **slow day**.*

Use adverbs of manner to describe verbs, to say how you do something or how something happens:

*My exams **went well** yesterday.*

*I'm **drinking** my coffee **slowly**.*

-ly adverbs

You can add -ly to many adjectives to make them into adverbs: *slowly → slowly, quick → quickly, quiet → quietly, loud → loudly, bad → badly*

Key spelling rules

Normally you add -ly to the adjective. Also note:

* adjectives ending in -l: *beautiful → beautifully* (not ~~beautifuly~~)
* adjectives ending in -y: *happy → happily*
* adjective ending in -ble: *horrible → horribly*

See page 233: Spelling rules

adjectives or adverbs?

Some adjectives and adverbs have the same form.

*I had a **late** night* (*late* is an adjective).

*I got up **late*** (*late* is an adverb).

Other adjectives / adverbs like this include:

*He's a **fast** runner. / Run **fast**!*

*She always has an **early** breakfast. / She gets up **early**.*

good or well?

Good is an adjective and *well* is the adverb: *My exam results were **good**. / My exams went **well**.*

However, *well* can also be an adjective (to talk about health): *I don't feel very **well**.* (= *I feel **ill**.*)

Position of adverbs of manner

An adverb of manner often comes …

* after the object: *He plays **the guitar brilliantly**.*
* after the verb if there is no object: *He can **play brilliantly**.* (don't say *He ~~plays brilliantly~~ the guitar.*)

With questions, the adverb comes after *how*: ***How well** can you play?*

See Unit 7 for more information on position of adverbs.

hard / hardly, late / lately

The adjectives *hard* and *late* have two different adverb forms:

hard → hard / hardly

*My father works **hard**.*

*My father **hardly** works.* (hardly = almost not at all)

late → late / lately

*This train always arrives **late**.*

*I haven't been on the train **lately**.* (lately = recently)

Exercises

1 **Choose the correct forms in this school report for a pupil.**

School Report

Peter is a (1)quiet/quietly boy but he participates (2)happy/happily in class and works (3)good/well with other students. This term he has produced some (4)excellent/excellently essays.

Unfortunately, he scored (5)bad/badly in his mathematics tests because he made some (6)simple/simply mistakes. Checking answers (7)careful/carefully at the end of a test will help!

Sometimes he can be (8)slow/slowly in class and he does not write (9)quick/quickly. However, he has made (10)reasonable/reasonably progress.

2 **Add -ly to the sentences where necessary.**

1 I can run fast. ____✓____

2 You need to come quick_ly____ !

3 That music is very quiet _____. Can you turn it up?

4 She sang so nice _____ at the school musical.

5 Be careful _____!

6 Can you lift that careful _____? It's very fragile.

7 I don't understand your English. Please speak slow _____.

8 You play the piano beautiful _____.

3 **Put the words in brackets in the correct place in the sentences.**

1 Your daughter sings _beautifully_. (beautifully)

2 I woke up _late_ this morning. (late)

3 How do you know Michelle? (well)

4 The Olympic swimmer Michael Phelps swims. (fast)

5 John plays the piano. (badly)

6 She speaks English. (very well)

4 **Complete the sentences with hard, hardly, late or lately.**

1 My mathematics homework has become really _____ since we got this new teacher.

2 Don't stay up too _____. You'll be tired in the morning.

3 Don't be _____ home. We've got guests for dinner tonight.

4 We _____ go away any more because petrol is so expensive.

5 I haven't see Richard for ages. Have you seen him_____?

6 How _____ did the other car hit you?

44 Modifying adjectives and adverbs
very, really, quite, not very, enough, too

A: How did your fishing trip go?

B: Really well! I caught a really big fish!

A: How big?

B: Oh, VERY big!

A: Can I see it?

B: Oh, it was too big to fit in my car! The boot isn't big enough. I threw it back.

Presentation

very, really, quite and *not very*

Use the words *very, really, quite* and *not very* to modify the meaning of adjectives or adverbs:

*I caught a **really big** fish.*

*My fishing trip went **really well**.*

The words can make the meaning of the adjective or adverb stronger or weaker:

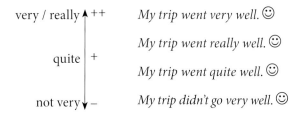

very / really ▲ ++   *My trip went very well.* ☺

                       My trip went really well. ☺

quite │ +   *My trip went quite well.* ☺

not very ▼ −   *My trip didn't go very well.* ☺

TIP Modifiers can answer the question
How + adjective …? / How + adverb …?:

*How big was it? It was **very big**!*

*How well did you do in the exam? Not **very well**.*

too and *very*

You can use *too* as a modifier. It makes the adjective or adverb stronger. It means *more than necessary*.

*The fish was **very** big (but I could fit it in my car).*

*The fish was **too** big (so I couldn't fit it in my car).*

enough and *not enough*

You can use *enough* and *not enough* to say you have (or don't have) the correct or sufficient quantity:

*My car was big **enough** to take six people.*

*My car wasn't big **enough** to fit the fish in.*

Notice the word order!

enough comes *after* the adjective or adverb:

Say *My car was big enough*. (don't say *My car was enough big*.)

Say *He was driving slowly enough*. (don't say *He was driving enough slowly*.)

Exercises

1 Read the report on customer feedback and complete sentences 1–6.

Answer the following questions about service at this shop:

0 = Not very 1 = Quite 2 = Very	Mr Ross	Mrs Slater	Ms Turnball
How polite were the staff?	2	2	1
How quickly could you find what you wanted?	0	1	1
How satisfied were you with the choice and range?	2	2	2
How efficiently were you served at the checkout?	0	0	1

1 Two customers thought the staff were
   very polite ....

2 Mr Ross couldn't find what he wanted
   ....

3 Two other customers found what they wanted
   ....

4 Everyone was .... with the choice and range.

5 Two customers weren't served .... at the checkout.

6 One customer was served .... at the checkout.

2 Complete the sentences with *too, very* or *enough*.

1 This coat is .... big for me. Can I have a size smaller?
2 I'm .... well today, thanks.
3 You need to send this back .... quickly.
4 These curtain aren't long ....
5 You always do things .... quickly and then you make a mistake.
6 Are you sure this coat is big .... for him?

3 🔊 1.48 Complete the conversations with the words in the boxes. Then listen and check.

Conversation 1

enough   quite   really   wasn't

A: How was your holiday?

B: It was ¹ .... good! It was so relaxing!

A: How about the weather?

B: It rained for the first couple of days but after that it was ² .... sunny.

A: Was your hotel close to the beach?

B: No, it ³ .... , but it was close ⁴ .... to a swimming pool so we went there most days.

Conversation 2

enough   too   very

C: What did you think of the film?

D: Daniel Craig was great but the plot was ⁵ .... complicated. I couldn't understand it at all.

C: I agree. I thought the whole story was ⁶ .... badly written.

D: Me too. It wasn't exciting ⁷ ....

45 Review of units 41 to 44

Grammar

1 Complete the sentences with the words in brackets.

1 How much did that ^lovely green coat cost you?   (lovely)

2 It's the large brick building on the right.   (red)

3 They've found an Egyptian temple in the desert.   (ancient)

4 Who does this new grammar book belong to?   (green)

5 All these modern designs are stunning.   (Italian)

6 You quite rudely to her.   (spoke)

7 He works and he never takes a break.   (hard)

8 How can your daughter play the flute? Is she any good?   (well)

9 Have you seen Malcolm?   (lately)

10 How do you think she will be?   (late)

11 I've met them once before so I know them.   (hardly)

12 He fell down and broke his leg badly.   (quite)

13 The twins are excited about their birthday.   (really)

14 You finished that very!   (quickly)

15 Don't be angry with him.   (too)

16 He's working hard at school to pass this course.   (enough)

17 The recording isn't clear.   (enough)

2 Correct the mistakes.

1 This TV show is really amusing. It always makes me laugh.   ✓

2 What's so ~~depressed~~? Why do you look sad?
   depressing

3 I'm not really convincing by this idea. I don't think it'll work.

4 My ex-boyfriend is sitting over there. If he sees me, it'll be very embarrassing.

5 Travelling by plane makes me tiring.

6 Aren't you bored of working here? Get another job!

7 I'm interested in apply for the position of receptionist.

8 This leather feels quite softly.

9 The two children are getting on really good.

10 There's been a lot of rain late, hasn't there?

11 This orchestra plays Mozart so beautiful.

12 This is totally confusing. Please explain it again.

3 A school teacher is talking to a parent. Choose the correct words.

Mother: So how is Francesca doing?

Teacher: She gets on [1]good / well with other students and is always [2]happy / happily.

Mother: What about her test scores?

Teacher: She scored [3]bad / badly. I'm afraid, Francesca is an [4]intelligent / intelligently girl but she's also very [5]lazy / lazily.

Mother: Is she [6]slow / slowly?

Teacher: No, in fact she writes [7]quick / quickly, but she needs to be more [8]careful / carefully and check her writing for mistakes.

4 Complete the second sentence so that it has the same meaning as the first sentence.

1 Jane's a really good tennis player.
   Jane plays tennis really well.

2 The violence in the film was worrying.
   I _____ about the violence in the film.

3 Alan is a quick learner.
   Alan learns _____.

4 Felicity was annoyed by her brother's behaviour.
   Felicity's brother's behaviour was _____.

5 The winner was a fast runner.
   The winner ran _____.

6 This coffee's too cold!
   This coffee isn't _____.

Grammar in context

5 Complete the three reviews with the correct form of the word in brackets.

HOTWORK COOLS OFF WITH NEW ALBUM

I was very ¹ <u>excited</u> to receive the new album from *Hotwork*. When the band (EXCITE)

released their first album, the world went ² _____ crazy and (REAL)

it will be ³ _____ to see if they can do it again. The new album is (INTEREST)

good but I wasn't ⁴ _____. Many of the tracks are too similar. (AMAZE)

DILLON BACK IN ACTION!

Daniel Dillon is back as the superhero and he still looks ⁵ _____. In this (AMAZE)

sequel - he gets the bad guys, and he also gets the girl played by the ⁶ _____ (BEAUTY)

actress, Meg Carter. However, you'll be ⁷ _____ by the strange plot ... (CONFUSE)

A NEW NOVEL FROM SINGH

Mary Singh is an ⁸ _____ new novelist. When you read her books, she seems (EXCITE)

to write very ⁹ _____. With her new novel, *The Exile of Kashmir,* you turn every (EASY)

page ¹⁰ _____ because you want to know what happens next ... (QUICK)

Pronunciation: stressing modifiers

6 (1.49) Listen and underline the word with the most stress. Listen and repeat.

1 I'm really sorry.
2 We're very happy for you.
3 That is not very good behaviour!
4 That's too hot!
5 I suppose it's quite nice.

Listen again

7 (1.50) Listen to someone talking about their holiday. Are these statements true (T) or false (F)?

1 She relaxed on holiday. ....
2 She did some work while she was away. ....
3 She liked everyone she met. ....
4 One person talked too much. ....
5 She really liked one person she met. ....
6 She isn't very happy to be home. ....

46 Comparatives
Adjectives and adverbs

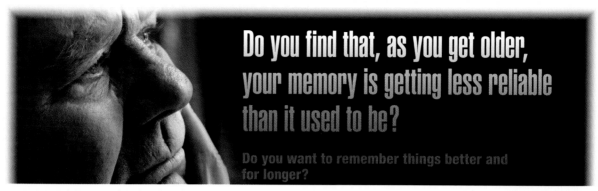

Do you find that, as you get older, your memory is getting less reliable than it used to be?

Do you want to remember things better and for longer?

Try our five-day starter course and your memory will immediately be more efficient. With each exercise your memory will get stronger and stronger until you find that you can think more clearly, study harder and work more efficiently than ever before.

MEMORY
TRAINING COURSES

Presentation

Use the comparative form …

- to make comparisons: *This course is **better than** the last one.*
- to describe the results of a change: *Your memory will be **more efficient*** (than it was before).
- to describe how something is in the process of changing: *Your memory is getting **less reliable.***

Adjectives

To form comparative adjectives, use *-er* or *more / less*.

Short adjectives (one syllable or two syllables ending in -*y*)	Long adjectives (two syllables or more)
adjective + -*er*	*more / less* + adjective
old → older, easy → easier, big → bigger	*efficient → more efficient / less efficient*

Some adjectives have two possible comparative forms: *more quiet / quieter, more gentle / gentler*
Some adjectives are irregular: *good → better, bad → worse, far → further*
The spelling sometimes changes when we add *-er*: *big → bigger, silly → sillier*
See page 233: Spelling rules

Adverbs

Form comparative adverbs in the same way as comparative adjectives, using *-er* or *more / less*.

Short adverbs (one syllable)	Long adverbs (two syllables or more)
adverb + -*er*	*more / less* + adverb
hard → harder, fast → faster	*efficiently → more efficiently / less efficiently*

Some adverbs are irregular : *well → better, badly → worse*

than

Use the preposition *than* to link the two objects, people or situations that you are comparing:
*My memory is less reliable **than** it used to be.*

Exercises

1 Complete the text with the correct comparative form of the adjectives and adverbs. Use *-er*, *more* or *less*.

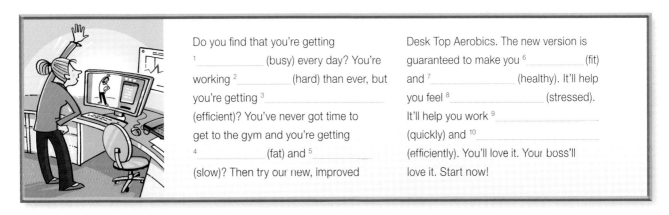

Do you find that you're getting
¹ _____ (busy) every day? You're working ² _____ (hard) than ever, but you're getting ³ _____ (efficient)? You've never got time to get to the gym and you're getting ⁴ _____ (fat) and ⁵ _____ (slow)? Then try our new, improved

Desk Top Aerobics. The new version is guaranteed to make you ⁶ _____ (fit) and ⁷ _____ (healthy). It'll help you feel ⁸ _____ (stressed). It'll help you work ⁹ _____ (quickly) and ¹⁰ _____ (efficiently). You'll love it. Your boss'll love it. Start now!

2 🔊 **1.51** Complete the texts using the comparative form of the adjectives and adverbs in the boxes. Then listen and check.

good grey long stressed

I hate my job! I'm working
¹ _____ hours
than ever and the wages aren't getting any ² _____ .
I'm ³ _____ than
I've ever been before. My hair's getting ⁴ _____ by
the day! I don't think I can take it anymore!

happy healthily short stressed

I love my new life. I can relax now so I'm ⁵ _____
than before. I'm working
⁶ _____ hours. I'm
eating ⁷ _____ .
I'm ⁸ _____ and
enjoying life more than I ever have before.

3 Write sentences that give your opinion. Use a comparative form using *-er*, *more* or *less*.

1 pizza / ice-cream   (tasty)   I think *ice-cream is tastier than pizza.*
2 work / studying   (stressful)   I think _____
3 listening to music / doing sport   (relaxing)   I think _____
4 travelling by car / travelling by train   (fast)   I think _____
5 dancers / golfers   (fit)   I think _____
6 teachers / lawyers   (work hard)   I think _____

4 Complete these sentences so that they are true for you.

1 I am less _____ than I was five years ago.
2 I think _____ is more important than _____ .
3 _____ is easier than _____ .
4 _____ is better for you than _____ .
5 I'd like to be more / less _____ than I am at the moment.

47 Superlatives
Adjectives and adverbs

Zurich, Switzerland's largest city, has been voted the best city in the world to live in. Zurich's parks make it one of the greenest cities in the world, its air is the least polluted and it's one of the cities where you can travel most comfortably. And with the third lowest crime rate, it is certainly one of the safest.

Presentation

Use the superlative form to show that one thing or person in a group has got more or less of a quality than all the others in the same group: *Zurich is Switzerland's largest city.* (= no other city in Switzerland is larger.)

Adjectives

To form superlative adjectives, use *-est* or *most / least*.

Short adjectives (one syllable or two syllables ending in -y)

adjective + *-est*
large → largest, green → greenest
big → biggest, easy → easiest
pretty → prettiest

Long adjectives (two syllables or more)

most / least + adjective
expensive → most expensive, exciting → most exciting, polluted → least polluted

Some adjectives have two possible superlative forms: *most polite / politest, most gentle / gentlest*

Some adjectives are irregular: *good → best, bad → worst, far → furthest*

See page 233: Spelling rules

the and possessive adjectives

You often use *the*, a *possessive* or *possessive 's* before a superlative adjective: *The best city, its best attraction, Switzerland's largest city.*

Common expressions

Superlative adjectives are often used with …

- one / some of the … : *one of the greenest cities, some of the cleanest water*
- the second / third etc. … in … : *the third lowest in Europe*
- the most … ever … : *the most exciting city you'll ever visit*

Adverbs

Form superlative adverbs in the same way as superlative adjectives, using *-est* or *most / least*.

Short adverbs (one syllable)

adverb + *-est*
hard → hardest, fast → fastest

Long adverbs (two syllables or more)

most / least + adverb
safely → most / least safely
comfortably → most / least comfortably

Some adverbs are irregular: *well → best, badly → worst*

We can use superlative adverbs both with and without *the*:

*It's the city where you travel **most comfortably** / **the most comfortably**.*

Exercises

1 Complete the text by adding *most* or *-est* to the adjectives in brackets. Make any necessary spelling changes.

Tierra del Fuego is one of the [1] _____ (fascinating) places on earth. Its snowy mountains offer some of the [2] _____ (spectacular) views you will ever see. The [3] _____ (high) peak stands at 2448 m above sea level. The [4] _____ (easy) access to Tierra del Fuego is from Argentina, and Ushuaia is the [5] _____ (popular) destination with tourists. But the [6] _____ (southern) town in South America, and the world, is Puerto Toro, Chile. It is also one of the [7] _____ (small) towns in South America with a population of under fifty people. A visit to Puerto Toro will certainly be one of the [8] _____ (unforgettable) experiences of your life.

2 Complete the sentences using *most, least* or *-est* and the adjectives and adverbs in the box.

cold   expensive   fast   high   hot   northern   small   visited

1 Ulaan Batar, Outer Mongolia, is the _____ capital city in the world. It has an average temperature of −1.3° C.

2 Bangkok is the _____ city in the world, with an average temperature of 30° C all year round.

3 Chonqing, China, is probably the _____ growing city in the world. Experts believe its size will double from ten million to twenty million in the next thirteen years.

4 Paris is the _____ city in the world. It has over thirty million tourists a year.

5 The Vatican City is probably the world's _____ capital city. Just under 1000 people live inside its walls.

6 La Paz, Bolivia, situated at 3640 m above sea level, is the _____ capital city in the world.

7 Asuncion in Paraguay is possibly the _____ capital city in the world. The cost of living in Asuncion is only a third of the cost of living in New York.

8 Hammerfest, Norway, situated just outside the Arctic Circle, is one of the _____ cities in the world.

3 🔊 **1.52** Complete the conversations with the comparative or superlative form of the adjectives in brackets. Then listen and check.

Conversation 1

A: So, what did you think of Prague?

B: Amazing. It's definitely [1] _____ (beautiful) than any of the other cities I've visited so far. But, I must admit, the food is [2] _____ (good) in Paris.

Conversation 2

C: What's [3] _____ (good) way to get to London?

D: Well, the train probably gets you there [4] _____ (quick). It's definitely [5] _____ (fast) than going by car.

Conversation 3

E: What was the hotel like?

F: Well, it wasn't [6] _____ (comfortable) hotel I've ever stayed in! It was on one of [7] _____ (busy) streets in the town – it was really noisy. And the second night was [8] _____ (bad) than the first. The air-conditioning wasn't working and there was a party going on in the street. That was probably [9] _____ (bad) night's sleep I've ever had!

48 Modifying comparatives and superlatives

Don't miss our special online offers!
Travel much further, spend much less!

Shooting the rapids in Chile
£1,500 £1,000

This one is a little more expensive than the others, but it looks much more exciting.

Horseback trekking in Mexico
£1,250 £800

What about this one? It's a little less expensive, and it still looks pretty good.

Book much more cheaply and quickly online

Paragliding in southern Spain
£850 £550

Look at this one! It's easily the best. It's a lot cheaper than the other two and it looks as if it's even more fun!

Presentation

Modifying comparatives

Use modifiers such as *a bit, a little, much more,* in comparisons to show the degree of difference between the things being compared.

- small difference: *This holiday is **a little less expensive**.*
- big difference: *You can book **much more cheaply** online.*

Use the same modifiers with both adjectives and adverbs.

Small differences

a bit	cheaper
a little	more / less expensive
slightly	more / less cheaply

Big differences

much	cheaper
a lot	more / less expensive
far	more / less cheaply

A bit is more informal than *a little* or *slightly*.

TIP When using *fun* in a comparison, say *more fun than* (don't say ~~funner~~.)

*This one's **more fun** than the other one.*

Modifying superlatives

Use modifiers with superlative expressions to say that something has much more of a certain quality than all the other things that it is being compared to.

Modifier	Superlative form + *the*
easily	the best
by far	the most exciting
	the least interesting

This is by far the best film. (= much better than anything else.)
This is easily the most exciting holiday. (= much more exciting than anything else.)
This is by far the least interesting book. (= much less interesting than anything else.)

Exercises

1 Look at the table and use the notes to write sentences. Use the modifiers in the boxes.

Top three honeymoon destinations of the month

	New York	The Maldives	Finland
Price	$$$$$$$$	$$$$	$$
Length of stay	5 days	10 days	2 weeks
Weather	☼ ☼	☼ ☼ ☼ ☼	☼
Adventure	☺	☺ ☺	☺ ☺ ☺ ☺
Romance	♥♥♥♥	♥♥♥♥♥♥	♥♥♥

> a bit / far

1   weather / New York / better / Finland *The weather in New York is a bit better than the weather in Finland.*
2   weather / the Maldives / better / Finland

> a little / much

3   Finland / exciting / New York
4   New York / exciting / the Maldives

> easily / slightly

5   the Maldives / romantic choice
6   Finland / romantic / New York

2 🎧 **1.53** Choose the correct modifiers. Then listen and check.

A: How was your trip to Finland?

B: Amazing! It's a really beautiful place. It was ¹ *a bit / much* greener than I'd imagined. I thought it was covered in snow all year and that there was no grass or plants. But, of course, in summer there's no snow. And it was ² *slightly / a lot* warmer than I thought as well. We took heavy winter clothes with us, but we were in shorts and T-shirts most of the time. We went swimming in one of the lakes one day. The water was just ³ *a little bit / a lot* colder than I'd like but not much. But we soon got warm again in the sun.

A: Sounds good. Did you go up to the Arctic Circle?

B: Yes, we did. That was ⁴ *by far / far* the most interesting part of the trip. It was definitely ⁵ *easily / much* colder there! And the mosquitoes were incredible. There were thousands of them. That was ⁶ *a little / easily* the worst thing about the whole trip! Everyone says that ⁷ *a lot / by far* the best time to go is early spring, when there are no mosquitoes, and if you're lucky you can see the Northern Lights.

49 *as … as …*

> It looks like a normal sports car, it's **as fast as** a normal sports car, it drives **just as well as** a normal sports car, but it isn't a normal sports car. It's 100% electric. It may be **twice as expensive** to buy **as** a traditional sports car, but it's a hundred times more ecological and it isn't **nearly as expensive** to run. With this car, saving the planet isn't **nearly as difficult as** we thought – and it's much more fun!

Presentation

Use *as … as …* to compare two things and say that they are similar:

*It's **as** fast **as** a normal sports car.* (= Sports cars are fast. This car is equally fast.)

Use *just* with *as … as …* to emphasise the similarity:

*It drives **just as** well **as** a normal sports car.*

Use *not as … as …* to compare two things and say that they are different, and that one possesses less of a certain quality and ability than the other:

*It **isn't as** expensive to run **as** a traditional petrol-fuelled car.* (= It's cheaper to run than a traditional petrol-fuelled car.)

(not) as	adjective adverb	as	noun

*It's **as** cheap **as** a bicycle.*

*It drives **as** well **as** a normal sports car.*

Also use *not as … as…* to explain that an object, person or situation has less of a quality than you imagined:

*It **isn't as** difficult **as** we'd expected.*

Modifying *as … as …*

You can modify expressions using *(not) as … as …* to show the degree of similarity or difference.

- small difference: *This one is **almost as** exciting **as** that one.*
- big difference: *This one is **twice as** expensive **as** that one.*

Small differences

almost	as exciting as
nearly	as cheaply as
not quite	

Big differences

twice / three times …	as expensive as
not nearly	as cheaply as

Common expressions

As … as … is used in a lot of common fixed expressions: *as soon as possible, as quickly as I can, as good as new, as good as gold, as old as the hills*

Exercises

1 Put the words in order. Start with the phrase which is underlined.

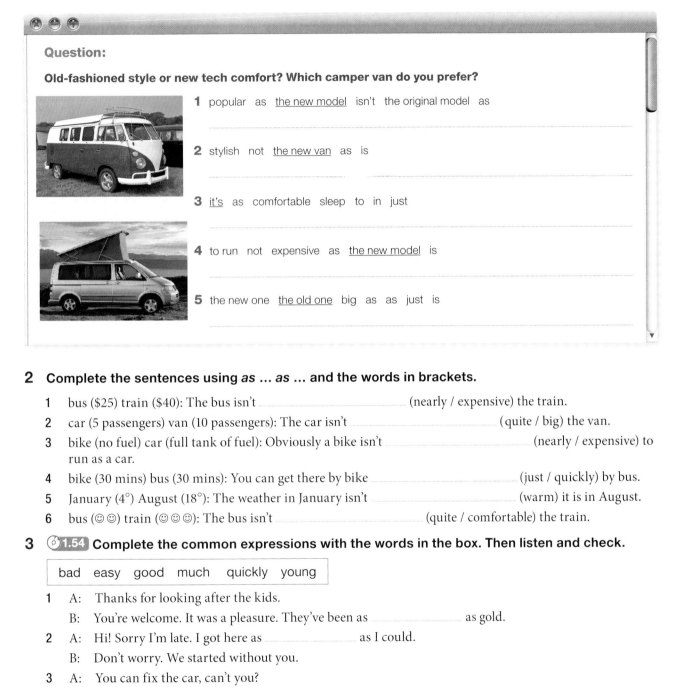

Question:

Old-fashioned style or new tech comfort? Which camper van do you prefer?

1 popular   as   <u>the new model</u>   isn't   the original model   as

_____

2 stylish   not   <u>the new van</u>   as   is

_____

3 <u>it's</u>   as   comfortable   sleep   to   in   just

_____

4 to run   not   expensive   as   <u>the new model</u>   is

_____

5 the new one   <u>the old one</u>   big   as   as   just   is

_____

2 Complete the sentences using *as ... as ...* and the words in brackets.

1 bus ($25) train ($40): The bus isn't _____ (nearly / expensive) the train.
2 car (5 passengers) van (10 passengers): The car isn't _____ (quite / big) the van.
3 bike (no fuel) car (full tank of fuel): Obviously a bike isn't _____ (nearly / expensive) to run as a car.
4 bike (30 mins) bus (30 mins): You can get there by bike _____ (just / quickly) by bus.
5 January (4°) August (18°): The weather in January isn't _____ (warm) it is in August.
6 bus (☺☺) train (☺☺☺): The bus isn't _____ (quite / comfortable) the train.

3 (🔊1.54) Complete the common expressions with the words in the box. Then listen and check.

bad   easy   good   much   quickly   young

1 A: Thanks for looking after the kids.
   B: You're welcome. It was a pleasure. They've been as _____ as gold.
2 A: Hi! Sorry I'm late. I got here as _____ as I could.
   B: Don't worry. We started without you.
3 A: You can fix the car, can't you?
   B: Mmm ... I'm not sure. It isn't as _____ as it looks.
4 A: Help yourselves to some food. Take as _____ as you want.
   B: Thanks! It looks delicious!
5 A: Look at this! It's ruined!
   B: Let me see. No, it isn't as _____ as you think. It'll come out in the wash.
6 A: Ouch! I'm not as _____ as I used to be!
   B: Watch out Fred. You're showing your age!

50 Review of units 46 to 49

Grammar

1 Choose the correct option.

1 Russia is the *larger / largest* country in the world.

2 Canada has got *by far / slightly* the longest coastline of any country in the world.

3 Russia is much *bigger than / as big as* China.

4 The Democratic Republic of the Congo is the *three / third* biggest country in Africa.

5 Luxembourg is one of the *smallest / most small* countries in the world and it is also one of the *richest / most rich*.

6 The United States is *by far / far* more popular with visitors than the UK.

7 The population of Liberia is growing *more fast / faster* than that of any other country in the world.

8 English is not nearly *as / more* important on the internet as it used to be.

2 Add one word from the box to each sentence. You can use some words more than once.

a	as	by	more	than	the

1 Jake is politer ^than^ his sister.

2 This is far the most delicious meal I've ever eaten!

3 Green tea is much better for you black tea.

4 This is one of most difficult exams I've taken so far.

5 It's far difficult than all the others.

6 This is worst car in the whole world. It's always breaking down.

7 This flat looks good. It's just as big as the other one, but it's lot cheaper.

8 This is boring! It isn't nearly as much fun it looks on the TV.

3 Write sentences using the prompts.

1 this TV programme / lot / funny / that one
   This TV programme is a lot funnier than that one.

2 this TV programme / not / funny / that one

3 this TV programme / funny / I've ever seen

4 this phone is / just / expensive / that one

5 these phones are / cheap / the phones in the shop

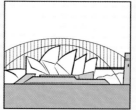

6 Sydney / far / hot / London

7 Sydney / as cold / London in winter

8 Sydney / hot / place / I've ever visited

110

Grammar in context

4 Read about Death Valley and complete the text. Write one word in each gap.

Death Valley, California, is a place of extremes. It is [1]_____ of the hottest and driest places on earth. [2]_____ second highest recorded temperature in the world (57°C) was recorded in Death Valley in July, 1913. Daytime temperatures are higher [3]_____ 40°C for at least four months of the year.

In most desert regions, night time temperatures are [4]_____ lot cooler than day time temperatures. Although this is also true in Death Valley, in summer it makes very little difference. With night time temperatures hardly ever dropping lower [5]_____ 30°C that often means that the nights can feel almost [6]_____ hot as the day.

Fewer [7]_____ 5 cm of rain fall per year on average, and some years there's no rain at all. It is also a place of extreme differences. Badwater, a dry salt lake at the floor of the valley, is [8]_____ lowest point of land in the USA.

Thanks to these extremes, Death Valley has become the home of what is by [9]_____ the world's toughest foot race, the Death Valley Ultramarathon. The [10]_____ extreme of all physical challenges, the race covers 135 miles in 45°C, from Badwater, Death Valley, at 82 m below sea level to Whitney Portal at 2,500 m. There is a time limit of just 60 hours to finish the race. [11]_____ fastest runner did it in just over 22 hours.

Pronunciation: sentence stress 1

5 🔊 **1.55 Read the information. Listen and repeat.**

1   Notice how the main stress falls on the **adjective**.

   *Badwater is the **hott**est place in North America.*

2   Notice how the main stress now falls on the **modifier**.

   *Badwater is **eas**ily the hottest place in North America.*

6 🔊 **1.56 Mark the main stress in the sentences. Listen and repeat.**

1   January is the coldest month.

2   August is far hotter than May.

3   The Ultramarathon is much more challenging than I thought.

4   The Ultramarathon is more than three times as long as a standard marathon.

Listen again

7 🔊 **1.57 Listen to Jay describing his holiday in Finland. Match 1–6 to a–f.**

1 Finland in summer	☐	**a** good time to go
2 the weather	☐	**b** cold
3 the water in the lakes	☐	**c** green
4 the Arctic Circle	☐	**d** incredible
5 the mosquitoes	☐	**e** interesting
6 spring	☐	**f** warm

51 *going to* and present continuous
Plans, intentions and arrangements

Presentation

going to

You can use *be + going to + infinitive* to talk about intentions or plans for the future:

I'm going to stay single.

I'm never going to get married.

Affirmative and negative

I	'm / 'm not		
He / She / It	's / isn't	going to	get married.
You / We / They	're / aren't		

Question

	Am	I		
(When)	Is	he / she / it	going to	invite Harry?
	Are	you / we / they		

Present continuous

You can use the present continuous to talk about arrangements in the future:

Paula and I are getting married on 1st May.

I'm meeting Harry tomorrow night at eight.

See also Units 8 and 9.

Present continuous or *going to*?

You can use either form to talk about plans and arrangements in the future:

We're playing tennis tomorrow.

We're going to play tennis tomorrow.

When you use the present continuous to talk about the future you normally use a specific future time expression:

We're playing tennis tomorrow.

If you don't use a future time expression (or the time is not obvious), the present continuous refers to the present time:

We're playing tennis tomorrow. (= future)

We're playing tennis. (= now at the moment of speaking)

go and *come*

You normally use the verbs *go* and *come* in the present continuous, not with *going to*:

Who's coming to your wedding? (not *Who's ~~going to come~~ to your wedding?*)

Who's going to the wedding? (not *Who's ~~going to go~~ to the wedding?*)

Exercises

1 **Look at the pictures and write sentences. Use *going to* and the phrases in the box.**

> become a firefighter   buy a Ferrari   get married   grow her own food   have a long holiday
> start his diet next week   ~~travel round the world~~   try something exciting

1 He's going to travel round the world.

2 He

3 They

4 She

5 He

6 He

7 She

8 She

2 **Tick the sentences where you can use the present continuous without changing the future meaning.**

1 We're going to speak to everyone in about an hour. ✓
2 I'm going to ask him to call you back. ✗
3 Lucinda isn't going to arrive until three.
4 Is she going to explain how to answer these questions?
5 I'm going to tidy my room. I promise I will.
6 The children are going to start school at the end of August.
7 Everyone is going to meet in the town square at midnight.
8 They're going to rebuild that old house.
9 Are you going to tell her how you really feel? She needs to know.
10 The whole family is going to spend their next holiday on the beach.

3 **Complete these sentences about your plans and intentions for the future.**

1 Next week I'm going to
2 Next month I'm going to
3 Next year I'm going to

52 *will* and *going to* 1
Decisions

A: It's Sandra's birthday tomorrow. I'm going to buy her a scarf.

B: Oh, I didn't know it was her birthday! I'll get her some jewellery or something.

Presentation

Use *will* and *going to* to talk about decisions:

I'm going to buy her a scarf.

I'll buy her some jewellery or something.

going to

Use *going to* to talk about a decision made before the conversation:

It's Sandra's birthday tomorrow. I'm going to buy her a scarf.

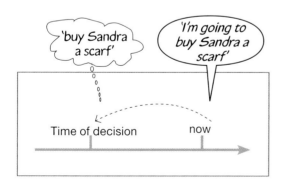

will

Use *will* to talk about a decision made during the conversation (while we are speaking or making the decision):

I didn't know it was her birthday! I'll buy her some jewellery or something.

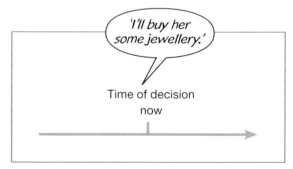

Rule of form for modal verbs

Will is a modal verb and follows the rules of form for all modal verbs.

- The third person singular has no -s: *John will be here at 9 o'clock.* (not *He ~~wills~~ be here at 9 o'clock.*)

- The auxiliary verbs *do* and *does* are not used in questions or negatives: *Will he be here at 9 o'clock?* (not *~~Does he will~~ be here at 9 o'clock?*)

- It is followed by the bare infinitive of the verb. *He'll be here at 9 o'clock.* (not *He'll ~~to~~ be here at 9 o'clock.*)

You normally use the contracted form *'ll* in conversation.

Exercises

1 Put these words in the correct order to make sentences or questions.

1 are fun you something to going do for your birthday?

    _____ ?

2 going birthday are you to what buy for her?

    _____ ?

3 as soon back as call you possible I'll

4 next you do will what?

    _____ ?

5 do to won't be that we able

6 Laura and decide today to are going Mike

2 ⊙ 2.02 Tick the correct response, a or b. Then listen and check.

1 I'm really sorry. I've just broken the handle on the door.
   a: That's OK. I'm going to fix it later.
   b: That's OK. I'll fix it later.

2 Are you busy later? Can you help me with something?
   a: I can't, I'm afraid. I'll help Martin later on.
   b: I can't, I'm afraid. I'm going to help Martin later on.

3 I need someone to help me with something.
   a: I'll do it.
   b: I'm going to do it.

4 What are your plans for your retirement?
   a: I'm going to travel round the world on a cruise ship. I've already bought the tickets!
   b: I'll travel round the world on a cruise ship.

5 Are you going to join us later?
   a: Maybe later. I'm going to see a play at the theatre.
   b: Maybe later. I'll see a play at the theatre.

6 Is anyone going to come shopping with me? Why don't any of you want to?
   a: OK then. I'm supposed to be in class but I'm going to come.
   b: OK then. I'm supposed to be in class but I'll come.

3 Complete the emails with the *will* or *going to* form of the verbs in brackets.

📧 New   📧 Reply   📧 Forward   🖨 Print   🗑 Delete

Hi Mariana
I have a conference in Brazil next month and I ¹ _____ (stay) in Rio for three days so
we can meet!
Raul

Hi Raul
Great! The problem is I've already planned my holiday for next month - I ² _____
(travel) round Argentina with Lizzie for a couple of weeks and we ³ _____
(not return) until the 18th. Is that too late? I could change our flights I suppose.
M.

I'm not exactly sure about my dates yet so don't change anything. I ⁴ _____ (email)
again when I know for certain.
Raul

OK. I ⁵ _____ (not change) my flights until I hear from you.
M.

53 *will* and *shall*
promising, offering, requesting, suggesting

Man:	There's someone at the door! Shall I answer it?
Woman:	No, it's OK. I'll go. It's probably my taxi.
Man:	Where are you going?
Woman:	To see a friend. Don't worry. I promise I won't be late.
Man:	Shall I pick you up?
Woman:	That would be nice.
Man:	Will you phone me when you want to come home, then?

Presentation

will

You can use *will* for …

- Promising: *I promise I **won't** be late.*
- Offering: *I'll come and pick you up if you want.*
- Requesting: ***Will** you phone me, please?*

shall I / we:

Shall is a modal verb. See Unit 52 for notes on the rules of form for modal verbs.

You often use *Shall I …?* or *Shall we …?* for …

- Asking what to do: ***Shall I** answer it?*
- Suggesting: ***Shall we** go out later?*
- Offering: ***Shall I** pick you up?*

will or *shall*?

Questions with *Shall …?* and questions with *Will …?* have different functions:

offer | question about future

***Shall I** pick you up later or **will you** catch the bus?*

Exercises

1 Replace the words in bold with the words in the box.

> I'll   I won't   shall I   shall we   we'll   will you

1   **I promise not** to be late.

_____ be late.

2   **Why don't we** have some lunch here?

_____ have some lunch here?

3   **Can you** help me with something?

_____ help me with something?

4   **Do you want me to** speak to them?

_____ speak to them?

5   **Shall we** leave a message for them?

_____ leave them a message if you want.

6   The phone's ringing. **Let me** answer it.

The phone's ringing. _____ get it.

2 ⊚ **2.03** Complete the conversations with *shall*, *will/'ll*. Then listen and check.

1   A: _____ we start or do you want to wait for the others to arrive?

B: I _____ give them a call and see how long they're going to be.

2   A: This is my favourite song! _____ we dance?

B: No, I can't dance to this but I _____ dance if they play some Elvis.

3   A: _____ there be time for a break later on?

B: Unfortunately not, so _____ we take a break now?

4   A: The package is at the post office. _____ I go and collect it?

B: Don't worry. I _____ pick it up when I go for lunch.

5   A: _____ I carry your bags for you?

B: Oh. Thanks a lot. You take this one and I _____ carry the other.

6   A: _____ you carry my bag for me?

B: Sure. Give it here. _____ I take your coat as well?

3 Write a sentence for each situation. Use the word in brackets.

1   Promise your friend not to tell anyone his secret.
(won't) _____

2   Offer to make a cup of tea for someone.
(shall) _____

3   You bought an mp3 player but it doesn't work. Ask a shop assistant to change it for another.
(will) _____

4   You are with a group of friends. Suggest going to the park.
(shall) _____

5   A friend lends you his car. Promise to look after it.
('ll) _____

54 Present simple for future

Schedules, *when/as soon as*

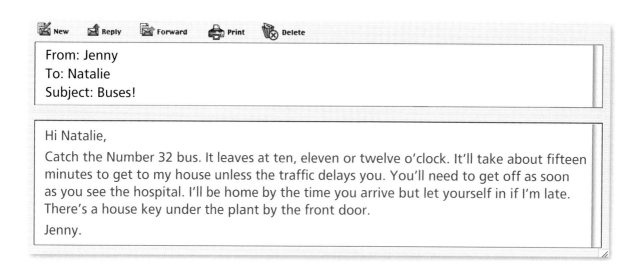

From: Jenny
To: Natalie
Subject: Buses!

Hi Natalie,

Catch the Number 32 bus. It leaves at ten, eleven or twelve o'clock. It'll take about fifteen minutes to get to my house unless the traffic delays you. You'll need to get off as soon as you see the hospital. I'll be home by the time you arrive but let yourself in if I'm late. There's a house key under the plant by the front door.

Jenny.

Presentation

Present simple for future

We can use the present simple to talk about timetables or scheduled events in the future:

*The bus **leaves** at ten o'clock.*

TIP You often use verbs such as *arrive, come, finish, go, leave, start* with the present simple for future reference.

Present tenses in future time clauses

You can talk about the future using a sentence with two clauses joined by time conjunctions such as *after, as soon as, before, if, when, by the time, unless, until.*

Main clause	time clause

*It'll take you about 15 minutes to get to my house **unless** the traffic delays you.*

Notice that the verb in the future time clause is in the present simple and not the future.

*You'll need to get off **as soon as** you **see** the sign for the park.*

*I'll be home **by the time** you **arrive**.*

Exercises

1 (●2.04) **Complete the conversation with the present simple form of the verbs in brackets. Then listen and check.**

A: Let's go and see *Live One More Time*.

B: Good idea. What time
¹_____ (it start)?

A: Erm. It ²_____ (start) at six fifty-five. If we ³_____ (catch) the bus from Suffolk Street at twenty-five to seven, it'll arrive at the cinema in time.

B: But I ⁴_____ (not finish) work until seven. Is there a later showing?

A: It ⁵_____ (last) nearly three hours so it ⁶_____ (not start) again until ten.

B: Is there anything else we can see?

A: *Master of the World* ⁷_____ (begin) at seven.

B: That sounds terrible. What about *Love Interestingly*?

A: Err. There's a showing at eight twenty-five.

B: What time ⁸_____ (it end)?

A: It ⁹_____ (finish) two hours later.

B: Is there a bus home?

A: The bus ¹⁰_____ (leave) at ten twenty.

B: That's too late. Aren't there any other buses?

A: Yes, but the next bus
¹¹_____ (not leave) until eleven twenty.

B: That's OK. We can get something to eat afterwards.

2 **Which lines in this email are correct? Correct the mistakes.**

1   Our flight ~~leave~~ Rome at five in the morning   *leaves*

2   so when we land it will be about six thirty   ✓

3   unless they will delay the flight – they   _____

4   often do! The first airport bus don't leave   _____

5   until seven. It will be seven by the time we'll   _____

6   get through passport control and customs.   _____

7   If we will catch this bus, we'll get to the city   _____

8   centre at half past. What time do you leaves   _____

9   for work? Will you be there when we arrive?   _____

3 **Combine the two sentences to make one sentence. Use the words in bold in your new sentence.**

1   They'll get here soon. Let's eat then.

as soon as   Let's eat *as soon as they get here.*

2   Everybody will arrive. The meeting will begin.

when   The meeting will begin _____

3   The taxi will arrive. We'll be ready.

by the time   We'll be ready _____

4   I'll speak to my parents tonight. Don't mention it to anyone until then.

until   Don't mention it to anyone _____

5   Jean might bring his car. If not, I'll drive us to the movie.

if   I'll drive us to the movie _____

55 Review of units 51 to 54

Grammar

1 Match 1–5 to a–e.

1 We're going ☐
2 We're ☐
3 The bus ☐
4 Shall we ☐
5 I'll ☐

a meet at your house?
b meeting Lisa at her house.
c meet you at your house.
d to move house in a year.
e goes past your house.

2 Choose the correct forms.

1 *Are they ever going to finish / Are they ever finishing* building the new road?

2 You don't need to call me when you land unless the plane *is / will be* late.

3 A: Has Dorothy sent us an email with the directions to her house?
   B: I don't know. I *check / 'll check* my inbox.

4 A: This soup is cold.
   B: *Will / Shall* I heat it up again for you?

5 You *'ll join / 're going to join* the army! When did you make that decision?

6 Let's clean the house before your parents *get / are getting* home.

7 A: *Shall we try / Are we trying* the new Greek restaurant at the end of the road?
   B: Good idea.

8 Sandy and Michelle *come / are coming* on holiday with us. Is that OK?

3 Complete the telephone conversation with the present simple or present continuous form of the verbs in brackets.

A: Hi Frank. It's Eugenia.

B: Oh hi Eugenia. How are things?

A: Fine. [1] _____ you _____ (do) anything this Friday evening? There's a new film at the cinema by that Chinese director we like – Zhang Yimou.

B: Sorry, but Malcolm and I [2] _____ (go) to the mountains this weekend. We [3] _____ (ski) all day on Saturday and Sunday.

A: Sounds great! What about the following Monday?

B: What time [4] _____ the film _____ (start)?

A: At five thirty.

B: That's going to be difficult. I [5] _____ (meet) with my boss until five. It's about a pay rise so it's important. The bus from my office to the city centre is at quarter past the hour so if I [6] _____ (take) it, I'll probably be late.

A: Don't worry. I [7] _____ (come) in my car so I'll pick you up as soon as you [8] _____ (be) ready to leave.

4 There is one word missing in each sentence. Write it in.

1 Do you think it's going to rain today?

2 I let you know as soon as I hear something.

3 I won't come if you want me to.

4 When the visitors arriving?

5 He coming for dinner. He had to cancel because his mother is ill.

6 The film start until half past seven. We've still got time to get there.

7 My son says he is going make a million dollars before he's thirty!

Grammar in context

5 Complete the email with the correct answer a, b or c.

To: Marty

From: Rosie

Hi Marty,

Well, I've booked my tickets to Kathmandu and I ¹ .... on the 19th. ² .... you meet me off the plane? You'd better! The flight is eighteen hours long with a six-hour stop in Karachi so as soon as I ³ .... I'll need some sleep. Anyway, I'm so excited. ⁴ .... you anything in particular from England? I ⁵ .... some space in my luggage because I'm going to buy loads of new clothes when I ⁶ .... there. By the way, ⁷ .... carry everything in a suitcase or a backpack? Which is better? I suppose when we ⁸ .... trekking it's better to have a backpack. Anyway, let me know what you think.

Rosie.

1	a comes	b 'm coming	c will come
2	a Shall	b Will	c Are
3	a land	b will land	c am landing
4	a Shall I bring	b Will I bring	c Am I bringing
5	a 'm having	b 'll have	c have
6	a 'm going	b 'm getting	c get
7	a will I	b shall I	c am I going to
8	a go	b will go	c are going to

Pronunciation: going to

6 🔊 **2.05** **There are two ways to pronounce *going to*: /ɡəʊn tə/ and /ɡɒnə/. Listen to six sentences and tick the pronunciation of *going to* that you hear.**

1 /ɡəʊn tə/   /ɡɒnə/
2 /ɡəʊn tə/   /ɡɒnə/
3 /ɡəʊn tə/   /ɡɒnə/
4 /ɡəʊn tə/   /ɡɒnə/
5 /ɡəʊn tə/   /ɡɒnə/
6 /ɡəʊn tə/   /ɡɒnə/

Listen again

7 🔊 **2.06** **Listen to the conversation and answer the questions.**

1 What time does *Live One More Time* start?
   ....

2 What time does the bus leave in order to see this film? ....

3 How long does the film last? ....

4 What time does *Master of the World* begin?
   ....

5 What time does *Love Interestingly* begin?
   ....

6 Which bus do they decide to catch after the film?
   ....

56 *will* and *going to* 2
Predictions

It's going to rain. Let's take an umbrella.

Man: Do you think it'll be cold in Rome at this time of year?

Woman: What? In May? No, it'll be warm and sunny. I don't think you'll need that jumper.

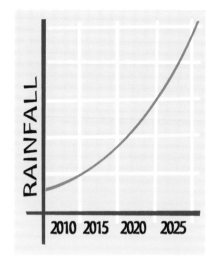

Countries in the north of Europe will have more and more rain over the coming years.

Presentation

You can use both *going to* and *will* to make predictions about the future:

*It's **going** to rain.*

It'll be warm and sunny.

going to or *will*?

You can often use both forms with very little difference:

*Do you think it'**ll** rain this afternoon?*

*Do you think it's **going** to rain this afternoon?*

You tend to use *going to* when you make a prediction based on information in the present situation:

There are big, black rain clouds in the sky. It's going to rain soon.

You often use *will* with *I think / don't think, I'm sure, I expect*:

***I don't think** it'll rain.*

***I think** she'll win the election.*

***I'm sure** they'll be very happy.*

TIP You usually say *I don't think it'll rain.* (not *I think it won't rain.*)

You tend to use *will* for long-term predictions:

*Global temperatures **will** rise by two or three degrees over the next ten to twenty years.*

Exercises

1 **Write sentences to describe what is going to happen in the pictures.**

 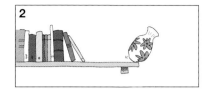 

1 car / crash into / wall *The car is going to crash into the wall.*

2 vase / fall off / shelf

3 she / have a baby

4 cat / catch / mouse

5 they / play tennis

6 branch / break

2 **Complete the sentences using *will, 'll* or *won't*.**

1 They make a great couple. I think they _____ be very happy together.

2 I don't think he _____ be very pleased when he finds out they've stolen his bicycle.

3 Why don't you ask her out for a drink? I'm sure she _____ say yes.

4 Do you think I _____ get into the football team this year?

5 _____ they want to see our passports, do you think?

6 Don't worry. I'm sure it _____ be as difficult as you think.

7 They _____ get married until Luis finds a job.

8 We _____ all be a lot happier when the exams are over.

3 **Answer the questions with your own predictions. Write full sentences with *will, 'll* or *won't*.**

1 Do you think it'll rain tomorrow?

No, it won't rain tomorrow. It'll be warm and sunny.

2 Who do you think will win the next election in your country?

3 What kind of job do you think you'll have in ten years' time?

4 Will you have (more) children in the next five years?

5 Where will you live in ten years' time?

6 Do you think you will live to be 100?

57 *will/won't + probably/possibly/certainly/definitely*

The future is in mobile phones

Mobile phones will continue to play an important part in our lives. They will possibly become the most important thing we possess. They will certainly be more important than computers. We definitely won't need computers for internet access and emails. Most people will use their phones instead, and personal laptop computers will probably become a thing of the past.

Presentation

You often use the adverbs *certainly, (almost) definitely, possibly* and *probably* with *will* to make predictions:
*Computers **will probably** become a thing of the past.*
*Mobile phones **will certainly** be more important than computers.*

certainty / uncertainty

The adverbs show whether you think something is more or less certain to happen.

	The speaker is . . .
certainly / definitely	100% certain it will happen
almost definitely	90% certain it will happen
probably	more than 50% certain it will happen
possibly	less than 50% certain it will happen

When you use these adverbs with *will* they come between *will* and the main verb.
*They **will certainly be** more important that computers.*
*They **will possibly become** the most important thing we possess.*
When you use the adverbs with *won't* they come before *won't*.
*We **definitely won't** need computers for internet access.*
*We **probably won't** use computers for sending emails.*

Exercises

1 Complete the sentences with the adverb in brackets.

1 Computers in the future will look very different. (probably)

2 In fact, they won't look anything like computers as we know them today. (probably)

3 But they will be part of everything we use. (certainly)

4 Our televisions will include computer technology that can download films and programmes directly from the internet. (definitely)

5 We won't see any difference in our personal music players. (possibly)

6 And we won't change the way we use them. (definitely)

7 But new technology will make it possible to download music directly onto the players without using a computer. (probably)

2 ⊚2.07 Raymond Lacey is a futurologist. His job is to predict the future. Read this interview with him about transport in the future. Choose the correct options. Then listen and check.

Interviewer:	Good morning Doctor Lacey. In one of your articles you say we [1] *definitely / possibly* won't have cars by the end of the century. Why are you so sure?
Lacey:	Actually I didn't say that. I said we [2] *will definitely / definitely won't* have cars that use traditional fuel. There isn't enough oil in the world. But it's difficult to say what we will use in its place. We'll [3] *possibly / certainly* use water or air but it's hard to predict exactly what will happen.
Interviewer:	What about aeroplanes? How do you think they'll be able to fly without oil?
Lacey:	Well, cars will almost [4] *possibly / definitely* fly in the future, so the car and the aeroplane will be the same vehicle.
Interviewer:	Really? When do you think this will happen?
Lacey:	It [5] *probably / definitely* won't happen in my lifetime – I have no doubt about that – but my grandchildren [6] *will probably / probably won't* fly the car to the shops once a week or fly to work.
Interviewer:	And what about travel through time?
Lacey:	No, that's impossible. That will [7] *definitely / probably* never happen.

3 Look at these predictions about the future. Decide if you think they will happen before the end of this century. Add *certainly, definitely, probably* or *possibly* to the sentences. You can change *will* to *won't* if you want.

1 Cars will fly.

2 We will eat pills instead of traditional food.

3 Tourists will travel to the moon.

4 Robots will do all the housework for us.

5 People will live to be 150.

6 Water will become more expensive than gold.

4 Write three more sentences with your own predictions.

1 _____ .

2 _____ .

3 _____ .

58 *may, might, could*
Speculating about the future

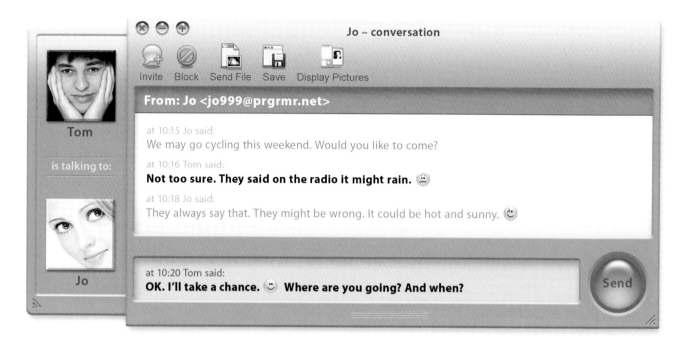

Presentation

You use *may, might* and *could* to show that you think something is possible, but you're not certain.

It **may** / **might** / **could** rain. (= It's possible that it'll rain, but it's also possible that it won't.)

I / You / He / She / It / We / They	may / might / could	go cycling.
	may not / might not / could not	be wrong.

may not / might not

You use *may not* and *might not* to say that you think it is possible that something is not true, or is not going to happen:

It **may not** rain after all.

Be careful – you can't use *could not* with the same meaning.

He **may not** come. = (future, it's possible that he won't come.)

He **couldn't** come. = (past, he wasn't able to come.)

May, might and *could* are modal verbs. See Unit 52 for notes on the rules of form for modal verbs.

Exercises

1   Rewrite the sentences using the modal verb in brackets.

1   It's possible that Sue will get a new job. (may)

Sue ....

2   I don't think I'll go to the meeting tomorrow. (might)

I ....

3   There's a possibility that it will rain during the night. (could)

It ....

4   It's possible that Luis won't be here tomorrow. (may)

Luis ....

5   There's a chance Jess and Marcos won't get married this year (might)

Jess and Marcos ....

6   The economic situation will possibly get worse next year. (could)

The economic situation ....

7   We're thinking of asking Katie to look after the children. (may)

We ....

8   We probably won't take a summer holiday this year. (might)

We ....

2   ⊙2.08 Look at the conversations. Change the words in bold to *might / might not* where possible. Then listen and check.

Conversation 1

Ana: Are you going to the party tonight?

Ben: I don't know. I think I ¹ **won't**   *might not*   be able to go. I need to ask Jan.

Ana: Why, what's Jan doing?

Ben: She ² **'ll** .... have a parents' meeting after work. I'm not sure. If she does, I ³ **'ll** .... definitely need to stay at home to look after the kids.

Conversation 2

Jake: Do you think it ⁴ **'ll** .... rain tomorrow?

Suzy: I don't know. Just a second, I ⁵ **'ll** .... look at the weather forecast on the internet. … Yes, I'm afraid it ⁶ **'ll** .... definitely rain. It says here that there's a 100% chance of it!

Jake: Oh dear! I don't think we ⁷ **'ll** .... go to the beach then!

Conversation 3

Lee: Hello? Bob? Listen, I'm really sorry, but I ⁸ **won't** .... have time to finish that job today.

Bob: Oh no! But I really need it for tomorrow afternoon.

Lee: I think I ⁹ **'ll** .... be able to do it by midday. I ¹⁰ **'ll** .... try my best, at least.

Bob: Thanks, Lee. I really appreciate it.

3   Complete the sentences so that they are true for you.

1   I may .... at the weekend.

2   I might not .... this evening.

3   It could .... later today.

59 *may, might, could, must, can't, couldn't*
Speculating about the present

Bigfoot

A mysterious creature that may live in the forests of north-west Canada. Some theories suggest that the creature might be a bear, and others that it could be a giant ape similar to a gorilla. Similar stories are also told in Indonesia and Australia and many say there must be some truth to them. Others say the creatures can't possibly exist as no one has ever been able to find a body or the remains of a body.

Presentation

You can use *may, might, could, must, can't* and *couldn't* to discuss possible and probable explanations of present situations:

*It **may** live in the forests of north-west Canada.*

*The creature **might** be a bear.*

*It **could** be a giant ape.*

*Many say there **must** be some truth to the stories.*

*Others say they **can't** possibly exist.*

may, might and *could*

You use *may, might* and *could* to say that you think something is possible but that you cannot be certain that is true:

*The creature **may** / **might** / **could** be a bear.*

may not and *might not*

You use *may not* and *might not* to say that you think it is possible that something is not true:

*It **may not** exist.*

can't and *couldn't*

You use *can't* and *couldn't* to say that you think something is impossible:

*It **can't** be true.*

must

You use *must* to say that you believe very strongly that something is true:

*There **must** be some truth to the story.*

You do not use *mustn't* to say that something is impossible:

Say *It **can't** be true.* (don't say *It ~~mustn't~~ be true.*)

May, might, could and *must* are modal verbs. See Unit 52 for notes on the rules of form for modal verbs.

Exercises

1 **Choose the correct modal verb. Sometimes both are possible.**

The Yeti, or Abominable Snowman

Another mysterious creature, similar to Bigfoot, that may or ¹*can't / may not* live in the Himalayas. Some theories suggest that the creature ²*could / may* be an ape and others say it ³*might / must* be an enormous grey wolf. Locals say there ⁴*must / couldn't* be some truth to the story and point to giant footsteps as proof of its existence. Scientists argue that it ⁵*can't / mustn't* possibly be true as no real evidence has ever been found.

2 **Complete the second sentence using the word given in brackets so that it has the same meaning as the first sentence.**

1 That man looks just like John. It's obviously his brother.

(must) That man _____ John's brother, they look so similar.

2 I'm sure that answer's wrong.

(can't) That answer _____ right.

3 They live in the same street. Perhaps they know each other.

(might) They live in the same street. They _____ each other.

4 He looks too young to drive a car.

(can't) He _____ old enough to drive a car.

5 It's possible that the footprints belong to a large bear.

(may) The footprints _____ to a large bear.

6 They've got three houses. They're obviously very rich.

(must) They've got three houses. They _____ very rich.

3 (2.09) **Complete the sentences with *might, must* or *can't*. Then listen and check.**

1 Is that Rose over there? No, it _____ be. She's gone to visit her mother.

2 You've been working since six o'clock this morning. You _____ be exhausted.

3 You're going in the sea? You _____ be serious! It's too cold.

4 Sue _____ want us to bring some food to the party. I'll phone and ask her.

5 He _____ love his job. He's always at the office.

6 He works so hard, he _____ spend much time with his family.

7 That's the phone. I'll get it. It _____ be my mother. She sometimes phones around this time.

8 Jamie's so happy these days. He's always smiling and singing to himself. He _____ be in love!

60 Review of units 56 to 59

Grammar

1 Correct the mistakes.

1 I've got an exam on Monday. I'm going _{to} study really hard over the weekend.

2 Oh no! Look out! It going to fall!

3 I really think our team will to win this time.

4 Take an umbrella with you. It must rain later today.

5 Tom doesn't will be able to come to dinner tonight. He's too tired.

6 The next exam won't definitely be as difficult as the last one!

7 That mustn't be true! It's impossible!

8 They probably'll buy a house when Fran gets a new job.

2 Choose the correct option. Sometimes both are possible.

1 Do you think *we'll ever find / we're ever going to find* intelligent life in space?

2 You *can't / mustn't* be serious! That's a totally crazy thing to do!

3 He *might / couldn't* change his mind. I've no idea.

4 With Tony around, you really don't know what *might / mustn't* happen!

5 We'll *be probably / probably be* back by seven o'clock.

6 I *won't definitely / definitely won't* do that again. I promise!

7 *I'm probably going to / I'll probably* take some time off work next week.

8 That *may / might* be James over there – in the taxi. Look!

3 Rewrite the sentences using the verbs in the box. Use some verbs more than once.

can't going to might must 'll won't

1 He'll probably want something to eat when he gets home.

He might want something to eat when he gets home.

2 I really don't think that's John. He's away on holiday.

That _____. He's away on holiday.

3 There's definitely something wrong. Sally's never late.

Sally's never late so there _____.

4 There's a strong possibility of rain. Look at those clouds.

Those are storm clouds over there. It _____.

5 It's my 30th birthday on Saturday.

I _____ on Saturday.

6 I don't believe they're going to close the station. Too many people depend on it.

They _____. Too many people depend on it.

7 We possibly won't see you again until next year.

We _____.

8 Watch out for that glass! There's a danger of it falling off the table.

Watch out for that glass! It _____ off the table.

9 I can't find my wallet anywhere. I definitely left it at home.

I can't find my wallet anywhere. It _____ be at home.

10 I think it's very unlikely I'll be able to come tonight.

I really don't think I _____ tonight.

Grammar in context

4 Read the article and put the words in bold in the right order.

The future of teaching?

Classrooms of the future [1] **certainly look will** very different from the one in the photo! In fact, most children [2] **may go not** to school at all. They [3] **go will probably** to virtual, 3D schools on their computers or mobile phones. They [4] **may to choose** log on at home in the comfort of their bedrooms. But most [5] **to prefer will** log on in public places, at a café, in a shopping centre or in a park. These online learning centres will offer students freedom, choice and variety. But parents are worried that [6] **will there be** too much choice – and too much freedom. 'They [7] **serious be can't** about this, surely? How [8] **know they will** that the kids are learning and not just playing?' said one concerned parent. But that's the key. The new digital generation is already learning through playing and sharing and communicating in virtual worlds. Teachers [9] **need to going are** to learn how to use these virtual worlds. As one teacher said, 'If it means the kids are having fun as they learn, then [10] **must it be** a good thing!'

1	will certainly look	6	
2		7	
3		8	
4		9	
5		10	

Pronunciation: contracted forms

5 🔊2.10 Listen to five sentences. Are the verb forms contracted or full? Tick the sentences you hear.

1 It can't be true.
   It cannot be true.

2 It mightn't open until later.
   It might not open until later.

3 It couldn't possibly happen.
   It could not possible happen.

4 I definitely won't forget.
   I definitely will not forget.

5 I'll do it tomorrow, I promise.
   I will do it tomorrow, I promise.

Listen again and repeat the sentence you hear.

Listen again

6 🔊2.11 Listen to the interview with Doctor Lacey. Tick the predictions he makes.

1 We won't have cars by the end of the century. ☐

2 Cars may use air or water instead of oil. ☐

3 Aeroplanes will continue to use oil. ☐

4 Cars will be able to fly. ☐

5 Time travel may become possible one day. ☐

61 *can* and *could*
Ability and possibility

Incredible but true

Aron Ralston was climbing in Blue John Canyon, Utah, when his arm became trapped under an enormous rock. He couldn't move. He couldn't call for help. He waited for five days. Finally, he cut off part of his arm with a pocket knife. He lost his arm, but saved his life. But this didn't stop him from climbing. With his new prosthetic arm, he can climb just as well now as he ever could before.

Presentation

Use *can* and *could* to talk about ability and possibility.

can

Use *can* and *can't* (*cannot*) to talk about ability and possibility in the present:

*He **can** climb just as well now as he could before.*

*I **can't** come tomorrow. I'm busy.*

***Can** he climb with his prosthetic arm?*

See Units 59, 62 and 66 for other uses of *can* and *can't*.

could

Use *could* and *couldn't* to talk about general ability and possibility in the past:

*He **could** climb much better than any of the other children in his class.*

*He **couldn't** swim until he was ten.*

***Could** he call for help?*

See Units 58 and 59 for other uses of *could* and *couldn't*.

Exercises

1 Choose the correct form.

1 He's always loved the water. He *can / could* swim when he was three.

2 She teaches French and she *can / can't* speak fluent Chinese as well.

3 When he lost his driving licence, he *could / couldn't* drive for two years.

4 We're a bit worried about Jake. He's six years old, but he still *can't / couldn't* read.

5 You *can / could* see the sea from here before they built that hotel.

6 He was heart-broken and he *could / couldn't* understand why she left him.

7 *Can / Could* you read that poster, over there? Wow! Your eyesight is very good!

8 *Can / Could* you speak Spanish before you moved to Spain?

2 Correct the mistakes. Three sentences are correct.

1 I'm really sorry we ~~could~~ come to the party last night. couldn't

2 My father's going to give me some money so I can buy my first car. ✓

3 Which one of you could run the fastest? Let's have a race to find out!

4 I can speak Spanish really well when I was at school.

5 I really can't believe he's forgotten your birthday!

6 She could believe her eyes when she saw the beautiful flowers.

7 I'm sorry, I don't think I can help you with that. Maybe you should ask Seb?

8 It was a long time before he couldn't walk again after the accident.

3 Look at the pictures. Which do you think are possible? Write sentences using *can, can't, could* or *couldn't* and the verbs in the box.

colours fly jump see sleep ~~sleep standing up~~ swim

1 Horses can sleep standing up.

2 Elephants

3 Penguins

4 Snails

5 Bulls

6 The Tyrannosaurus Rex

4 Complete the sentences so that they are true for you.

1 I can .... but I can't ....

2 When I was .... I could ....

3 I couldn't .... until I ....

62 can/can't, allowed to
Permission and prohibition

Presentation

can / can't

Use *can* and *can't* to talk about permission:

*We **can** usually stay up late at weekends.* (= we have permission to stay up late)

You also use *can* to ask for and give permission.

- asking for permission: ***Can** we stay up late tonight?*
- giving permission: *You **can** stay up late tonight.*
- refusing permission: *You **can't** stay up late tonight because you have to go to school tomorrow.*

be allowed to

You can also use *be allowed to* to talk about permission:

*Are you **allowed to** stay up late at weekends?*

*We're **allowed to** stay up late at the weekend, but we aren't usually **allowed to** watch TV in the evening.*

Exercises

1 **⏺2.12** **Choose the correct forms. Then listen and check.**

A: Thanks for offering to look after the kids.

B: You're welcome. What time do they usually go to bed?

A: They [1] *can / can't* stay up until nine o'clock. They aren't normally [2] *allowed to / can* stay up so late, but there's no school tomorrow.

B: [3] *Can / Can't* they watch TV before they go to bed?

A: Yes, they're [4] *allowed to / can* watch TV, but they [5] *aren't allowed / can't* play any computer games.

B: Will they want me to read them a bedtime story?

A: No, but they [6] *can / are allowed* to read in bed for half an hour before you turn out their lights.

2 **Write sentences to explain the signs using *can* and *can't*.**

1   You can't eat or drink here.
2
3

4
5
6

3 **Complete the conversations. Use the correct form of *can* or *allowed to*.**

Conversation 1

A: I'm sorry, you [1]_____ to smoke here. It's a no-smoking area.

B: Oh. [2]_____ I smoke in the bar?

A: Yes, you [3]_____ .

Conversation 2

C: [4]_____ we [5]_____ to take grammar books into the exam?

D: No, I'm afraid you [6]_____ . But you [7]_____ take your dictionary.

Conversation 3

E: [8]_____ I bring my dog in here?

F: No, sorry. Dogs [9]_____ to come into the hotel. It'll have to stay in the car.

4 **Write three things you can do in your classroom or at work and three things you can't.**

Yes ☺

1   We can _____ .
2   We're allowed _____ .
3   We _____ .

No ☹

4   We can't _____ .
5   We aren't _____ .
6   We _____ .

63 *must, have to, need to*
Obligation, prohibition, no necessity

Tips for running your first marathon

You don't have to be a world-class athlete to run a marathon. You don't even need to be super fit. But you do have to follow a good training programme. And you must start training several months before your first race.

For a few days before the big race, you must make sure you rest well and eat lots of carbohydrates. During the race itself, remember to drink lots of water. You mustn't get dehydrated.

Presentation

must, have to, need to

Use *must, have to* and *need to* to say that it is obligatory or very important to do something. There is very little difference between the three verbs in the affirmative.

Must suggests that the speaker thinks something is necessary: *I must get up early tomorrow morning.* (= I think it's very important.)

Have to and *need to* suggest that somebody else has made the decision: *My trainer says I have to / need to get more practice over the full distance.*

You can also use *must, have to* and *need to* to give advice:

You must start training as soon as possible. (= this is my advice.)

mustn't

Use *mustn't* to express prohibition, or to say that it is very important not to do something:

You mustn't get dehydrated. (= It's very important that you don't get dehydrated.)

Spectators must not cross the road when the race is on. (= This is not permitted.)

don't have to, don't need to

Use *don't have to* and *don't need to* to show that …

- something is not important or essential: *You don't have to / don't need to be a world-class athlete to run a marathon.*

- you can choose not to do something if you want: *You don't have to / need to get up early to train; you can train in the evenings instead.*

don't have to, mustn't

Notice the difference between *don't have to* and *mustn't*:

You don't have to run every day. You can take a day off from time to time. (= There's no obligation, it's your choice.)

You mustn't run every day. You aren't fit enough. (= It's a really bad idea, it's prohibited.)

Obligation / Necessity	must	You must start training several months before your first race.
	have to	You have to follow a good training programme.
	need to	You need to run a distance of ten miles at least three times a week.
Prohibition	mustn't	You mustn't get dehydrated.
No obligation / No necessity	don't have to	You don't have to be a world-class athlete to run a marathon.
	don't need to	You don't need to be super fit.

Exercises

1 Choose the correct form.

1 You *have to / mustn't* train really hard if you want to run a marathon.

2 You *need to / don't have to* follow the advice of an expert if you haven't run a marathon before.

3 You *mustn't / must* run for at least two hours three or four times a week.

4 It can be quite hard at times but you *don't need to / mustn't* stop.

5 I *need to / don't need to* get up really early in the morning if I want to go running before work.

6 You *mustn't / don't need to* run every day if you don't want to, but I think it helps.

7 You *mustn't / don't have to* run the whole race. You can walk some of the way if you want.

8 You really *must / mustn't* be careful not to run too far when you first start training.

2 ⟨♪2.13⟩ Complete the texts using *have to*, *don't have to* and *mustn't*. Then listen and check.

I like my job. I ¹_____ wear a uniform. I can work in jeans and a T-shirt. I ²_____ get up early. I start work at 12. But I ³_____ be late! The boss gets really angry if I'm late.

I love chess. You ⁴_____ be tall, or fast or strong to play! Of course, you ⁵_____ be quick and intelligent. And you ⁶_____ let yourself get distracted. That's a sure way to lose the game!

3 Complete the second sentence using the word given so it has the same meaning as the first sentence.

1 It is essential that you answer all the questions on the exam paper.
(must) You _____ all the questions on the exam paper.

2 It isn't necessary for you to take me in the car. I can go by bus.
(need) You _____ me in the car. I can go by bus.

3 It is sometimes necessary for us to work at weekends.
(have) We _____ at weekends.

4 Smoking is not allowed in the school buildings.
(must) You _____ in the school buildings.

5 It is essential that you go to the front desk when you arrive.
(must) You _____ to the front desk when you arrive.

6 You must get a good night's sleep before an exam.
(need) You _____ a good night's sleep before an exam.

4 Write three things that you *have to do* and three things you *mustn't do* in your flat or house.

have to do

1 _____ .

2 _____ .

3 _____ .

mustn't do

4 _____ .

5 _____ .

6 _____ .

64 could/couldn't, had to/didn't have to, wasn't/weren't allowed to

Permission, prohibition, obligation, no necessity in the past

> My parents sent me away to school when I was twelve. It was a very strict school. We had to wear a uniform all the time – even at weekends. We weren't allowed to wear make-up or jewellery. We couldn't listen to music or read comics. Our parents could only come and visit us on Sundays and we were only allowed to go home for the weekend once a month. I hated it! I was so happy when my parents said I didn't have to go back after the summer.

Presentation

You can talk about permission, prohibition, obligation and necessity in the past with *could, was allowed to, had to,* and *didn't have to*:

Permission	could	Our parents could come and visit us on Sundays.
	was / were allowed to	We were allowed to go home for the weekend once a month.
Prohibition	couldn't	We couldn't listen to music.
	wasn't / weren't allowed to	We weren't allowed to wear make-up.
Obligation / Necessity	had to	We had to wear a uniform.
No obligation / No necessity	didn't have to	I didn't have to go back after the summer.

Notice that there is no past form of *must* and *mustn't*. Use *had to, couldn't* and *wasn't / weren't allowed to*.

'You **must** be in bed by ten.' → We had to be in bed by ten.

'You **mustn't** leave the room!' → We couldn't / weren't allowed to leave the room.

Exercises

1 Match 1–6 to a–f.

1	I had to be home by eleven o'clock during the week.	☐	a	Because our flat was too small.
2	I could borrow my mother's car at the weekends.	☐	b	And sometimes we had parties.
3	I didn't have to work in the school holidays.	☐	c	If she wasn't using it, that is.
4	I wasn't allowed a pet.	☐	d	Sometimes, at weekends, I could stay out until midnight.
5	I couldn't go out much on my own.	☐	e	So I always went out with my big brother.
6	I was allowed to invite friends to my home.	☐	f	But I had to look after my little sister.

2 Choose the correct forms. Sometimes both forms are possible.

A: Hi, how's your new job going in the restaurant?

B: Not too bad. You worked there last year, didn't you?

A: Yes, I did.

B: ¹ *Could you / Did you have to* work in the mornings?

A: No, we didn't. But we ² *could / had to* stay after the restaurant closed to clean up and wash the floors.

B: That's changed. We do that in the morning now. ³ *Did you have to / Were you allowed to* ask for time off?

A: Yes, we ⁴ *could / were allowed to* have two days a week, but we ⁵ *could / couldn't* ask for a Saturday or Sunday.

B: That's still the same. But I don't think it's fair!

A: Yeah, but that's always the busiest time. I remember that the only person who ⁶ *couldn't / didn't have to* work at the weekend was the boss!

3 ⊘2.14 Complete the text with the words in the box. Then listen and check.

could   couldn't   had to   didn't have to   were allowed   weren't allowed

My secondary school was really easy-going. We ¹_____ wear a uniform. We ²_____ wear almost anything we liked. There were a few rules. We ³_____ to wear football shirts unless we were playing official games. And the girls ⁴_____ wear make-up, especially not lipstick. But that was about it. We ⁵_____ to listen to our mp3 players when we were studying if we wanted. But we ⁶_____ to switch off our mobile phones in our exams.

4 Write sentences about you when you were ten years old.

1 I wasn't allowed to _____ .

2 I couldn't _____ .

3 I had to _____ .

4 I didn't have to _____ .

65 Review of units 61 to 64

Grammar

1 **Do these sentences have the same meaning (S) or a different meaning (D)?**

1   A: We don't have to go to bed early tonight.

    B: We can stay up late tonight if we want.

2   A: You can't park your car outside the door.

    B: You mustn't leave your car outside the door.

3   A: You don't have to tell him about your new job.

    B: You mustn't tell him about your new job.

4   A: We were allowed to stay in the classroom to do extra homework.

    B: We had to stay in the classroom to do extra homework.

5   A: You don't need to lock the door.

    B: You can't lock the door.

2 **Correct the sentences. Four sentences are correct.**

1   I mustn't forget to send my mother a birthday card.

2   The doctor says I must lift heavy objects because it's bad for my back.

3   My parents have said we can't have a pet if we promise to look after it ourselves.

4   I had to work in a bar when I was a student to pay for my studies.

5   I can't drive my dad's car until I was 21.

6   We weren't allowed to play football during the break at school.

7   I'm happy I didn't have to go away to school when I was a child.

8   You're allowed to smoke in most public places. It's forbidden by law.

3 **Write the words in bold using the past tense.**

1   Sorry, I **can't come** to the party.

2   We **aren't allowed** to ride our bikes in the school yard.

3   We **must take** the dog for a walk every night.

4   They **can speak** Portuguese very well.

5   We **mustn't use** our mobile phones during the concert.

6   He **has to learn** to control his anger.

7   I **must study** hard to pass my driving test.

8   They**'re allowed to take** laptops into the exam.

4 **Rewrite the sentences using the correct form of the words in brackets.**

1   John doesn't know how to swim.   (can)

2   Is it OK if I smoke here?   (can)

3   Sarah didn't start talking until she was three.   (could)

4   We can't park outside the main offices.   (allowed)

5   There was no need for me to get up early.   (have to)

6   It's very important that you remember to bring your passports.   (must)

Grammar in context

5 Read the article. Then cross out which of the three options (a–c) below cannot be substituted for the words in red.

The world's strangest laws

1 **You can't** call a pig Napoleon in France.

2 **It is illegal to** die in the Houses of Parliament.

3 In Miami, Florida, **you mustn't** skateboard in a police station.

4 In London, **you don't have to** pay to take a flock of sheep across London Bridge.

5 In Florida, unmarried women **can't** parachute on Sundays.

6 **It's illegal to** play golf on the streets of New York.

7 In Kentucky the law still says that everyone **must** have a bath at least once a year.

8 In seventeeth-century Russia, **you couldn't** grow a beard unless you paid a special tax.

9 In fifteenth-century England, **it was illegal for men to** wear a moustache.

10 In the USA in the eighteenth century, **bars couldn't** sell soda water on Sundays.

	a	b	c
1	It is illegal to	It is forbidden to	~~It is allowed~~
2	You must	You mustn't	You aren't allowed to
3	it is illegal to	you're allowed to	it's against the law to
4	it isn't necessary to	it isn't essential to	it isn't allowed to
5	aren't allowed to	mustn't	have to
6	You don't have to	You mustn't	You can't
7	has to	can	needs to
8	you had to	you weren't allowed to	it wasn't possible for you to
9	men weren't allowed to	men couldn't	men didn't have to
10	it was illegal for bars to	bars weren't allowed to	it was possible for bars to

Pronunciation: *to* /tə/

6 (2.15) **Listen to the sentences below. Notice how *to* is not stressed and is pronounced /tə/. Listen again and repeat.**

1 I have to go to the dentist.

2 I don't have to work late tomorrow.

3 I had to get up early this morning.

4 I need to buy a new computer.

5 We weren't allowed to keep pets.

Listen again

7 (2.16) **Listen and tick the things the children can do and put a cross next to the things they can't do.**

1 Stay up until 9 p.m. on weekdays. ☐

2 Stay up until 9 p.m. at the weekend. ☐

3 Watch TV in the evening. ☐

4 Play computer games in the evening. ☐

5 Read in bed. ☐

66 *can, could, may, would, will*
Requests 1

Presentation

You use *can, could, may, would* and *will* for making different types of requests.

Requesting people to do things

You use *can, could, will* and *would* to ask people to do things.

Can	
Could	
Will	you fill in this form, please?
Would	

Requesting things

You use *can, could* and *may* to ask for things.

Can	
Could	I have a wake-up call at seven?
May	

Requesting permission (and offers)

We use *can, could* and *may* to ask permission to do something:

Can	
Could	I take your bag?
May	

You can also use these verbs to make offers:
A: *Can I take your bag?*
B: *Thanks.*

Formality

* *can* and *could*

  could is slightly more formal and less direct than *can*:

  ***Can** you fill in this form, please?* → ***Could** you fill in this form, please?*

* *will* and *would*

  would is more formal and less direct than *will*:

  ***Will** you carry my bag, please* → ***Would** you carry my bag, please?*

* *may*

  may is less common than *will, would, can* or *could* for requests. It is often used for formal requests.

  ***May** I see your passport, please?*

Can, could, may, would and *will* are all modal verbs. This means:

* The third person singular form requires no *-s*.
* The auxiliary verbs *do* and *does* are not used in questions or negatives.
* Modal verbs are followed by the bare infinitive of the verb.

See Unit 52 for notes on the rules of form for modal verbs.

Exercises

1 Choose the correct verbs. Sometimes both forms are possible.

1 *Can / Will* you carry that for me?
2 *May / Can* you take a message?
3 *May / Would* I borrow a pen, please?
4 *May / Could* you answer the phone?

5 *Could / Would* you tell Martha I'll be late?
6 *Can / Could* you move a little, please? I can't see.
7 *Could / Would* I have another glass of water?
8 *Could / Will* you post these letters for me?

2 🔊 2.17 Underline five mistakes in the conversations. Then listen and check.

Conversation 1

Guest: Good evening. Will I have a room for one night?
Receptionist: Yes, of course. Can you to fill this form in, please?
Guest: Certainly. Can I pay with American Express?
Receptionist: I'm sorry. Only Mastercard or Visa.

Conversation 2

Barman: Good evening. Could I get you a drink?
Guest: Yes. May I have a bottle of red wine, please?
Barman: Of course. Would I put that on your room bill?
Guest: Actually, will I pay for it now?
Barman: Sure.

Conversation 3

Guest: Hi. I haven't seen you for ages. May you have dinner with me?
Friend: That would be nice.

3 Write a request for each situation.

1 You need to borrow ten euros from a colleague at work.
Would .... ?

2 You walk into a shop and ask for a kilo of apples.
Can .... ?

3 You ask your teacher if you can leave her lesson early today.
Could .... ?

4 It's hot in the room. A good friend is sitting next to the window. Ask her to open it.
Will .... ?

5 You're sitting on a train. The person next to you has a newspaper. You want to read it.
May .... ?

6 You've hurt your knee. Ask someone to drive you to the hospital.
Would .... ?

7 You want to have lunch early. Ask your boss for permission.
Could .... ?

67 Could you possibly... ?, Would / Do you mind... ?
Requests 2

Presentation

Could you possibly ... ?

You can make *could* in requests more formal and less direct with *possibly*:

Could you move your head to one side, please? → ***Could you possibly*** move your head to one side, please?

Would / Do you mind ... ?

Use questions beginning with *Would you mind ... ?* or *Do you mind ... ?* to make polite requests:

Would you mind *if I sat here?*

Do you mind *if I sit here?*

Do / Would you mind *talking somewhere else?*

Follow with *if* for requests where **the speaker** wants to do something.

Would	you mind if I	opened*	the window?
Do		open*	

*Notice the use of the past simple with *would*.

Follow with the *-ing* form for requests where the speaker wants **the other person** to do something.

Would	you mind	opening	the window?
Do			

Responding to requests

Positive:
Certainly. / Sure. / Of course. / No problem. / Not at all.

Negative:
Actually ... / I'm sorry but ...

The verb *to mind* means *to object*:

Would / Do you mind ... ? = Would / Do you have an objection ... ?

So the normal response to a request with *Would you mind ... ? Do you mind ... ?* is *No*. This shows you are happy to do something.

Would / Do you mind *filling in this form?*

Say *No, not at all.* (= I'm happy to do it.) or *I'm sorry but I can't.* (= I'm not happy to do it.)

Don't say ~~Yes, I do mind.~~ (= I don't feel happy about doing it.)

Exercises

1 **Look at the pictures and write requests.**

1 would / help / lift / box

2 possibly / move / bag

3 do / if / borrow / phone

4 would / copy / answers

5 do / post / parcel for me

2 **Rewrite the requests using the words in brackets.**

1 Will you buy me some milk at the shop?
(possibly)

2 Would you ask Peter to come into my office?
(mind)

3 Can I sit here?   (do)

4 Do you mind helping Rachel with the cleaning?
(could)

5 Do you mind if my brother comes with us?
(would)

6 Would you mind if we met at the café?
(meeting)

3 🔊 **2.18** **Choose the correct responses. Then listen and check.**

1 A: Do you mind if we go in front of you to buy a ticket? Our train is about to leave.
   B: *I'm sorry but / Of course* my train goes in three minutes!

2 A: Would you mind if I left a few minutes earlier today? I have an appointment at the dentist's.
   B: *Yes, I mind. / No, not at all.*

3 A: Could we possibly sit by the window?
   B: *Yes, of course. / No, not at all.*

4 A: Could I possibly talk to you about my salary? I think I deserve an increase.
   B: *No, I couldn't. / I'm sorry but I'm just leaving.* Can we talk about it tomorrow?

5 A: Do you mind turning that music down? I'm trying to write an essay.
   B: *Sorry. Of course I'll turn it down. / Yes, I do.*

68 Making suggestions
Could, should, let's, shall, how about, what about, why don't we, why not

Father:	How about buying Jimmy a pet for his birthday?
Mother:	That's not a bad idea. We could get something small.
Father:	What about getting him the puppy?
Mother:	But who's going to walk it every morning?
Father:	True. Maybe we should choose something that's easy to keep.
Mother:	Why don't we buy the goldfish?
Father:	You must be joking!
Mother:	Why not?
Father:	They don't do anything. They're SO boring.
Mother:	OK. I agree. Shall we buy Jimmy one of those? They're small, easy to keep and cute.
Father:	Agreed. Let's buy him the hamster.

Presentation

should, could, let's, shall

You can use *should*, *could*, *let's* and *shall* + bare infinitive to make suggestions:

We should choose something that's easy to keep.

We could get something small.

Let's buy the hamster.

Shall I / we buy a hamster?

See Unit 53 for more on *Shall I / we … ?* for suggestions.

TIP With the verbs *could* and *should*, you often add the words *maybe* or *perhaps*:

Maybe we should choose something that's easy to keep.

Perhaps we could get something smaller.

How about, What about, Why don't we, Why not

You also use the questions *How about … ?*, *What about … ?*, *Why don't we … ?*, *Why not … ?* to make suggestions:

How / What about buying a pet?

Why don't we / Why not buy the goldfish?

We can use a noun or a verb after *How about … ?* and *What about … ?*. Use the verb in the -*ing* form.

How about	a pet?	
What about	a puppy?	
How about	buying	a pet?
What about	getting	a puppy?

You use the bare infinitive with *Why don't we … ?* and *Why not … ?*

Why don't we		
Why not	buy	a pet?

Exercises

1 Choose the correct options. Sometimes both forms are possible.

1 We *should / could* get some pizza.

2 *We could / Let's* go out for the day.

3 *Why not / What about* driving to the mountains?

4 *How about / Why don't we* working on it in the evening?

5 *Let's / We could* stay in on Saturday.

6 *Why don't / Why not* you do it after lunch?

2 Add suggestions from exercise 1 to the conversation.

A: Are you doing any work over the weekend?

B: Yes, I've got to finish this report. But I don't want to spend all weekend on it.

A: Well, ¹ _____ 5 _____ and do it then?

B: No, I promised to play tennis with Neil on Saturday morning.

A: Well, ² _____ ?

B: No, I always feel really tired after lunch. It really isn't a good time to get any work done.

A: OK, ³ _____ . I'll cook and you can work while I watch the football.

B: ⁴ _____ instead. Then you wouldn't have to cook.

A: Sounds like a good idea to me! And then on Sunday ⁵ _____ . ⁶ _____ and going for a walk. We haven't done that for ages.

B: Sounds like a good plan.

3 Write suggestions for each of these people. Use the words below.

1 don't / cycle / work _____

2 could / use / stairs _____

3 let / have / drink _____

4 perhaps / try walking _____

5 how / take / holiday? _____

6 what / this one? _____

69 should, ought to, had better
Expressing opinions and giving advice

Presentation

You use *should*, *ought to* and *had better* to express opinions and give advice.

should

Use *should* to ask for and give advice in specific situations:

Should I buy her some flowers, do you think?

You should definitely take a present.

You shouldn't worry about taking a present. She won't be expecting one.

You also use **should** to talk about what is generally accepted to be the right thing to do:

What should you do when you're invited to dinner at someone's house?

You should always take a present when you're invited to dinner at someone's house.

You shouldn't arrive too early. Your hosts may not be ready.

ought to

Ought to is similar to *should*. You use it to give advice in both specific and general situations:

You ought to take a present.

Ought I to buy flowers?

You oughtn't to be late you know.

Ought to is less common than *should*, especially in questions and negatives.

had ('d) better

You use *had ('d) better* to give strong advice in specific situations:

You'd better hurry up or you'll be late.

With *had better*, the consequence of not following the advice is often said (or implied):

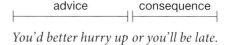

You'd better hurry up or you'll be late.

Notice that in negative sentences *not* comes after *better* and not *had*.

Say *You'd better not forget.* (don't say *You hadn't better forget.*)

hadn't you better ... ? / had you better ... ?

You use the negative form of the question to give advice. It is more common in everyday speech than the affirmative form of the question:

Hadn't you better leave it until tomorrow?

You often use the question form to give advice. Form the question by inverting *have* with the subject:

Had you better leave it until tomorrow?

Exercises

1 Choose the correct form of the verb.

1 I think you *should / shouldn't* do more exercise. You're putting on a bit of weight.

2 Parents *ought / oughtn't* to let their children run around like that!

3 They *'d better / 'd better not* call for a taxi. It's getting late.

4 People *ought / oughtn't* to keep their dogs under control in public places.

5 He *should / shouldn't* talk to her like that. She'll get really angry.

6 You *ought / oughtn't* to talk to her about it. She needs to know the truth.

7 You *'d better / 'd better not* stay much longer. You have to get up early tomorrow morning.

2 🔊 **2.19 Complete the conversations with the positive or negative form of the words in brackets. Then listen and check.**

Conversation 1

A: It's my mum's birthday on Friday. I really
  ¹ _____ (should) buy her something
  in town tomorrow and post it to her.

B: It'll take too long. You ² _____
  (better) get her something online. It's quicker.
  What about flowers?

A: Yes, that's a good idea, and maybe I
  ³ _____ (ought) to get her a book as
  well.

B: I ⁴ _____ (should) worry about a
  book. I'm sure she'll be happy with flowers.

Conversation 2

A: Jack's arguing with the boss again.

B: He ⁵ _____ (better) argue too much
  or he'll lose his job.

A: Yes. I really think he ⁶ _____ (ought)
  to try and relax about things.

B: Right. ⁷ _____ (we / better) say
  something to him?

A: No, we ⁸ _____ (ought) to get involved.
  It could make everything worse.

3 Write advice for these people.

1

2

3

1 You should _____

2 You ought to _____

3 You'd _____

70 Review of units 66 to 69

Grammar

1 Match 1–7 with a–g.

1 Would you like to come to my birthday party on Saturday? __b__

2 Would you mind closing the window, please? It's really cold in here. _____

3 Do you mind if I leave the room for a moment? I need to make a phone call. _____

4 Have you got any money? Could you lend me some? _____

5 Is that the phone ringing? _____

6 What are we going to do this weekend? _____

7 This cake is delicious. I wonder if the lady next door likes cake. _____

a I think so. Shall I answer it?

b ~~I'd love to, but I might have to work this weekend.~~

c No, not at all. There's an empty room next door. Use that.

d No, not at all. Is that any better?

e Why don't you offer her some?

f Sorry, no. I've got nothing till pay day.

g Why don't we have a party?

2 Complete the sentences with the correct form of the verb in brackets.

1 Would you mind _____ (wait) for five minutes?

2 Do you mind if I _____ (sit) here?

3 Why don't we _____ (order) a take-away pizza?

4 What about _____ (ask) Tim to do it for you?

5 You _____ (have) better leave now if you want to catch the train.

6 Why not _____ (give) your old bicycle to your brother?

7 Do you mind if another friend _____ (come) with us to the theatre?

3 There is one word missing in each sentence. Write it in.

1 Do you mind I use your phone?

2 You look exhausted. Why don't take a holiday?

3 If you want to bring a present, why buy flowers? She loves flowers.

4 You ought tell your parents the truth about last night.

5 How about to the cinema tonight?

6 Would you switching your mobile phones off, please?

7 You possibly stand over here while I move these boxes?

8 Hadn't you tell your parents you'll be late?

4 Complete the second sentence so that it has the same meaning as the first sentence.

1 Could we invite Julian?
Would you mind if _____?

2 Would you mind taking the rubbish outside, please?
Could you possibly _____?

3 Would you explain to the man that I don't speak Japanese?
Do you mind _____?

4 We could stop in Paris on the way to Barcelona.
How about _____?

5 What about trying the fish?
Why don't we _____?

6 You had better not walk home. It's very late.
You ought _____.

7 Should you be leaving soon?
Hadn't you _____?

Grammar in context

5 **Complete the text with the correct answer a, b or c.**

The young man drove up to the hotel in a limousine.

'¹ _____ you possibly take these for me, please?' he said to the doorman as he handed him his coat and hat.

'² _____ take your bag for you, sir?' said the porter, as he walked up to reception. Was he the same man? The smiling figure next to the dead body. I turned and asked Joe what he thought.

'It could be. We ³ _____ to talk to him.' Joe suggested.

'Why don't I ⁴ _____ to him alone. Two of us might scare him.'

'I'll be outside if you need me.' Joe left.

I watched the young man start to light a cigarette.

'Do you mind if I ⁵ _____ ?' he asked the receptionist.

'⁶ _____ .' The receptionist pointed at the No Smoking sign.

He slowly turned around and his eyes looked directly at mine. He walked towards me.

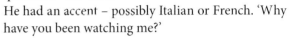

'⁷ _____ ask you a question?' he said.

He had an accent – possibly Italian or French. 'Why have you been watching me?'

'⁸ _____ invite me for a drink,' I said. 'And we can talk about it.'

He was amused by the suggestion. 'Sure. ⁹ _____ go to the bar.' He smiled. At that moment – at that smile – I was certain he was the same man.

1	**a** Do	**b** Shall	**c** Could
2	**a** Do you mind	**b** Why not	**c** May I
3	**a** possibly	**b** ought	**c** should
4	**a** talk	**b** to talk	**c** talking
5	**a** smoke	**b** smoked	**c** smoking

6	**a** No, not at all	**b** I'm sorry	**c** Of course
7	**a** Could I	**b** Would you mind	**c** Let's
8	**a** Why you don't	**b** Why don't you	**c** Why you not
9	**a** Will we	**b** How about	**c** Let's

Pronunciation: intonation in requests

6 (♪ 2.20) **We use intonation to make requests more polite. Listen to this polite intonation:**

1 Can you **help** me? (polite)

Listen to another request. The speaker sounds less polite and the listener might think he is rude:

2 Can you **help** me? (impolite)

7 (♪ 2.21) **Listen to the requests and tick when the speaker is polite.**

1 Would you mind turning off your mobile phone? ✓

2 Do you mind not smoking?

3 Could you possibly say that again?

4 Can I get past you?

5 May I see your ID card?

6 Will you close the door?

8 (♪ 2.22) **Listen to the requests again. They now all have polite intonation. Listen and repeat.**

Listen again

9 (♪ 2.23) **Listen to a man and woman planning their weekend. Complete the diary with their plans.**

71 Infinitive of purpose and adjective + infinitive

It's easy to save the planet ... and save money!

1. Turn down the heating and put on an extra sweater to keep warm.
2. To save energy, switch off the TV and computer at the wall.
3. Recycle glass, plastic and paper in order to reduce waste.
4. When you go shopping, take your own bags in order not to use supermarket plastic bags.
5. Don't wait to fix a dripping tap. If you're afraid to do it yourself, call a plumber.

Presentation

Infinitive of purpose

You use the infinitive of purpose to talk about why a person does something:

*Turn down the heating and put on an extra sweater **to keep warm**.*

***To save energy**, switch all electrical devices off at the wall.*

*I'm waiting **to see my teacher**.*

in order to ... / in order not to ...

You can also use *in order to*. It is often used in more formal writing such as instructions:

*Recycle glass, plastic and paper **in order to** reduce waste.*

*Click here **in order to** back up your computer.*

When the infinitive of purpose is negative, use *in order not to* ... :

Say *Take your own bags **in order not to** use supermarket plastic bags.*

(don't say *Take your own bags ~~not to use~~ supermarket plastic bags.*)

adjective + infinitive

You can use the infinitive form after adjectives:

*It's easy **to save** the planet.*

*I'm pleased **to meet** you.*

*Sometimes English is difficult **to learn**.*

*He's mad **not to go** to the dentist.*

You often use the infinitive with adjectives that describe ...

- feelings: *You're afraid **to do** it yourself. / I'm happy **to be** here.*

- opinions of other people's behaviour: *You're silly **not to see** a doctor. / He's right **to recycle** everything.*

TIP Note the word order for negatives:

Say *You're silly not to see a doctor.* (don't say ... *to ~~not~~ see a doctor.*)

Exercises

1 Match 1–7 to a–g.

1	Look the word up in a dictionary	☐	a	to get there on time.
2	Put your credit card in the machine	☐	b	to visit another country.
3	Turn the key	☐	c	to start the car.
4	You need to leave now	☐	d	in order to understand it.
5	Carry a passport	☐	e	to listen to the news.
6	Take an umbrella	☐	f	to get money out.
7	You can switch the radio on	☐	g	in order not to get wet.

2 Combine the two sentences using the words in brackets.

1 We employ over 200 people. They answer customer calls. (to)
We employ over 200 people to answer customer calls.

2 We provide training to every employee. This helps guarantee quality. (to)

3 Our factories use the latest technology. This improves production. (in order to)

4 We check each product. This is so that we don't sell any that don't work. (in order not to)

5 We own twenty delivery lorries. These deliver our products to your local supermarket. (to)

6 We offer some of the lowest prices. We don't want to be uncompetitive. (in order not to)

3 Complete the sentences with the pairs of words in the box.

afraid + meet   crazy + buy   easy + make   nice + meet   right + be   sad + see

1 How do you do? It's _____ to _____ you.

2 You're _____ to _____ angry. I would be too!

3 Are you _____ to _____ my father?

4 The instructions say it's _____ to _____ .

5 And at this price, you'd be _____ not to _____ it today!

6 We're _____ to _____ you go.

4 Complete the sentences so that they are true for you.

1 I'm always happy to _____ .

2 It's very difficult to _____ .

3 Humans are crazy not to _____ .

4 I think the government is right to _____ .

72 Verb patterns

How do you learn new words?

Tick (✓) the techniques you use for learning new words in English.

A I translate it in my notebook in case I want to read it again later.

B I practise repeating the word a few times.

C I learn by listening to the new word.

D I need to write a sentence with it.

E I keep using it in conversation for the rest of the day.

How many did you tick? Can you think of any other techniques? Why not try all of them?

Presentation

The **main verb** in a sentence is sometimes followed by a second verb. This verb can be an infinitive or the *-ing* form.

*I **want** to read it again.*

*I **keep** using it in conversation.*

The choice depends on the main verb. Some verbs are always followed by a *to*-infinitive; some verbs are followed by the *-ing* form.

See Unit 73 for information about verbs that are followed by both forms.

verb + *to*-infinitive

Certain verbs are always followed by the *to*-infinitive form:

*I want **to read** it again later.*

Common verbs followed by *to*-infinitive: *agree, decide, expect, hope, learn, manage, need, offer, plan, promise, seem, want*

verb + *-ing* form

Certain verbs are always followed by the *-ing* form:

*I keep **using** it in conversation for the rest of the day.*

Common verbs only followed by the *-ing* form: *consider, dislike, enjoy, finish, imagine, involve, keep, mind, postpone, practise, suggest*

verb + preposition + *-ing* form

When a preposition follows the first verb, the next verb uses the *-ing* form:

*Which of these techniques do you use for **learning** new words in English?*

*I learn by **hearing** the new word.*

Common verbs followed by a preposition + the *-ing* form: *apologize for, learn by / from, plan on, stop from, thank for, think of / about, use for, worry about*

verb + bare infinitive (infinitive without *to*)

You use the bare infinitive (infinitive without *to*) with *do / does / did* when you form negatives and questions and with modal verbs, e.g. *can, must, will*:

*How do you **learn** new words?*

*How many did you **tick**?*

*Can you **think** of any other techniques?*

Exercises

1 Complete the sentences with the correct words a, b or c.

1 I never learn by _____ words down.

   a write   **b** to write   **c** writing

2 Can we _____ that film again? It's great!

   a watch   **b** to watch   **c** watching

3 Don't keep _____ your music up so loud.

   a turn   **b** to turn   **c** turning

4 Did the owners of the company agree _____ us more money?

   a pay   **b** to pay   **c** paying

5 I hope _____ a professional football player after school.

   a become   **b** to become   **c** becoming

6 How many new words do you _____ a day?

   a learn   **b** to learn   **c** learning

7 My neighbour paid me for _____ his car.

   a clean   **b** to clean   **c** cleaning

8 Let's postpone _____ out tonight. I'm too busy.

   a go   **b** to go   **c** going

9 This mp3 player doesn't seem _____ .

   a work   **b** to work   **c** working

10 Are you going to apologise for _____ your little sister?

   a hit   **b** to hit   **c** hitting

2 Cross out *to* where necessary.

1 Can you to help me?

2 Can you to stay late at work tonight?

3 They've decided to get married.

4 When do they to plan to get married?

5 Do you want to try that exercise again?

6 How long did you to work here?

7 Did you want to speak to someone?

8 Will you to be able to finish the project on your own?

9 You mustn't to drive so fast on this road.

10 I don't expect to be back here for a while.

3 ⏸2.24 Complete the text with the correct form of the verbs. Then listen and check.

Good morning everyone and thank you for [1] _coming_ (come) today. Do you dislike [2] _____ (look) for new words in a thick, heavy dictionary? Can you imagine [3] _____ (have) instant access to the world's biggest dictionary in every language? Well, today I want [4] _____ (present) the latest in electronic dictionaries, the XtraLingo. It's so simple that anyone can [5] _____ (use) it. First of all, you need [6] _____ (press) the ON button. Then you begin by [7] _____ (type) in a word in English and the machine will automatically [8] _____ (give) you the translation in any language. And don't worry about [9] _____ (carry) it around because the XtraLingo is the size of a mobile phone.

73 Verb + -ing form or to-infinitive
Change of meaning / no change of meaning

Presentation

verb + -ing / to-infinitive

You can follow some verbs with the *to*-infinitive form or the *-ing* form.

*She's started **to cross** the road. / She's started **walking** again.*

*She's stopped **to look** in a shop window. / She's stopped **looking** in the shop.*

No change of meaning

With some verbs there is little or no important change in meaning:

*She's started **to cross** the road. = She's started **crossing** the road.*

*I love **shopping**. = I love **to shop**.*

Common verbs which can be followed by either form: *continue, begin, hate, like, love, prefer, start*

would ('d) + like / prefer / hate to ...

When you use *would* ('d) with the verbs *like, prefer, love, hate,* use the *to*-infinitive form, not the *-ing* form.

Say *I'd like **to go** shopping.* (don't say *I'd like ~~going~~ shopping.*)

Say *We'd prefer **to go** out later.* (don't say *We'd prefer ~~going out~~ later.*)

Change in meaning

Some verbs can be followed by the *to*-infinitive or the *-ing* form but the meaning changes.

stop, remember, forget

Use a *to*-infinitive with *stop, remember* and *forget* when the action happens <u>after</u> the speaker *stops, remembers* or *forgets*:

*She's **stopped to look** in a shop window.* (She was walking but stopped and looked in a shop window.)

*I **remembered to switch** my phone off.* (I remembered my phone was on so I switched it off.)

*I forgot **to look** at her.* (I was supposed to look at her but I didn't.)

Use *-ing* with *stop, remember* and *forget* when the action happens <u>before</u> the speaker *stops, remembers* or *forgets*:

*She's **stopped looking** in the shop window.* (The reason she stopped walking was to look in a shop window.)

*I **remember switching** my phone off.* (I had to switch it off and I did.)

*I'll never **forget looking** at her for the first time.* (I'll always remember looking at her for the first time.)

Exercises

1 **Choose the correct forms. In some sentences, both forms are possible.**

1 We like *going out* / *to go out* on a Saturday night.

2 Would you like *going out* / *to go out* next Saturday night?

3 The dog began *chasing* / *to chase* the cat across the road.

4 I think I'd prefer *drinking* / *to drink* tea this afternoon.

5 My father hates *waiting* / *to wait* for other people.

6 I've never been skiing but I'd love *trying* / *to try*.

7 They love *skiing* / *to ski*. They go every year.

8 If you continue *driving* / *to drive* like this, you'll have an accident.

2 **Rewrite the sentences using the verbs in brackets. Add *would* where necessary.**

1 I enjoy doing any kind of exercise. (like)
   I _____

2 How about trying one of these cakes? (like)
   _____

3 I dream of travelling around the world one day. (love)
   _____

4 My brother often goes sailing. He really enjoys it. (love)
   _____

5 I don't like eating seafood. It's horrible. (hate)
   _____

6 I wouldn't want to see your mother get angry! (hate)
   _____

3 **⊘ 2.25 Match the responses (A and B) to the pairs of sentences. Then listen and check.**

1 They've stopped to talk. _____

2 They've stopped talking. _____

A: Why, what's the matter? Have they had an argument?

B: Well, tell them to hurry up. We're late already.

3 I remembered to turn left at the traffic lights this time. _____

4 I remember turning left at the traffic lights last time I came. _____

A: Great, I'm glad you found our house!

B: Are you sure, because there aren't any houses on this street?

5 I'll never forget going to the dentist's as a child. _____

6 I forgot to go to the dentist's. _____

A: You'd better call and make another appointment.

B: Me neither. I hated it.

4 **Complete the sentences with the *-ing* form or *to*-infinitive form of the verbs in the box.**

come feed fly have see tell

1 This restaurant looks nice. Let's stop _____ some lunch.

2 Why did you stop _____ to the yoga classes? We all miss you.

3 a: Did you remember _____ the cat before we left?
   b: Yes, don't worry. I left enough for two days.

4 I don't remember _____ Joel at the party. Was he there?

5 I won't ever forget _____ over the Andes. The views were incredible.

6 Don't forget _____ Roger that his wife called.

74 Verb + object + infinitive

To do this week!

- Remind Petra to stay late on Thursday.
- I'd like Marcus to plan the next office party – tell him to arrange a planning meeting.
- Tell everyone to meet me at 2 p.m.
- Let the managers know about next month's visit from head office.
- Ask my manager to give me a pay rise!

Presentation

verb + object + *to*-infinitive

You can follow some verbs with an object + *to*-infinitive:

verb	object	*to*-infinitive
Remind	Petra	to stay late on Thursday.
I'd like	Marcus	to plan the next office party.
Ask	my manager	to give me a pay rise!

These verbs include: *advise, ask, expect, hate, help, instruct, invite, like, love, need, order, prefer, remind, request, teach, tell, want, would like, would prefer*

verb + object + bare infinitive

You can follow some verbs with an object + bare infinitive:

verb	object	bare infinitive
Make	everyone	hand in their time sheets.
Let	the managers	know about next month's visit from head office.

These verbs include: *let, make, see, hear, feel, watch, notice*

Exercises

1 The word *to* is missing five times in this list. Write it in.

> To do list
> • Advise Martin apply for a different job!
> • Invite all the staff attend the annual party.
> • Ask reception take all phone calls between 2 and 4.
> • Remind the local sandwich shop make a plate of sandwiches for today's meeting.
> • Let Sally leave an hour early on Friday.
> • Teach the employees how use the new software.

2 Put the words in order.

1 you a copy to make I'd like of this letter
I'd like you to make a copy of this letter.

2 me the police to drive more slowly told

3 when do expect you to arrive them?

4 to clean up the children remind afterwards

5 taught my grandfather to play chess us

6 do you to Harry help need?

7 make wash the children their hands

3 Combine the sentences using verb + object + *to*-infinitive or bare infinitive.

1 Do your own homework. Don't tell other people to do it.
Don't .... homework.

2 Gina wants to make her own decisions now she's eighteen. So let her.
Let .... now she's eighteen.

3 I read English. My mother taught me.
My mother ....

4 Where's your homework? Hand it in by tomorrow at the latest.
I want .... by tomorrow at the latest.

5 Everyone is late. I don't like it.
I like .... on time.

75 Review of units 71 to 74

Grammar

1 Add the words in brackets to the sentences.

1 Do you want ^to call me back later? (to)

2 It works pressing this button. (by)

3 He isn't enough to accept the job. (interested)

4 Can you remind to sign this? (her)

5 Let the boys TV for a while. (watch)

6 Let's take a taxi in order to be late. (not)

7 I'm going to Paris to the Eiffel Tower. (see)

2 Complete the sentences with the correct answer a, b or c.

1 _____ Julian do his homework.
   a Make   b Ask   c Suggest

2 Would you _____ to help me?
   a hating   b like   c to enjoy

3 Billy _____ playing with the toy car you gave him.
   a would like   b wants   c keeps

4 _____ Billy clean his room right now!
   a Remind   b Make   c Tell

5 You need to _____ playing your piano music before the performance.
   a practise   b work   c learn

6 I _____ to tell you but you failed the exam.
   a dislike   b hate   c don't enjoy

7 With my new job, I _____ to have six weeks' holiday a year.
   a plan   b can   c enjoy

8 You _____ visit us next time you are here.
   a consider   b expect   c must

3 Which sentences are correct? Correct the mistakes.

1 Do you remember being thirteen years old? ✓

2 I'll never forget ~~to get~~ my first bike when I was six.
   getting

3 When did you begin learning English?

4 When did you begin to learn Chinese?

5 The politicians have stopped to take a quick break from their discussions.

6 Have you heard Michelle to play the guitar?

7 We're really sad seeing you go.

8 Would you like trying some of this cake?

9 Ask someone in the office to photocopy this.

10 Turn all the taps off in order not to waste water.

Grammar in context

4 Complete the review with the correct form of the verbs in brackets.

What (and how) is your child reading?

We often hear that children and teenagers have stopped
¹ _____ (read) books because of computers.
Kids prefer ² _____ (use) the internet these
days and many parents say it's impossible to make
their children ³ _____ (pick) up a novel. But do
we need ⁴ _____ (worry)? In my opinion, it's
wrong ⁵ _____ (suggest) that we are reading
less. Every day, we read in order ⁶ _____ (work)
with a computer or ⁷ _____ (find) information
quickly online. And if you want to read a novel, you
can buy an electronic reader in order ⁸ _____
(download) novels and newspapers from the internet.
⁹ _____ (use) the e-reader, you read the novel
from a screen that you can carry around with you in
your pocket – it could be the perfect answer for parents
and children.

Pronunciation: sentence stress 2

5 *2.26* **Listen and underline the stressed words in these sentences. Then listen and repeat.**

1 I'm pleased to meet you.
2 It's difficult to learn.
3 It's easy to play.
4 I'm afraid to go.
5 You'd be mad to disagree.
6 We're happy to do it.
7 You're right to worry.
8 It was nice to see you.

Listen again

6 *2.27* **Listen to someone talking about a modern dictionary. Tick the features he mentions.**

1 Access to the world's biggest dictionary ☐
2 Tells you how to pronounce a new word ☐
3 Immediately gives you a translation of any word ☐
4 Small and easy to carry around ☐
5 Buttons and controls are easy to use ☐
6 Battery powers lasts up to fifty hours ☐
7 Costs less than fifty dollars ☐

76 all, most, some, none/no, every, each, both, either/neither

Results of customer survey

We interviewed all the customers that visited the store between 10 a.m. and 11.30 a.m. on 30th May. Every customer who took part tried both products. Three customers refused to try either product. In total we interviewed 100 customers. Some of them were shopping with their partner or in small groups but each of them wrote their own individual comments on separate survey forms.

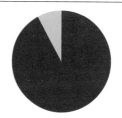

92%
Most customers preferred Product A.

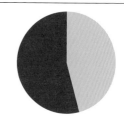

46%
Some of the customers said they would also buy Product B.

Product A   **Product B**

4%
Four customers liked neither Product.

Presentation

all, most, some, none / no

You use *all, most, some, no / none* to talk about the quantity of people or things.

all = ◯   most = ◯   some = ◯   no/none = ◯

You use *all, most, some, no* in front of a noun:

All/Most/Some/No customers preferred Product A.

You can use *all* with *the + noun*:

All the customers preferred Product A.

You can use *all, most, some, none + of* in front of:

• *the + noun: We interviewed all of the customers.*

We interviewed all the customers.

• an object pronoun: *Some of them were shopping alone.*

(don't say *No of the customers / No of them.*)

all, every, each

You use *all, every* and *each* to talk about all the members of a group of people or things:

• Use *all* with a plural noun: *All of the customers have tried the same products.*

• Use *every* and *each* with a singular noun: *Every / Each customer has tried both products.*

You can use *all* and *each* with *of*: *All of them have filled out a separate form. Each of them has filled out a separate form.*

You cannot use *every* with *of*.

Say *Every customer filled out a separate form.* (don't say *Every of them filled out a separate form.*)

both, neither, either

Use *both / both of* to say two people or things are the same: *Their comments were positive about both products.*

Use *neither / neither of* to make a negative sentence: *Four customers liked neither product.*

Use *either* to say the choice between two people or things is not important: *They would buy the ketchup in either bottle.*

You can use *not ... either* instead of *neither*:

Four customers didn't like either product.
(= Four customers liked neither product.)

Both is followed by a plural noun: *both products*

Either / Neither is followed by a singular noun: *either product, neither product*

Exercises

1 **(2.28)** Look at the results of a leisure survey. Complete the text with the determiners in the box. Then listen and check.

> all of them   most   none of them   some of   some

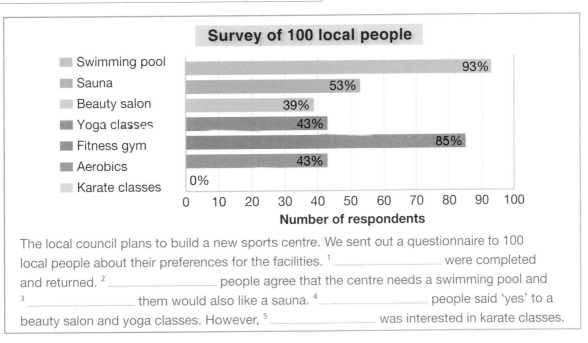

Survey of 100 local people

- Swimming pool — 93%
- Sauna — 53%
- Beauty salon — 39%
- Yoga classes — 43%
- Fitness gym — 85%
- Aerobics — 43%
- Karate classes — 0%

Number of respondents (0 10 20 30 40 50 60 70 80 90 100)

The local council plans to build a new sports centre. We sent out a questionnaire to 100 local people about their preferences for the facilities. ¹_____ were completed and returned. ²_____ people agree that the centre needs a swimming pool and ³_____ them would also like a sauna. ⁴_____ people said 'yes' to a beauty salon and yoga classes. However, ⁵_____ was interested in karate classes.

2 **Complete the sentences using _both, neither_ or _either_.**

1 Make the twins pasta for lunch. _____ of them will eat that.

2 I'll sit in _____ chair. I don't mind where I sit. You choose.

3 A: How was your tennis match?
   B: Not very good. _____ of us was playing very well today.

4 We can turn left or right. We'll get home just as quickly on _____ road.

5 We interviewed two people but _____ of them was very impressive. Let's advertise the job again.

6 Cricket and baseball have some similarities. For example, with _____ sports you use a bat and a hard ball.

3 **Complete the sentences about these groups or pairs.**

1 tennis, boxing, judo, badminton: All_____ of them are sports with two people.

2 butter, milk, cheese, chicken, yoghurt: Most _____ of them are dairy products.

3 London, New York, Sydney, Paris, Venice, Moscow: _____ of them are capital cities.

4 Bill Clinton, George Bush: _____ of them have been Presidents of the USA.

5 cigarettes, alcohol: _____ is good for your health.

6 Penélope Cruz, Antonio Banderas: _____ are Spanish actors.

7 elephants, lions, giraffes: _____ of them live in Africa.

8 Italy, Germany, Spain, Poland, Sweden, Mexico, China: _____ of them are members of the European Union.

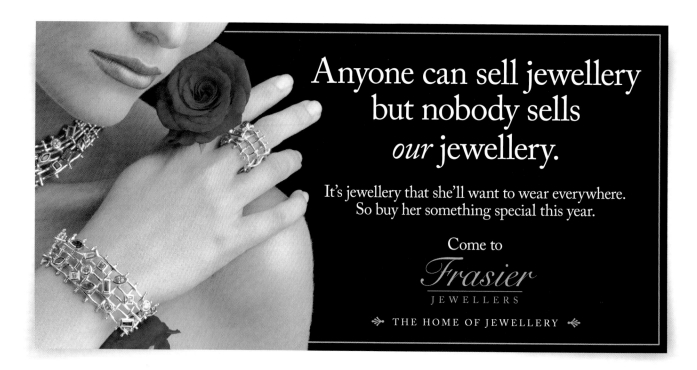

Presentation

You can combine *any, every, no* and *some* with *thing, where, one* and *body* (e.g. *anybody, everywhere, nothing, someone*) to talk in general about things, people or places.

	-thing	-where	-one	-body
any-	anything	anywhere	anyone	anybody
every-	everything	everywhere	everyone	everybody
no-	nothing	nowhere	no one	nobody
some-	something	somewhere	someone	somebody

When a word with *any-/every-/no-/some-* is a subject, the verb is in the singular form:

*Nobody **sells** our jewellery.*

*Everything **is** good at this shop.*

-one / -body

There is no difference between the words ending in *-one* and *-body*.

*Any**one** can sell jewellery but no**body** sells our jewellery. = Any**body** can sell jewellery but no **one** sells our jewellery.*

not any- / no-

not any (*-thing/-where/-one/-body*) and *no* (*-thing/ -where/-one/-body*) have the same meaning:

*There is**n't anything** in the cupboard. = There's **nothing** in the cupboard.*

TIP Notice the spelling: *no one* (not ~~noone~~)

Word order with adjectives

Notice that the adjective comes **after** *something, anywhere* etc., and **not** before.

*Buy her **something** <u>special</u> this year.*

*We didn't go **anywhere** <u>interesting</u> at the weekend.*

Exercises

1 Complete the second half of each pronoun with *thing*, *where*, or *one*.

① There isn't any _____ in the world as beautiful.

② DO SOME _____ INTERESTING WITH YOUR LIFE. JOIN THE ARMY.

③ No _____ will know it isn't real!

④ They're delicious. But don't tell every _____. They'll all want one, or two, or three...

2 Complete the first half of each pronoun with *any*, *every*, *no* or *some*.

① You'll never drive _____ thing like it again in your life.

② Buy it for _____ body special in your life.

③ Go _____ where with this bag. It's an essential.

④ $ALE PAY NO MORE THAN A DOLLAR. _____ thing at our shop costs more than a dollar!

3 Complete the sentences.

1 I'm sure you'll meet _____ special one day.

2 The museum is so boring. Can we go _____ more interesting today?

3 Why is _____ tired today? Did you all stay out late last night?

4 There isn't _____ left in the kitchen cupboards. I need to go to the shop.

5 There's _____ new in my department. We've all been here for years.

6 A: Do you ever go _____ abroad for your holidays?
   B: No. I like having my holidays at home.

4 Complete these sentences so that they are true for you.

1 I'd like to live somewhere _____ .

2 Everybody in my class is _____ .

3 I won't eat anything _____ .

4 Nobody knows this about me: I _____ .

78 Defining relative clauses 1
who, which, that, whose, where, when

Man:	Oh look! It's that actor whose films we love!
Woman:	Are you sure?
Man:	Yes, he's the one who's always in films with Julia Roberts.
Woman:	I don't recognise him.
Man:	Don't you remember his film about the bank robbery which goes wrong? It was hilarious!
Woman:	Oh, I know the one. So, is that his girlfriend?
Man:	Yes, but it isn't the same girlfriend that he brought last year.
Woman:	Really? What happened!
Man:	Well, the newspapers say he wouldn't answer the phone one day when she called him.

Presentation

Use *who, which, that, whose, where* and *when* to introduce defining relative clauses. These clauses give us essential information about people, things, possessions, places or a time.

• Use *who* for people: *He's an actor **who** makes science-fiction films.*

• Use *which* for things: *I only watch films **which** make me laugh.*

• Use *whose* for possessions: *That's the actor **whose** new film we saw last week.*

• Use *where* for a place: *That's the town **where** we met.*

• Use *when* for a time: *He wouldn't answer the phone one day **when** she called him.*

You can also use *that* for people or things instead of *who* or *which*:

*It isn't the same girlfriend **that** he brought last year.*

*It isn't the same girlfriend **who** he brought last year.*

Exercises

1   Match 1–6 to a–f.

1	He's the person	☐	a who's always late for work.
2	He only does jobs	☐	b job I want.
3	I saw him at the weekend at that café	☐	c when we normally break for coffee.
4	Ten thirty is the time	☐	d which he likes doing.
5	That's the manager whose	☐	e works in accounts!
6	He came to the office to see the new girl that	☐	f where we often go after work.

2 (2.29) **Complete the conversation with the words in the box. Then listen and check.**

| when | where | which | who | whose |

A: This is the villa ¹ _____ we stayed. It was next to the sea.

B: Looks nice.

A: It was. And these are the people ² _____ car we borrowed. They were very generous.

B: Yes, they were. Who's this?

A: He's the man ³ _____ showed us round the island. He was a really good tour guide. One day we went to a parade ⁴ _____ always takes place at the end of the summer. Here's a photograph of it. It's a special day ⁵ _____ everyone dresses up and walks through the streets.

3 **Which answers in exercise 2 can you replace with *that*?** _____

4 **Complete the sentences with *who, which, whose, where* or *when* and the phrases in the box.**

| controls the traffic | new song we like so much | stores information | you can relax | you feel a little special |

1 It's something _____

2 It's a place _____

3 That's the band _____

4 It's someone _____

5 It's the one day in the year _____

5 **Complete these sentences so that they are true for you.**

1 A good teacher is someone who _____ .

2 The best part of the year is the period when _____ .

3 Home is a place where _____ .

4 I usually read books which _____ .

5 _____ is a singer whose music I really like.

79 Defining relative clauses 2
Combining sentences / omitting the relative pronoun

Stratford-upon-Avon

THE HOME OF *Shakespeare*

Stratford-upon-Avon is an old English town which attracts about three million visitors every year. Stratford is famous because of the playwright who lived there.

This is the house where Shakespeare was born.

This is one of the three pictures we have of Shakespeare from his life.

Presentation

Combining sentences

You can use *which, who, where, whose, when* and *that* to combine sentences:

Stratford-upon-Avon is an old English town. Stratford-upon-Avon attracts three million visitors every year.

*Stratford-upon-Avon is an old English town **which** attracts three million visitors every year.*

Omitting the relative pronoun (*which, who, that*)

Subject of the relative clause

You always use *which, who* and *that* when it is the subject of the defining relative clause (i.e. when it is followed by the verb).

Say *Stratford-upon-Avon is famous because of the playwright **who** lived there.*

(don't say *Stratford-upon-Avon is famous because of the ~~playwright lived~~ there.*)

Object of the defining relative clause

You don't have to use a relative pronoun (*who, which, that*) when it is the object of the relative clause (i.e. when it is followed by a noun or pronoun).

Say *This is one of the three pictures **which we** have of Shakespeare.*

Say *This is one of the three pictures **we** have of Shakespeare.*

Exercises

1 Combine the sentences using the words in brackets.

1 Picasso was an artist. He was able to paint in many different styles. (who)
   Picasso was an artist who was able to paint in many different styles.

2 Paris is a popular tourist destination. It attracts 15 million visitors per year. (which)

3 4th April is the date. People in the USA remember Martin Luther King. (when)

4 Elvis lived in a house. It was called Graceland. (that)

5 Midnight on 31st December is a special time. Many people let off fireworks. (when)

6 The card is from a friend. She lives in Italy. (who)

7 The Louvre is an art gallery. Many people go to see the Mona Lisa. (where)

8 Switzerland is a country. It has four national languages. (which)

2 Cross out the relative pronoun where possible.

1 This is the school uniform ~~which~~ I wore as a child.
2 That's the same man who we talked to earlier.
3 She's the actress that was in that other film with Hugh Jackman.
4 Over there is the factory which is going to close down.
5 This tree is the first of many which we hope to plant around the town.
6 Aren't you the student who asked to change classes?

3 Add the missing relative pronoun (*who, which, whose, where*) to the sentences where necessary.

1 It isn't a book I've read. ✔

2 It isn't a book ˄*which* interests me.

3 My grandfather is one of those people never seems to look older.

4 She's a TV presenter I can't stand watching!

5 *Gone with the Wind* is a film lasts for over four hours.

6 He's the man bag we found.

7 That's a nightclub lots of students like to go to on a Friday night.

8 The piano is an instrument I'd like to be able to play.

80 Review of units 76 to 79

Grammar

1 Put the words in order.

1 for them dinner coming are of some

2 speak language either can I

3 good you're anything hungry tastes if

4 have I go anywhere don't to this afternoon

5 take special them let's something

6 train which we is the catch this

7 whose is my neighbour is missing that dog

8 the person are you left a message that this morning?

2 Choose the correct options. In some sentences, both answers are possible.

1 This room is full of boxes. We need to move *all of / all* them.

2 I don't like *neither / either* colour for this room.

3 *Every / Each* student has to pass this exam.

4 This is the house *where / which* Elvis lived.

5 All our products *is / are* good quality.

6 There*'s no / isn't any* milk in the fridge.

7 Nobody *make / makes* these kinds of printers anymore.

8 Is there *anywhere / everywhere* near here we can go for lunch?

9 Are you the person *who / that* I'm supposed to speak to about a job?

10 There's a place *where / that* we can buy some water.

11 Are you the person *who's / whose* car is in front of my house?

12 Johnny Depp is an actor *who / that* I'd like to meet.

3 Correct the mistakes.

1 Neither film ~~are~~ very good.
  is

2 Every customers complained about this product.

3 Did you buy her nice something for her birthday?

4 Everybody leave work at five.

5 There isn't nobody old enough to drive in my class.

6 Michael Phelps is the swimmer won eight Olympic gold medals in Beijing.

7 Is that the town which you grew up?

8 This is the person who car we borrowed.

4 Rewrite the sentences using the words in bold.

1 There isn't anybody at the door.
  nobody .

2 No staff work here at the weekend.
  no one .

3 Let's go to a quiet restaurant for dinner.
  somewhere .

4 I've been all over the world.
  everywhere .

5 Why will nobody come out with me tonight?
  anybody .

6 All people like chocolate!
  everyone .

7 I think there's a person at the door.
  someone .

8 There's nothing left to eat.
  anything .

Grammar in context

5 **Complete the text with the correct answer a, b or c.**

Visit Hampton Court Palace

Are you looking for ¹ _____ to do this weekend? Visit Hampton Court ² _____ is one of England's oldest and most beautiful royal palaces. Its most famous resident was King Henry VIII ³ _____ lived here 500 years ago. ⁴ _____ part of the palace has a special story. It was the palace ⁵ _____ Henry's first and only son was born. You might even meet the two palace ghosts. ⁶ _____ of them walk along the corridors at night.

Apart from the ghosts, ⁷ _____ lives here now though the palace still belongs to the Queen of England. Luckily, it's open to ⁸ _____ throughout the year and there's ⁹ _____ here for the whole family. As well as looking at the beautiful architecture and paintings inside, walk around the gardens and of course ¹⁰ _____ will want to miss a visit to the famous maze.

1	a something	b anywhere	c somewhere
2	a who	b where	c which
3	a who	b where	c which
4	a All	b Each	c Either
5	a who	b where	c which
6	a Both	b Most	c Neither
7	a anybody	b nobody	c everybody
8	a each one	b all of them	c everyone
9	a nothing	b anything	c something
10	a anyone	b no one	c someone

Pronunciation: vowel sounds 3

6 🔊 **2.30** **Write these words in the table according to their vowel sound. Then listen and check.**

all	<u>a</u>ny	both	<u>e</u>very	most	none	some

/e/	/ɔ:/	/əʊ/	/ʌ/

Listen again

7 🔊 **2.31** **Listen again and answer the questions.**

1 What is the local council planning to build?

2 How many people received the questionnaire?

3 Does everyone want a swimming pool?

4 Does everyone want a beauty salon and yoga classes?

5 Is anyone interested in karate classes?

81 The passive 1: present simple, past simple, *by*

Apples – the world's favourite fruit

- More than 50 million tonnes of apples are grown every year.
- The first apples were grown in central Asia.
- The first apple tree was brought to Europe by Alexander the Great.
- Apples were introduced to the Americas by Europeans in the 1600s.
- Today, most apples are produced in China.
- Apples aren't usually found in tropical countries.

Presentation

You can use the passive to talk about facts and processes.

Most apples **are grown** *in China.*

The passive focuses attention on an action or the object of the action. The object of the action becomes the subject of the verb.

	action	object	
People	grow	apples	*in China.*

	subject	verb	
	Apples	are grown	*in China.*

To form the passive, use the verb *be* + past participle.

See page 235 for a list of common irregular past participles.

Affirmative and negative – present simple and past simple

This apple juice	is / was isn't / wasn't	made	
			in China.
These apples	are / were aren't / weren't	grown	

Questions – present simple and past simple

	Is / was	this apple juice	made	in China?
Where	are / were	these apples	grown?	

by

When you want to say who or what was responsible for the action (the subject or agent of the action) you use *by*:

Apples were introduced to the Americas **by** *Europeans in the 1600s.*

You may not want to say who or what did the action. You can also say:

Apples were introduced to the Americas in the 1600s.

You don't normally use *by* when the agent is …

- obvious and therefore unnecessary:

  The first apples were grown in central Asia ~~by Asian farmers~~.

- unknown:

  An apple was left on my desk. (I don't know who left it there.)

Exercises

1 Complete the sentences with the present simple passive or the past simple passive form of the verb in brackets.

Banana facts

The first bananas [1] _____ (grow) in Papua New Guinea.

Now bananas [2] _____ (produce) in over 100 tropical countries all over the world.

Green bananas [3] _____ (use) for cooking and yellow bananas [4] _____ (eat) uncooked. Banana skin [5] _____ (use) for making paper.

The banana tree [6] _____ (introduce) to the east coast of Africa by Muslim Arabs.

The first bananas [7] _____ (bring) to the Americas by Portuguese sailors in the 6th century AD.

Hundreds of accidents [8] _____ (cause) every year by people slipping on banana skins.

2 Complete the second sentence so that it has the same meaning as the first sentence. Use a passive verb.

1 People in the west buy too much food.

Too much food _____ in the west.

2 We do not eat all the food we buy.

Not all the food we buy _____ .

3 Last year we threw away more than six million tonnes of food.

More than six million tonnes of food _____ last year.

4 The 'Love Food Hate Waste' organisation started a campaign to stop waste.

A campaign to stop waste _____ by _____ .

5 The campaigners persuaded thousands of people to waste less food.

Thousands of people _____ .

3 🔊 2.32 **Cross out the phrases with *by* where they are not necessary. Then listen and check.**

1 Pasta was first brought to Italy by Marco Polo.

2 Pasta is now eaten by people all over the world.

3 Tomatoes were first grown in South America by tomato growers.

4 The first cookbook with tomato recipes was written in Naples by a writer.

5 Parmesan cheese is made in Italy by the cheese makers of Parma.

6 The cheese is made by cheese makers with cow's milk.

82 The passive 2: passive or active

New bridge under construction

A new bridge is going to be built across the bay of Cádiz.

"We're building a second bridge across the bay. The bridge will be completed by this time next year."

The mayor announced today that the new bridge will be ready for use in twelve months' time.

Presentation

In a sentence with an active verb, the subject of the verb is the person or thing responsible for the action:

We are building a second bridge across the bay.

In a sentence with a passive verb, the subject of the verb is the object of the action:

*A **new bridge** is going to be built across the bay.*

The choice between active and passive depends on what or who you want to focus on.

The bridge was designed by a local architect. (You are focusing attention on the bridge.)

A local architect designed the bridge. (You are focusing attention on the architect.)

You can form the passive with *be* in a variety of tenses.

Present perfect	We've built a bridge. → A bridge **has been** built.
Present continuous	We're building a bridge. → A bridge **is being** built.
Past continuous	They were building a bridge. → A bridge **was being** built.
Past perfect	They had built a bridge. → A bridge **had been** built.
Going to	We're going to build a bridge. → A bridge **is going to be** built.
Will	We'll build a bridge. → A bridge **will be** built.
Can / must / may / might	We can / must / may / might build a bridge. → A bridge **can / must / may / might be** built.

Exercises

1 Choose the correct form of the verb.

Tower Bridge is probably the most famous bridge in London. It [1] *calls / is called* Tower Bridge because it [2] *locates / is located* near the Tower of London. The City of London first [3] *started / was started* to plan a new bridge across the Thames in 1876. A public competition [4] *organised / was organised* to choose the best design. More than 50 designs [5] *received / were received* and it [6] *took / was taken* eight years for the judges to choose the winning design. The bridge [7] *finally completed / was finally completed* in 1893. The bridge [8] *still uses / is still used* today. More than 40,000 people [9] *cross / are crossed* the bridge every day.

2 Write one active and one passive sentence to describe each picture. Use the verbs in the box.

> break   cut   eat   paint

1   The men are _____ .
    The house is _____ .
2   The woman is _____ .
    The grass is _____ .
3   The children have _____ .
    All the cakes have _____ .
4   The boys have just _____ .
    The window has just _____ .

3 Rewrite the sentences using the words below. Use the passive or active form. Do not include the agent in the passive sentences.

1   The local council are building new houses on the edge of town.
    New houses _____ .
2   The houses will be finished in two years' time.
    The builders _____ .
3   The company has opened five new shops this year.
    Five new shops _____ .
4   Three more shops might be opened next summer.
    They _____ .
5   Local residents are going to hold a protest about road works in the town centre.
    A protest _____ .
6   The roadworks will affect local businesses.
    Local businesses _____ .

83 The passive 3: verbs with two objects

High school girls win gold!

Here's a photo of the lucky winners! The members of the winning team were given gold medals and a prize of £1,000 was awarded to the winning school.

Congratulations girls!

Presentation

Some verbs can have two objects: a direct object and an indirect object (see Unit 39):

	direct object		indirect object
The organisers gave	medals	*to*	the girls.
They awarded	a prize	*to*	the winners.

When a verb has two objects, you can form two passive sentences …

- either with the **direct object** of the action as the subject of the passive verb:
  Gold medals *were given to the girls.* **A prize of £1,000** *was awarded to the school.*
- or with the **indirect object** of the action as the subject of the passive verb: **The girls** *were given gold medals.*
  The school *was awarded a prize of £1,000.*

Use of prepositions

When the passive sentence starts with the direct object of the action, you use a preposition with the indirect object:

direct object		indirect object
Gold medals	*were given to*	the girls.
A prize of £1,000	*was given to*	the school.

When the passive sentence starts with the indirect object of the action, you don't need a preposition:

indirect object		direct object
The girls	*were given*	gold medals.
The school	*was given*	a prize of £1,000.

Passive sentences with verbs with two objects that start with a personal pronoun are common:

They were promised a lot of things.

I was sent some information by email.

We were shown some plans for the stadium.

Here are some verbs that can have two objects and are commonly used in the passive: *buy, give, leave, lend, pay, promise, send, show, teach, tell.* (See also Unit 39.)

Exercises

1 **Write two passive sentences for each of the active sentences below. Do not include the agent.**

1 The organisers gave all the boys new football shirts.
   a All the boys were given new football shirts.
   b Football shirts were given to all the boys.

2 The bank is going to lend the school £10,000 for new sports equipment.
   a The school
   b £10,000

3 They paid the gallery a lot of money for the painting.
   a The gallery
   b A lot of money

4 The organisers will send a letter to all the participants.
   a All the participants
   b A letter

5 The older pupils showed the new sports hall to the visitors.
   a The visitors
   b The new sports hall

6 The sports teachers are going to teach the children a new dance routine.
   a The children
   b A new dance routine

2 **Add *to* to the sentences where necessary.**

1 He was given a new bicycle for his birthday.

2 An urgent letter was sent her family by the director of the school.

3 A £100 reward was promised the person who found the missing cat.

4 The visitors were offered traditional flowers as they arrived.

5 He was paid a lot of money for his work.

6 The photographs were shown the press.

7 He was left over a million pounds by his grandfather.

8 Bedtime stories were always read her by her father.

3 **Rewrite the sentences in exercise 2.**

1 A new bicycle was given to him for his birthday.
2 Her family
3 The person who found the missing cat
4 Traditional flowers
5 A lot of money
6 The press
7 Over a million pounds
8 She

84 *have/get something done*

Presentation

Use *have / get* + object + past participle to talk about things other people do for you:

A: *Did you cut your own hair?*

B: *No, I* **got** */* **had** *my hair* **cut** *at the salon across the road.* (= a hairdresser cut it for me.)

You can use *have / get something done* in a variety of tenses:

I (don't) **get** */* **have** *my hair* **cut** *very often.*

Where do you **get** */* **have** *your hair* **cut**?

I'm **having** *my car* **repaired** *today.*

I'll **get** *my suit* **cleaned** *tomorrow.*

Have *you* **had** *your ears* **pierced**?

The neighbours **haven't had** *their house* **painted** *for ages.*

TIP *Get something done* is more informal than *have something done.*

Exercises

1 **Match 1–6 to a–f.**

1. I have my breakfast ☐
2. I get my letters ☐
3. I get my hair ☐
4. I have my nails ☐
5. I get all my clothes ☐
6. I have fresh flowers ☐

a. brought to my bedroom every morning.
b. brought to my house every day.
c. made for me by a designer.
d. manicured once a week.
e. read to me as I eat my breakfast.
f. styled by my personal hairdresser.

2 **Put the words in order.**

1. hair   cut   where   usually   your   get   do   you?

2. checked   I   my   had   yesterday   eyes

3. get   delivered   a   newspaper   don't   we   to   the   office

4. did   taken   photo   your   when   you   have?

5. painted   getting   I'm   my   nails   tomorrow

6. I   shaved   have   would   never   my   head

3 🔊 **2.33** **Complete the conversation using *have / get something done.* Use the words in brackets and sentences 1–6. Then listen and check.**

1	The builders put new windows in last week.
2	The decorators painted the living room walls yesterday.
3	They're doing the kitchen today.
4	The builders are putting the bookshelves up now.
5	And they're going to polish the floor tomorrow.
6	The furniture will be delivered on Monday.

A: Hi, how's it going?

B: Not too bad. We ¹ had new windows put in _____ (have) last week.

A: Oh, yes, very nice.

B: And we ² _____ (get) yesterday.

A: I love the colour!

B: We ³ 're _____ (get) today.

A: Yes, I saw the builders in there …. It looks great.

B: And, as you can see, we ⁴ _____ (have) now as well. Tomorrow we
⁵ _____ (have). We ⁶ _____
(get) on Monday – and the day after we'll move in!

A: Well done! I think you've done a great job!

85 Review of units 81 to 84

Grammar

1 Correct the mistake in each sentence.

1 Football ~~are~~ *is* played all over the world.

2 The modern version of association football first played in 1863.

3 The first official league matches was played between English teams.

4 The first World Cup was won for Uruguay in 1930.

5 The trophy was presented the winning team by the country's President.

6 The Olympic stadium are being rebuilt after an accident.

7 The building work might completed in the new year.

8 The team got made new shirts for the final.

9 He always has his hair cutting before a big match.

2 Complete the conversations with the verbs in brackets in the passive or active form.

Conversation 1

A: When [1] _____ (they / sell) the house?

B: It [2] _____ (sell) about two months ago, I think.

A: Who [3] _____ (they / sell) it to?

B: It [4] _____ (buy) by a family from New York.

Conversation 2

A: Have you heard the news? A new shopping centre [5] _____ (going to / build) in the old town.

B: Really? When [6] _____ (that / announce)?

A: Last night. They [7] _____ (announce) it on the local news.

Conversation 3

A: Did you hear the announcement about the underground? It said 'All services [8] _____ (cancel) on the Northern line.'

B: Oh no! That's terrible. They [9] _____ (do) that last week as well!

Conversation 4

A: Hey! When [10] _____ (you / get) your hair [11] _____ (do)?

B: I [12] _____ (have / it / do) last week at that new salon in the mall.

A: It looks great!

3 Complete the second sentence so that it has the same meaning as the first sentence.

1 Someone painted their house for them.
They had _____
_____ .

2 They grow a lot of potatoes in India.
A lot of _____
_____ .

3 People are buying more and more books online.
More and more books _____
_____
_____ .

4 The mayor is going to open the new town library.
The new town library _____
_____ .

5 The window cleaners wash our windows once a week.
We get _____
_____ .

6 All the pupils will be given new computers.
New computers _____
_____ .

Grammar in context

4 Complete the text with the phrases in the box.

a	as she is known in Italian	f	it is seen
b	by the French Government	g	the King of France
c	a special glass case	h	was moved
d	he was given	i	was found again
e	restoration work	j	wasn't finished

The Mona Lisa is probably the most famous painting in the whole world. It is owned ¹ _____ . It is on display in the Louvre museum in Paris where ² _____ by about six million people every year. The Mona Lisa, or the Giaconda ³ _____ , was painted by Leonardo da Vinci in the 16th century. He started painting it in 1503, but it ⁴ _____ until 1519. The painting was bought by ⁵ _____ and it was kept at the royal residence at Versailles until the French Revolution, when it ⁶ _____ to the Louvre. The painting was stolen in 1911 but it ⁷ _____ two years later. The thief was arrested and ⁸ _____ a short prison sentence. The painting has had ⁹ _____ done to it and the museum had ¹⁰ _____ made to protect it from future damage.

Pronunciation: word stress

5 Look at the past participles in the box. How many syllables does each one have?

completed (3) delivered directed introduced
located organised persuaded telephoned visited

6 2.34 Match each past participle to the correct stress pattern. Listen and check.

●●●	●●●	●●●
	completed	

Listen again

7 2.35 Listen and tick the things on the list that have already been done.

To do

1 Put in the new windows
2 Polish the floor
3 Paint the kitchen walls
4 Install the new kitchen
5 Paint the living room walls
6 Build the bookshelves
7 Get the furniture delivered

86 Direct speech

Alice in Wonderland
Chapter 3

The Caterpillar and Alice looked at each other.

'Who are you?' said the Caterpillar. Alice replied, 'Tell me who you are, first.'

'Why?' asked the Caterpillar.

'I don't have a good reason,' Alice thought and began to walk away.

'Come back!' shouted the Caterpillar. 'I've something important to say!'

Presentation

You use direct speech to report someone's …

- words:

  'Who are you?' said the Caterpillar.

  Alice replied, 'Tell me who you are, first.'

- thoughts:

  Alice thought, 'I don't have a good reason.'

Common reporting verbs are: *said, asked, replied, told (someone), shouted, thought*

When the direct speech is at the beginning of the sentence, you can put the reporting verb before the subject.

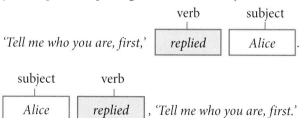

'Tell me who you are, first,' | verb: *replied* | subject: *Alice* .

subject: *Alice* | verb: *replied* , *'Tell me who you are, first.'*

If the subject is a pronoun (e.g. *she*), you always use subject + verb.

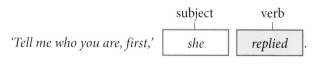

'Tell me who you are, first,' | subject: *she* | verb: *replied* .

TIP You often see direct speech in stories and fiction.

Punctuation rules

Quotation marks

Write quotation marks around the words spoken (or thought):

'Who are you?'

'Tell me who you are, first.'

Commas

Write a comma between the reporting verb and the direct speech:

Alice replied, 'Tell me who you are, first.'

If the direct speech comes before the reporting verb, you write a comma instead of a full stop:

'Tell me who you are, first,' Alice replied.

Full stops

Use a full stop (not a comma) when the direct speech ends the sentence:

Alice replied, 'Tell me who you are, first.'

Other punctuation marks

We often write *question marks* (?) or *exclamation marks* (!) in direct speech.

'Why?' asked the Caterpillar.

'Come back!' shouted the Caterpillar.

Don't write a comma after these punctuation marks.

Exercises

1 Write direct speech for each picture using the reporting verbs in the box.

| asked (×2)   replied   ~~said~~   shouted   thought |

1 He said, 'Hello, my name's Richard.'

2 She

3 The police officer

4 The girl

5 The passport officer

    The tourist

2 Rewrite sentences 1–6 in exercise 1. Put the direct speech first and then the subject and the verb.

1 'Hello, my name's Richard,' he said.
2
3
4
5
6

3 Add punctuation to the sentences.

1 Hello Michael said the woman's voice on the phone.
2 Who is this I asked.
3 The voice on the phone laughed and replied Don't you recognise my voice Michael
4 I said No
5 Are you sure the voice asked.
6 I thought It can't be her. Not after all these years.
7 Michael shouted the voice. You know who I am. And you remember what you did.
8 I thought I don't want to remember

87 Reported speech
(also called 'indirect speech')

'I have a dream . . .'

In 1963, Martin Luther King said that he had a dream . . .

Presentation

You use reported speech (or indirect speech) to report someone's words from the past:

'I have a dream.' → *In 1963, he said that he had a dream.*

that

You often use the conjunction *that* after the reporting verb. There is no difference.

*In 1963, he said **that** he had a dream.* ✓   *He thought **that** he could change people.* ✓

In 1963, he said he had a dream. ✓   *He thought he could change people.* ✓

Change in tense

When you report what someone said, you often move the tense 'backwards'.

present simple → past simple (I **have** a dream. → He said he **had** a dream.)

present continuous → past continuous (You**'re meeting** me at six. → You said you **were meeting** me at six.)

present perfect → past perfect (We**'ve finished** the book. → They said they **had finished** the book.)

will → *would* (I**'ll call** you back. → Gill said she**'d call** me back.)

can → *could* (We **can** help you. → They said they **could** help us.)

past simple → past perfect (We **wanted** more time. → They said they **had wanted** more time.)

Change in pronoun

Sometimes, you also need to change the pronoun. In this speech *I* becomes *he* because another person is talking about Martin Luther King:

Martin Luther King: *'**I** have a dream.'*

Other person: *In 1963, he said that **he** had a dream.*

Exercises

1 Rewrite these sentences using reported speech.

1 He said, 'I'm happy to help.'   Yesterday, he said that he <u>was happy to help.</u>

2 They said, 'We're going out at seven.'   They said that they _____ .

3 She said, 'I've done all my homework.'   She said that she _____ .

4 He thought, 'They have forgotten my birthday.'   He thought that they _____ .

5 The politician said, 'I want to improve people's lives.'   The politician said she _____ .

6 The team said, 'We aren't going to win.'   The team said they _____ .

7 She said, 'I'm busy so I won't come.'   She said that she _____ .

8 He said, 'I don't know if I can come.'   He said that he _____ .

2 🔊 **2.36 Complete the conversation. Use the words in bold and reported speech. Then listen and check.**

A: **Are** we **going out** with Peter and Nigella tonight?

B: No, they said that they ¹ <u>were going out</u> somewhere else tonight, so they **can't meet**.

A: Why didn't they tell us last week that they ² _____ ?

B: I don't know. Anyway, we**'re having** dinner together next Friday instead.

A: But you said that we ³ _____ dinner with your parents next Friday.

B: Yes, but they**'ll be** on holiday.

A: Really? You didn't tell me they ⁴ _____ on holiday.

B: Yes, I did. They**'ve booked** a holiday in France.

A: I thought they said they ⁵ _____ their holiday in Italy.

B: No, they said France.

A: So they **aren't going to** visit us before they go.

B: No. They said they ⁶ _____ have time to visit us.

3 Look at the before and after pictures. Then write sentences using direct speech.

1   You said that you knew how to drive it!
<u>'I know how to drive it'.</u>

2   He always said he was going to be an astronaut when he grew up.

3   You said you'd be home early.

4   I thought he said he could play the guitar.

88 Reported questions

Presentation

You use reported questions to report questions in the past.

What are you doing? → I **wanted** *to know what he was doing.*

Do you need any help? → I **asked** *him if he needed any help.*

Common reporting verbs for questions: *wanted to know, asked.*

Do not use question marks in reported questions:

I wanted to know what he was doing. (not *I wanted to know what he was doing?*)

wh- questions

When you report questions with *what, who, where, why, when, how,* the word order is the same as for an affirmative statement. The subject is before the verb:

What *are you doing?* → *I wanted to know what* **he was** *doing.* (don't say *I wanted to know what* ~~was he~~ *doing.*)

yes / no questions

When you report questions which need an answer *Yes* or *No,* use *if* or *whether* and do not use the auxiliary verb *do … ?*

Do you need any help? → *I asked him* **if** *he needed any help.* / *I asked him whether he needed any help.* (don't say *I asked him* ~~did he need~~ *any help.*)

Exercises

1 Put the words in order.

1 they wanted to were saying I know what

_____ .

2 me why she asked was I leaving

_____ .

3 they know if any you needed wanted to help

_____ .

4 you grew he where up asked

_____ .

5 we know when arrive he would wanted to

_____ .

6 the neighbours whether were we asked free next week

_____ .

7 wanted my mother to you had eaten know whether

_____ .

8 asked from driven where you'd she

_____ .

2 Write the journalists' questions as reported questions.

1 What is the name of your new film?
2 Are you happy with the film?
3 How long has it taken to make?
4 Who is the director?
5 Did you like the other actors?
6 Why are you visiting Europe?
7 Do you want to work with Tom Cruise again?
8 Are you going to make another film soon?
9 What will the next film be?
10 Will you film it in this country?

1 One journalist asked *what the name of her new film was.*
2 Another journalist wanted to know _____ .
3 They asked her _____ .
4 They also wanted to know _____ .
5 Someone asked _____ .
6 Another journalist asked _____ .
7 He also asked _____ .
8 Everyone wanted to know _____ .
9 Someone asked _____ .
10 Another journalist asked _____ .

3 Complete the sentences so they are true for you.

1 When I was younger, I wanted to know _____ .
2 In my last English lesson, I asked my teacher _____ .

89 *say, tell, ask*
Instructions, orders and requests

A: How was your journey?

B: Terrible. I got lost so I asked somebody to give me directions to King Street. She told me to turn left but it was a one-way street.

A: Oh no! What happened?

B: A police officer stopped me. He said it was a one-way street and he told me to turn the car around.

Presentation

say and *tell*

say SOMETHING

You often use the verb *say* to report someone's words:

'This is a one-way street.' → *The police officer **said** (that) it was a one-way street.*

tell SOMEBODY something

You can use *tell* to say who someone is talking to:

'This is a one-way street.' → *The police officer **told me** (that) it was a one-way street.*

(don't say *The police officer ~~said me~~ it was a one-way street.*)

say something TO somebody

You can use *say* to report who you said something to:

'This is a one-way street.' → *The police officer **said to** the driver (that) it was a one-way street.*

(don't say *The police officer ~~told~~ it was a one-way street.*)

tell and *ask*

tell / ask somebody TO DO SOMETHING

When you report instructions, orders or requests, you often use the reporting verbs *tell* and *ask* with the *to*-infinitive:

instructions

'Turn left.' → *He told me **to turn left**.*

orders

'Turn the car around.' → *The police officer told me **to turn** the car around.*

requests

'Can you give me directions to King Street?' → *I asked somebody **to give** me directions to King Street.*

Exercises

1 Complete the sentences using the correct form of *say, tell* or *ask*. Sometimes two answers are possible.

1 My dentist _____ me to come back in six months' time.
2 What a surprise! Everyone _____ you weren't coming to my party so it's nice to see you.
3 What did you _____ to me about the lesson next week? Is it cancelled?
4 The train driver _____ the passengers that the train wasn't stopping in Oxford.
5 We _____ someone where the theatre was but no one knew.
6 Arnold _____ he'd passed his exam! I'm amazed.
7 The boss has _____ a few people to work this weekend.
8 Why did you _____ Madeleine that I like her?
9 Your teacher looks angry. What did you _____ to him?
10 Why did you _____ Joanna to come with us? She's so irritating!

2 Report the words of the receptionist. Complete sentences 1–6 using the *to*-infinitive.

1 Can you sign this form, please?
2 Take a seat.
3 Please hold.
4 Turn left at the end of the corridor.
5 Take the lift to the second floor.
6 Can I take my lunch break?

1 The receptionist asked me _____ .
2 She told me _____ .
3 She asked the person on the phone _____ .
4 She told me _____ .
5 She told another visitor _____ .
6 She asked her boss _____ .

3 Write the direct speech as reported speech using the words in brackets.

1 'This is my house.' (he / say)
   He said (that) this was his house.

2 'I'm going to apply for the job.' (she / tell / me)
   _____ .

3 'It's true!' (I / say)
   _____ .

4 'Lunch is going to be at two.' (Gabi / tell / us)
   _____ .

5 'Press 100 on the machine for a coffee.' (he / tell / us)
   _____ .

6 'Slow down!' (my father / tell / me)
   _____ .

7 'Can you call me back later?' (Rita / ask / me)
   _____ .

8 'Do you mind turning your music down?' (they / ask / the people next door)
   _____ .

189

90 Review of units 86 to 89

Grammar

1 Match 1–6 to a–f.

1 The President told the reporters to ☐
2 The reporters asked him if ☐
3 Another journalist wanted to know ☐
4 The President said to ☐
5 The President asked ☐
6 The President ☐

a why the President hadn't met other world leaders.
b said that change would take time.
c come back at three.
d a reporter to repeat the question.
e the reporters he would talk to them again next month.
f he would spend more money on hospitals.

2 Correct the mistakes.

1 'No, I don't want to,' replied she.

2 The teacher asked why were you late today.

3 He wanted to know if you were doing tonight.

4 My manager asked I if you'd join us for lunch.

5 I told to the taxi driver that I needed to get out at the station.

6 My sister said us to stay out of her room.

7 They said us to wait for the next flight and we said we could.

3 Complete the report with the words in the box.

> asked   if   said   that   to (×2)   was   why

Report on management meeting

The meeting began at three. The company director thanked everyone for coming and said [1] .... everyone he understood how busy they had been in recent weeks. He explained [2] .... the company [3] .... currently having problems and that the aim of the meeting was to find solutions …

The company director asked his staff [4] .... they thought the company needed a new product. The Marketing Manager [5] .... that he thought they did and she also asked [6] .... the company hadn't introduced a whole new range of products for this year.

The company director ended the meeting by asking everyone [7] .... think about the discussion and [8] .... them all to come back next week at the same time with their ideas and solutions.

Grammar in context

4 (2.37) **There are words missing in the journalist's report about his interview with a popstar. Write them in. Then listen and check.**

So tell me about your new album. Is it different from your others?

Yes it is.

In what way?

I've used violins and an orchestra for the first time.

Do you think the change is because you're getting older?

Maybe. In the past, the words in my songs have been about love and teenage problems. I'm not interested in those issues any more.

And will you be performing live in our country this year?

No, I won't but I'm planning a world tour for next year, so come and see me then!

And, now music news! The singer Rick Shaw was visiting our city last week, so I met him in his hotel. I asked him to ¹ tell me about his new album. I asked him if ² _____. He said it ³ _____ because he ⁴ _____ violins and an orchestra for the first time. I also wanted to know if he ⁵ _____ that the change in the music was because he ⁶ _____ older. He replied that in the past the words in his songs ⁷ _____ about love and teenage problems but he ⁸ _____ interested in those issues any more. Finally I asked him if he ⁹ _____ live in our country. He told me he ¹⁰ _____ but that he ¹¹ _____ a world tour for next year, so he told us all to ¹² _____!

Pronunciation: contrastive stress

5 (2.38) **Listen to the conversations. Underline the main stress.**

1 A: This shirt was expensive.
   B: But you told me it was <u>cheap</u>.
2 A: It's a long journey.
   B: I thought you said it was quick.
3 A: I hate living here.
   B: But you said you were happy here.
4 A: Shall I ask them to stay?
   B: No, tell them to go.
5 A: Did you say anything to Petra?
   B: No, but I said something to Bill.

Then listen again and repeat part B with the main stress.

Listen again

6 (2.39) **Are the sentences true (T) or false (F)?**

1 Peter and Nigella said, 'We're going out somewhere else tonight.'
2 Peter and Nigella had told them they couldn't meet last week.
3 He thought that her parents were having dinner with them next Friday.
4 She had told him that her parents were going on holiday.
5 She didn't know why her parents weren't visiting them.

91 Real conditionals: *if* + present simple
Zero conditional and first conditional, *if, when, unless*

When it's sunny, we usually go to the beach. If it rains, we stay at home and read.

If it's sunny tomorrow, we'll go to the beach.

Presentation

If + present simple, present simple

You use *if* or *when* with the present simple followed by the present simple in the main clause to talk about facts and things which are generally true:

If it's sunny, we go to the beach.

When it's sunny, we go to the beach.

If it rains, we stay at home.

When it rains, we stay at home.

This is often called the zero conditional.

If + present simple, *will*

You can also use *if* with the present simple to talk about a possible future situation or action. You use *will / won't* in the main clause to talk about the result of that situation or action:

If it's sunny tomorrow, we'll go to the beach.

This is often called the first conditional.

Note that you use *if* with the present simple, <u>not</u> *will*, to talk about the future.

(don't say *If it will be sunny tomorrow, we'll go to the beach.*)

You can also use the present simple to talk about the future after time conjunctions. See Unit 54.

Position of *if*

You can use *if* in two possible positions.

- *if*-clause first: *If it rains, we'll stay at home.*
- main clause first: *We'll stay at home if it rains.*

When the *if*-clause is at the beginning of the sentence, you use a comma to separate it from the main clause.

If it's sunny, we'll go to the beach.

if or *when*?

When you talk about things that are generally true, you can use *if* or *when*. There's no difference.

If it's sunny / When it's sunny... If it rains / When it rains...

When you talk about situations in the future, there is a difference between *if* and *when*.

If I see Jim, I'll let him know. (You don't know if you're going to see Jim, but you know it's a possibility.)

When I see Jim, I'll let him know. (You know you are definitely going to see Jim.)

unless

unless = if … not

We'll go to the beach tomorrow unless it rains. = We'll go to the beach tomorrow if it doesn't rain.

Exercises

1 Match 1–6 to a–f.

1 I'll be really surprised   ☐   a   if he passes all his exams.
2 I'll take a break   ☐   b   when the teacher isn't in the classroom.
3 If you talk to Ruth,   ☐   c   they'll cancel the flight.
4 It's really cold   ☐   d   when I finish this exercise.
5 If the storm doesn't stop,   ☐   e   when the wind blows from the north.
6 The children always behave badly   ☐   f   will you tell her about the party?

2 🔊 2.40 Complete the conversation with the present simple or will future form of the verbs in brackets. Then listen and check.

Conversation 1

A: What do you usually do at the weekend?

B: If I ¹ _____ (not / have) any work to do, we ² _____ (often / go) away somewhere.

Conversation 2

C: What are you doing this weekend?

D: I'm not sure. If the weather ³ _____ (be) good, we ⁴ _____ (take) the kids to the zoo.

Conversation 3

E: Is Tim here today?

F: I don't know. I haven't seen him.

E: Well, if you ⁵ _____ (see) him, ⁶ _____ (you let) me know, please? I need to talk to him.

Conversation 4

G: The receptionist isn't here today. She's not well.

H: OK. I'll tell Laura. She ⁷ _____ (usually / cover) on reception if the receptionist ⁸ _____ (be) absent.

3 Complete the second sentence so that it has the same meaning as the first sentence.

1 You won't pass the exam if you don't study.
You won't pass the exam unless _____ .

2 We're going camping this weekend if it doesn't rain.
We're going camping this weekend unless _____ .

3 I'll drive you to the airport tomorrow if John doesn't want to.
I'll drive you to the airport tomorrow unless _____ .

4 We don't go out in the evenings unless we can get a babysitter.
We don't go out in the evenings if _____ .

5 That plant will die unless you water it.
That plant will die if _____ .

4 Complete these sentences so that they are true for you.

1 I'll probably _____ tomorrow, unless _____ .
2 If I have time this evening, _____ .
3 I don't usually _____ unless I really have to.
4 If I have any free time during the week, I usually _____ .

92 Real conditionals: use of modals and imperative
First conditional

If you go to London,

... you can try some traditional British food.

... you must visit the Houses of Parliament.

... you may see the Queen!

... don't forget to send me a postcard!

Presentation

When you talk about possible future situations, you can use the present simple form in the *if*-clause and a number of different modal verbs in the main clause.

	you can / could stay with my brother.
	you must / ought to / should visit the Tower of London.
If you go to London,	you may / might / could see the Queen.
	remember / don't forget to send me a postcard.

can

You use *can* to talk about the possible options you have to choose from. You can also use *could*:

*If you go to London, you **can** / **could** stay with my brother.*

See Unit 61 for more information about *can* and *could*.

must

You use *must* to …

• recommend an action. You can also use *should* or *ought to*:

*If you go to London, you **must** / **should** / **ought to** visit the Houses of Parliament.*

• say what is important or necessary:

*If you go to London, you **must** have a valid passport.*

See Units 63 and 69 for more information about *must*, *should* and *ought to*.

may

You use *may* to talk about events that are possible but not certain. You can also use *might* or *could*:

*If you go to Buckingham Palace, you **may** / **might** / **could** see the Queen.*

See Units 58 and 59 for more information about *may*, *might* and *could*.

Imperative

You can also use an imperative form in the main clause:

*If you go to London, **remember** / **don't forget** to send me a postcard.*

See Unit 36 for more information about imperative forms.

Exercises

1 **Complete the sentences with the verbs in the box.**

do some work   have some pizza   wake me up   watch the football

If I stay in tonight,

1   I can _____.

2   I must _____.

3   I may _____.

4   Don't _____
when you come in!

2 **Choose the correct verb. Sometimes both verbs are possible.**

1   You *can / should* come with us in our car, if you want.

2   If you're the last person to leave the office, you *may / must* remember to lock the door.

3   If you see Toni, please *don't / can you* tell her about the party – it's a surprise!

4   You *should / must* see a doctor if your back still hurts.

5   *Ask / You can ask* me if you need help.

6   If the phone rings, *could you / please don't* answer it.

7   If you get the chance, you really *should / may* visit the cathedral.

8   We *may / might* come round to see you tomorrow if that's OK.

3 **Complete the sentences so that they are true for your town.**

1   If you ever visit my town, you can _____.

2   You really must _____ and you should try to _____ if you've got time.

3   If you come in the spring, you may _____.

4   You could _____ as well, if you want.

93 Unreal conditionals: *if* + past simple
Second conditional

Presentation

You use *if* with the past simple to talk about situations that are …

- possible but not probable:
  If I won the lottery, … (I don't think it's very probable that I'll win the lottery.)

- impossible:
  If I were you, … (but I'm not and I never will be.)

You use the *if*-clause to describe the situation. You use *would/wouldn't* + infinitive in the main clause to talk about the imagined reaction to, or result of, the situation:

If I won the lottery, I'd buy a luxury yacht.

If I were you, I'd concentrate on my work.

You can also use *if* with the past simple to talk about …

- imagined present situations:
  If I had a lot of money, … (the real situation is that I don't have a lot of money.)

- imagined future situations:
  If I got a new job next week, … (I don't think I will get a new job.)

This is often called the second conditional.

If clause: *if* + past simple	Main clause: *would* + infinitive
If I had a lot of money, If he didn't have to work,	I'd (would) buy a yacht. he wouldn't (would not) get up so early.
If you won the lottery,	would you spend all the money? Yes, I would. / No, I wouldn't.

TIP The contracted form of *would* is *'d*. Do not confuse it with the contracted form of *had* in the past perfect. *Would* is followed by the infinitive. *Had* is followed by the past participle.
I'd go = I would go
I'd gone = I had gone (not ~~I would gone~~)

If I was or If I were?

When you use the verb *be* with *if* in the simple past, you can use *was* or *were* for *I, he, she* and *it*.

*If I **were** rich … / If I **was** rich …*

*If he **were** my husband … / If he **was** my husband …*

Were is more formal.

You often use *If I were you* to give advice. *If I were you* = If I was / were in your position. You use *would / wouldn't* for the advice.

If I were you, I'd get on with my work!

Exercises

1 Put the words in order.

1 the lottery give I to charity won I'd the money if
_____.

2 taller he'd were he be a great if basketball player
_____.

3 if I more energy did I'd some exercise have
_____.

4 asked for mind if wouldn't he you some help
_____.

5 if by bus I have go to work I'd didn't a car
_____.

6 worrying it stop if I about were I'd you
_____.

2 🎧 2.41 Choose the correct options. Then listen and check.

A: So, if you [1] *won / would win* a million pounds on the lottery, what [2] *did / would* you do with it?

B: I don't know. I think [3] *I bought / I'd buy* a house, and if my family [4] *needed / would need* some money,
[5] *I gave / I'd give* them some, of course.

A: [6] *Did / Would* you give any money to charity?

B: If [7] *I knew / I'd know* the money was going to help someone have a better life, well, yes, I [8] *did / would*. What about you?

A: If [9] *I had / I'd have* a million pounds, [10] *I started / I'd start* my own business. [11] *I opened / I'd open* an art gallery or something like that …

B: Nice idea. If [12] *I started / I'd start* a new business, I think [13] *I wanted / I'd want* to run a restaurant or a bar.

3 Complete the people's thoughts.

1 I have to work this morning. If I didn't have to work this morning, I'd have breakfast in bed.

2 I haven't got enough time. If I
_____ ,
to school on my bike.

3 I haven't got enough money. If I
_____ ,
that scooter.

4 I don't know how to drive. If I
_____ ,
a taxi driver.

1   2

3   4

4 Complete the sentences so that they are true for you.

1 If I had _____, I _____.
2 If I could _____, I _____.
3 If I didn't have to _____, I _____.

94 Real and unreal conditionals
First and second conditionals

Presentation

Real conditionals

You use *if* with a present tense followed by *will* in the main clause to talk about a real situation, i.e. a situation which is possible in the future:

If you forget something, I'll bring it along later. (The man thinks that it's possible that the woman will forget something.)

These sentences are often called first conditionals.

See Units 91 and 92 for more information about real conditionals.

Unreal conditionals

You use *if* with the past simple followed by *would* in the main clause to talk about an imagined situation in the present or the future, i.e. a situation that is either impossible or possible but not probable:

If I forgot her birthday, she'd never forgive me. (He doesn't think it's probable. He's imagining the situation.)

When you use the past simple with *if*, it <u>does not</u> refer to the past. It refers to the present or future.

These sentences are often called second conditionals.

See Unit 93 for more information about unreal conditionals.

Exercises

1 **Choose the correct option.**

1. If you wash the car,
   a I'd give you five pounds.　　　　b I'll give you five pounds.

2. I'll come into town with you
   a if you want.　　　　b if you'll want.

3. If she didn't like you,
   a she won't phone you.　　　　b she wouldn't phone you.

4. If he was really unhappy,
   a he'd left his job.　　　　b he'd leave his job.

5. If you want a good job,
   a you must pass your exams.　　　　b you'd need to study harder.

6. You definitely won't pass your exam
   a if you wouldn't study harder.　　　　b if you don't study harder.

7. If you hear a strange noise in the night,
   a you must call the police.　　　　b you'd have to call the police.

8. Please come straight back here
   a if you don't find him.　　　　b if you won't find him.

2 **Complete the sentences with the present simple, past simple, *will* or *would* form of the verb in brackets.**

1. If I don't see you later, I _____ (send) you a text message.
2. If you didn't have to work, what _____ (you / do)?
3. Jenny will be happy to help if you _____ (have) any problems.
4. If you _____ (wait) a minute, I can help you with those bags.
5. I wouldn't do that if I _____ (be) you.
6. They _____ (do) anything if you gave them enough money.
7. What _____ (you / do) if the bus doesn't come?
8. How would you react if it _____ (happen) to you?

3 **Write sentences about the situations using *if* and the words in bold.**

1. I don't have any money. I can't buy a car.　**had**
   If I had some money, I'd buy a car.

2. It may rain tomorrow. We may not play football.　**won't**
   _____

3. I like my job. That's why I do it.　**wouldn't**
   _____

4. I have to work tomorrow. I need to go to bed early.　**didn't**
   _____

5. I'll probably see Tom later today. I can tell him about the party.　**I'll**
   _____

6. I don't know if you have any money. I can pay the bill.　**don't**
   _____

95 Review of units 91 to 94

Grammar

1 Choose the correct option. In one question, both answers are possible.

1 If I were you, *I'd / I'll* ask for more money.

2 What would you do if you *would lose / lost* your job?

3 If you have enough time, you *can stay / don't stay* for dinner.

4 When the weather's bad, we usually *stay / stayed* at home and *watch / watched* TV.

5 You don't have to do it, unless you *don't want to / want to*.

6 I'll talk to my boss, *when / if* I'll see him.

7 If I see Jake, I *couldn't / could* ask him about the tickets.

8 If I had more time, *I learned / I'd learn* a new sport.

2 Correct the mistakes.

1 If the train will be cancelled, I can come and get you in the car.

2 When Bob gets home before 8 p.m. this evening, I'll ask him to call you.

3 Watch out! You'll fall and hurt yourself if you're careful.

4 If you can't come tomorrow, must you call to let me know.

5 If your company would offer you a job in another country, would you take it?

6 If it was an English-speaking country, I took the job.

7 If they was my children, I'd ask them to play more quietly.

8 If you need something, please to call me.

3 Complete the sentences with the correct form of the verb in brackets. Use the present simple, past simple, *will* or *would*.

1 If the market is closed, we _____ (go) to the supermarket later this afternoon.

2 You can't go kayaking if you _____ (not know) how to swim.

3 I hate living in the city! I _____ (be) much happier if I _____ (live) in the country.

4 If you can't come to the meeting, please _____ (let) us know.

5 I _____ (not do) that if I _____ (be) you. You'll get into trouble!

6 If our new house _____ (have) a big garden, we'll buy a dog.

4 Complete the second sentence so that it has the same meaning as the first sentence.

1 The last student to leave the room should close the windows.

If *you are the last student to leave the room, please close the windows.*

2 I'd like to travel but I don't have enough money.

If _____ .

3 My cousins may visit us this weekend. When they visit, we usually go hiking together.

If _____ .

4 There are often boat races in the port. At this time, the town gets very busy.

If there _____ .

5 You don't study enough. I don't think you'll pass your exams.

Unless you study more, _____ .

6 I don't have enough free time at the moment. I don't do any sport.

I'd _____ .

Grammar in context

5 **Choose the correct forms to complete the quiz.**

Are you a good language learner?

If you [1] **have / will have / would have** an hour free at the end of the day, do you …

A Do some grammar exercises? ☐

B Switch on the computer and read or watch something in English? ☐

C Switch on the TV and watch football? ☐

If a foreign visitor [2] **will approach / would approach / approached** you in the street and [3] **will speak / would speak / spoke** to you in English, would you …

A Try to help them and give them the information they wanted? ☐

B Stop and talk to them and maybe offer to buy them a coffee? ☐

C Cross to the other side of the street? ☐

If you [4] **win / won / would win** a week's holiday of your choice, what [5] **did / will / would** you choose?

A A week's intensive language course in New York ☐

B A week in a luxury hotel in one of the world's famous capitals ☐

C A week on the beach ☐

Results

Mainly **A**s: You are a great student, but don't you think studying [6] **is / will be / would be** more fun if you [7] **couldn't / didn't / wouldn't** always have your head in a grammar book?

Mainly **B**s: You know how to learn a language and have fun at the same time. If you [8] **continue / continued / will continue** like this, you'll soon be fluent!

Mainly **C**s: Somehow I don't think you're that interested in language learning. Maybe you should find something else to study!

Pronunciation: elision

6 (2.42) **Listen to the conversation. Notice the pronunciation of *would you* in the questions.**

Would you … ? /wʊdʒuː/

A: Would you cut all your hair off for £100?

B: Yes, I would. Would you?

A: No, I wouldn't. Not for £100 – but if they gave me £1,000, I'd do it.

Then listen again and repeat the conversation.

Listen again

7 (2.43) **Listen and tick the things the two people would do if they won a million pounds on the lottery.**

1 buy a car ☐
2 buy a house ☐
3 give money to charity ☐
4 help friends or family ☐
5 travel ☐
6 stop working ☐
7 start a business ☐

96 Subject and object questions

Policeman:	Who called the police?
Shop owner:	I did.
Policeman:	What happened?
Shop owner:	Someone broke into the shop.
Policeman:	When did it happen?
Shop owner:	In the middle of the night.
Policeman:	What did they take?
Shop owner:	They took some jewellery …

Presentation

You can ask questions about the subject or the object of the verb using *what / who / which / whose / how much / how many.*

Subject questions

In subject questions, the question word is the subject of the verb.

subject	verb	object
Who	*called*	*the police?*

The word order in a subject question is the same as in an affirmative sentence.

subject	verb	object
Who	*called*	*the police?*
The shop owner	*called*	*the police.*

You do not need an auxiliary verb (*do, does, did*) in present simple or past simple subject questions.

Say *What happened?* (don't say *What did happen?*)

What usually happens? (don't say *What does usually happen?*)

Object questions

In object questions, the question word is <u>not</u> the subject of the verb.

question word	auxiliary verb	subject	main verb
When	*did*	*it*	*happen?*

The word order in object questions is not the same as the word order in an affirmative sentence.

What did they take?

They took some jewellery.

In the present simple and past simple, you need to add an auxiliary verb (do, does, did) before the subject.

Say *What did you see?* (don't say *What saw you?*)

TIP You cannot form subject questions with *where, when, why* or *how.*

Say *Where do you live?* (don't say *Where you live?*)

Say *When did you start work?* (don't say *When you started work?*)

Exercises

1 Read an article about a robbery. Complete the questions 1–7 with *who*, *what* or *when* and an auxiliary verb where necessary.

A robber thought the robbery was going well when he ran from the chemist's with the money. But there was one problem. He had locked the car doors and the keys were inside. He couldn't open the doors, so when the police arrived he ran away. The police finally caught him later that night and he asked them, 'Would you mind taking care of my car, please? The keys are inside.' But the police were more interested in locking him up than unlocking his car.

1 _____ the robber think? The robbery was going well.
2 _____ he run from? The chemist's shop.
3 _____ he leave the car keys? Inside the car.
4 _____ arrived? The police.
5 _____ happened next? The robber ran away.
6 _____ the police catch him? Later that night.
7 _____ asked the police to take care of the car? The robber.

2 (2.44) Complete the conversation with subject or object questions. Then listen and check.

A: ¹ *What did you do* (you/do) last night?
B: I watched *Miami Police Team*.
A: Oh no! I always miss that show. ² _____ (what / happen)?
B: Well, you know Detective Sanchez's niece has joined the police force.
A: No. ³ _____ (when / she / join)? I missed that episode too.
B: Ages ago! She joined the police but he thought it was too dangerous for her. Anyway, she arrested someone for stealing a car, but it was an old boyfriend so then she released him.
A: Sorry, I don't understand. ⁴ _____ (who / think) it was too dangerous?
B: Her uncle, Detective Sanchez.
A: And ⁵ _____ (who / she / arrest)?
B: An old boyfriend from school.
A: And ⁶ _____ (who / release / the boyfriend)?
B: She did.
A: OK. And ⁷ _____ (what / Uncle Sanchez / say)?
B: Well obviously, he wasn't very happy.
A: ⁸ _____ (what / he / going to do) about it?
B: I think he's going to make her leave the police force.
A: I must watch it next week. What time is it on?
B: Nine o'clock.

3 Which questions in exercises 1 and 2 are subject questions and which are object questions? Write *S* or *O*.

Exercise 1

1_O_ 2____ 3____ 4____ 5____ 6____ 7____

Exercise 2

1____ 2____ 3____ 4____ 5____ 6____ 7____ 8____

97 Short answers

A: Hello, are you Mr Robertson?

B: Yes, I am.

A: Hello. I'm Mr Yao. I'm taking you to the hotel. Have you got all your luggage?

B: Yes, I have. It's just this one.

A: Can I carry it for you?

B: It's OK thanks. I can manage.

A: Did you have a good flight?

B: Yes, I did. I slept the whole way.

A: Was it long?

B: Yes, it was! About eighteen hours.

A: Oh dear. Are you hungry?

B: No, I'm not. I ate on the plane.

A: How about a drink? Would you like to have a coffee before we go to your hotel?

B: Yes, please. That would be nice.

Presentation

You can answer a question with the answer *yes* or *no*, but normally you also add a subject and an auxiliary verb:

Hello, are you Mr Robertson? Yes, **I am.**

Sometimes, you also add extra information after the answer:

Was the flight long? Yes, **it was! About eighteen hours.**

Use the auxiliary verb from the question in your answer:

Hello, **are** *you Mr Robertson?*	→ *Yes, I* **am.** */ No, I'* **m not.**
Have *you got all your luggage?*	→ *Yes, I* **have.** */ No, I* **haven't.**
Did *you have a good flight?*	→ *Yes, I* **did.** */ No, I* **didn't.**
Was *it long?*	→ *Yes, it* **was.** */ No, it* **wasn't.**
Will *the plane be late?*	→ *Yes, it* **will.** */ No, it* **won't.**

Do not use contracted forms in *yes* answers.

Say *Yes, I am.* (don't say *Yes, I'm.*)

Say *Yes, I have.* (don't say *Yes, I've.*)

Punctuation rule:

Put a comma after *yes* or *no*: *Yes, I am.*

TIP When you answer a request or offer, you can answer with *please/thank you* instead of the subject + auxiliary verb. This is often more polite:

A: *Can I carry it for you?*

B: *It's OK* **thank you***. I can manage.*

A: *Would you like to have a coffee before we go to your hotel?*

B: *Yes,* **please***. That would be nice.*

See Unit 67 for more on answering requests.

Exercises

1 Match the 1–7 to a–g.

1	Excuse me, is he your husband?	☐	**a** Yes, it was.
2	Has Millie telephoned you?	☐	**b** No, she hasn't.
3	Do you like this dish?	☐	**c** Yes, I will.
4	Will you call me when you arrive at the airport?	☐	**d** Yes, he is.
5	Would you like another cup of coffee?	☐	**e** No, thanks.
6	Was the hotel comfortable?	☐	**f** Yes, it did.
7	Did your dog come home last night?	☐	**g** No, I don't. It tastes awful!

2 ⓔ2.45 **Complete the conversation with auxiliary verbs. Then listen and check.**

A: Is this your bag, sir?

B: Yes, it ¹ _____ .

A: Did you pack it yourself?

B: Yes, I ² _____ .

A: Has it been with you at all times since you left home and at the airport?

B: Yes, it ³ _____ .

A: And has anyone else opened your bag since you left home?

B: No, no one ⁴ _____ .

A: Was it ever with someone else?

B: No, it ⁵ _____ .

A: OK. And do you have any dangerous objects in your bag? For example, a knife.

B: No, I ⁶ _____ .

A: Are there any electrical items?

B: Yes, there ⁷ _____ . There's an electric shaver and a mobile phone.

A: That's fine. Thank you.

3 Answer these questions with short answers so that they are true for you.

1 Are you busy today? _____ .

2 Have you got any spare time today? _____ .

3 Are you going out later? _____ .

4 Were you late for anything today? _____ .

5 Do you and your friends like to travel? _____ .

6 Have you finished all the exercises on this page? _____ .

98 Negative questions

Presentation

You can ask questions using the negative form of the verb:

Aren't we there yet?

Can't I sit in the front for a while?

When you use negative questions in spoken English, you normally use contracted forms.

Can't I sit in the front? (not *Can I not sit in the front?*)

You often use negative questions to …

- to complain or show surprise: ***Aren't*** *we there yet? We've been driving for hours.*
- suggest something: *Why* ***don't*** *we sing a song or play a game?*
- request something (often impolite or expecting a negative response): ***Can't*** *I sit in the front?*
- check some information or something you think is probably true: ***Isn't*** *that the name of the place we're going to?*
- exclaim about something: ***Don't*** *the mountains look wonderful!*

TIP When you use negative question forms for exclamations, you use an exclamation mark (!) not a question mark (?).

Answering negative questions

You can answer negative questions with *yes/no* answers:

Aren't we there yet? – ***Yes, we are. / No, we aren't.***

Can't I sit in the front? – ***Yes, you can. / No, you can't.***

Don't the mountains look beautiful! – ***Yes, they do. / No, they don't.***

Exercises

1 **Rewrite the questions as negative questions.**

1 Are you ready yet?

2 Can you come out tonight?

3 Is the word 'disappear' spelt with one *s*?

4 Did you study in Paris?

5 Does he want to go too?

6 Were the neighbours at home?

7 Should I help you?

8 Do you like sushi? It's delicious!

2 🔊2.46 **Complete the conversation with the negative form of the verbs in the box. Then listen and check.**

can	did	do	does	have	is	were	will

A: ¹ _____ you finished your Spanish homework yet? You've been doing it for hours.

B: I know! ² _____ you help me? It's really hard!

A: Sorry, I can't. I don't speak Spanish. ³ _____ your teacher explain it to you in class? Or ⁴ _____ you listening?

B: I was listening but I didn't understand it.

A: Why ⁵ _____ you phone a friend? ⁶ _____ Rachel in your class? She'll understand it.

B: But ⁷ _____ she think I'm stupid if I call her?

A: No, she won't. Anyway, ⁸ _____ she owe you a favour? You helped her last week with maths.

B: That's true. I'll call her now.

3 **Rewrite the sentences as negative questions.**

1 How about taking a boat across the sea?
   Why _____?

2 Won't you help me with some of the house cleaning?
   Can _____?

3 I think Kithnos is the name of the Greek island we're going to.
   Is _____?

4 Your new house looks great!
   Does _____!

5 I'm fairly certain this was the restaurant we went to last time.
   Was _____?

99 Indirect ways of asking questions

Excuse me. Could you tell me if the museum has a café?

Do you know what time the bus comes?

Sorry, but I was wondering whether I could have a look at your programme.

Have you any idea how old it is?

Presentation

You can ask questions in a more polite and less direct way by introducing them with certain expressions.

Does the museum have a café? → *Could you tell me if the museum has a café?*

Common expressions include:

- *Could you / anyone tell me …?*
- *Do you know / remember / think …?*
- *Do you have any idea …?*
- *Do you mind if …?*
- *Would you mind telling me …?*
- *I don't know … / I'd like to know …*
- *I wonder … / I was wondering …*

After the expressions, you can use …

- *wh-/how* questions:

*Do you know **what time** the bus comes?*

*Do you have any idea **how** old it is?*

- *if/whether* with *yes/no* questions:

*Could you tell me **if** the museum has a café?*

*I was wondering **whether** I could have a look at your programme.*

Word order

When you ask questions in this way, the word order is the same as an affirmative sentence. You do not need an auxiliary verb (*do, does, did*) in the present simple or past simple. The subject comes before the verb.

I'd like to know what time ~~does~~ the bus comes.

Punctuation

Some indirect questions have a question mark (?) and some do not. The punctuation depends on the phrase that introduces the indirect question. If it is a question, you use a question mark (?).

Could you tell me if the museum has a café?

If it is an affirmative phrase, you use a full stop (.).

I was wondering whether I could have a look at your programme.

TIP You often start a conversation by asking the question indirectly and then continue with direct questions:

A: *Excuse me, **could you tell me if the museum has a café?***

B: *Yes. It's downstairs.*

A: *Oh, thanks. **What time does it close?***

Exercises

1 Put the words in the correct order.

1 the you tell could station is me train where

_____?

2 do film you the when starts know

_____?

3 it's closing like why I'd to know early

_____.

4 the long journey you remember do how takes

_____?

5 how you would telling you are mind me old

_____?

6 Joel don't whether is I coming know too

_____.

2 Rewrite the direct questions as indirect questions.

1 When does the supermarket close?
  Could you tell me _when the supermarket closes?_

2 Is there another flight to Rome this evening?
  Do you know _____?

3 How long does this film last?
  Would you mind telling me _____?

4 Do they accept credit cards?
  Do you know _____?

5 Could I look at your newspaper?
  I was wondering _____.

6 Would your cousins enjoy this kind of music?
  Do you think _____?

3 Write an indirect question for each situation. Use the words in bold.

Situation 1: You are second in the queue for train tickets at a station but you want to buy your ticket next. Your train is leaving in four minutes. Ask the person in front.

Excuse me / do / mind / buy my ticket next

_____

Situation 2: You are looking for the departure lounge at an airport. Ask at the information desk.

Could / tell / where

_____

Situation 3: You are good friends with someone in your English class. You'd like to go out to dinner with them after class one evening. Invite them.

I / wondering / you'd like to go out

_____

Situation 4: You are on a tour of a palace. You want to know more about a painting. Ask the tour guide.

would / mind / tell / me more about

_____

100 Review of units 96 to 99

Grammar

1 Match 1–8 to a–h.

1	When did the accident happen?	☐	a	Sure. Let me find it.
2	Did anyone get hurt?	☐	b	At about three.
3	Wasn't he looking where he was going?	☐	c	Yes, I am. A bit later.
4	Is he OK?	☐	d	Yes, he is. He's fine.
5	What was he driving?	☐	e	Yes, he was, but the other driver wasn't.
6	Can I do anything to help?	☐	f	Thanks, but it'll be OK.
7	Aren't you going to see him?	☐	g	No, no one did. They were all OK.
8	Could you tell me what his number is?	☐	h	He was driving that red car.

2 Correct the mistakes.

Conversation 1

A: Who did tell you about the job?

B: I saw it on the company's website.

Conversation 2

A: Is not he coming with us?

B: No, he isn't. He's got other plans.

Conversation 3

A: Are you happy about the new job?

B: Yes, I'm.

Conversation 4

A: Why do we go somewhere different for our holiday this year?

B: That's a good idea.

Conversation 5

A: Could you tell me if is the plane on time?

B: Yes, it is.

3 Complete the second sentence so that it has the same meaning as the first sentence.

1 Can you tell me how long he's worked here?

   How long ....?

2 Do you know who scored the final goal?

   Who ....?

3 Are you coming with us?

   Aren't ....?

4 Why did Alex want to speak to you?

   I'd like to know ....

   ....

5 Your new hairstyle looks great!

   Doesn't ....!

   ....

6 We could use the money to buy a new car.

   Why ....?

4 Rewrite these direct questions as indirect questions.

1 How much do you earn?

   ....

   ....?

2 Why did you make your hair blonde?

   ....

   ....?

3 Are you going to be late again?

   ....

   ....?

4 Are you still married to Mike?

   ....

   ....?

5 Can I borrow fifty pounds?

   ....

   ....?

6 How long have you studied English?

   ....

   ....?

Grammar in context

5 Choose the correct option.

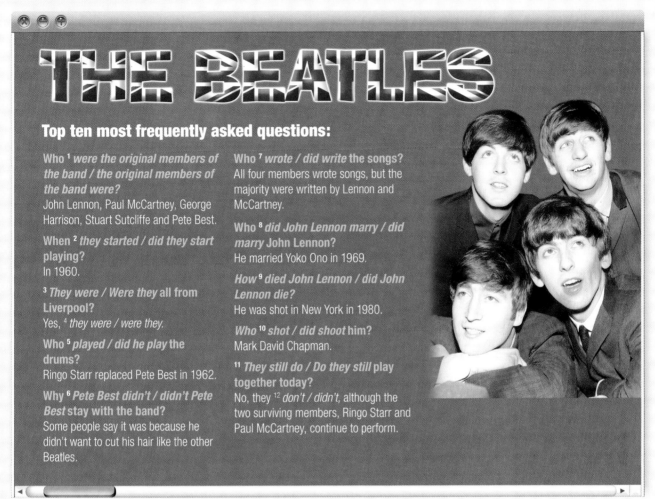

THE BEATLES

Top ten most frequently asked questions:

Who ¹ *were the original members of the band / the original members of the band were?*
John Lennon, Paul McCartney, George Harrison, Stuart Sutcliffe and Pete Best.

When ² *they started / did they start* playing?
In 1960.

³ *They were / Were they* all from Liverpool?
Yes, ⁴ *they were / were they.*

Who ⁵ *played / did he play* the drums?
Ringo Starr replaced Pete Best in 1962.

Why ⁶ *Pete Best didn't / didn't Pete Best* stay with the band?
Some people say it was because he didn't want to cut his hair like the other Beatles.

Who ⁷ *wrote / did write* the songs?
All four members wrote songs, but the majority were written by Lennon and McCartney.

Who ⁸ *did John Lennon marry / did marry* John Lennon?
He married Yoko Ono in 1969.

How ⁹ *died John Lennon / did John Lennon die?*
He was shot in New York in 1980.

Who ¹⁰ *shot / did shoot* him?
Mark David Chapman.

¹¹ *They still do / Do they still* play together today?
No, they ¹² *don't / didn't,* although the two surviving members, Ringo Starr and Paul McCartney, continue to perform.

Pronunciation: intonation on questions

6 ⏺**2.47** Intonation rises [↗] on *yes/no* questions and falls [↘] on the short answers. Listen and draw the arrows in 2 and 3. Then listen again and repeat.

1 A: Is this your bag, sir? [↗]
B: Yes, it is. [↘]

2 A: Did you pack it yourself?
B: Yes, I did.

3 A: Was it ever with someone else?
B: No, it wasn't.

Listen again

7 ⏺**2.48** Listen and answer the questions with short answers.

1 Has Detective Sanchez's niece joined the police force? ....

2 Did he want her to? ....

3 Did he think it was too dangerous? ....

4 Did she arrest her uncle? ....

5 Is the TV programme at 8 o'clock? ....

1 Progress test (units 1 to 10)

1 Rachel loves Martin and I think he loves _____ too.
   a herself   **b** she   **c** her

2 A: Who crashed my car?
   B: It wasn't me. It was _____ .
   a he   **b** him   **c** himself

3 Stop looking at _____ in the mirror! You're so self-obsessed!
   a myself   **b** yourself   **c** you

4 Is that your dog? _____ bit me!
   a It   **b** Itself   **c** Me

5 I think _____ would like to go skiing this winter.
   a we   **b** us   **c** ourselves

6 Bill and Ben looked at _____ and burst out laughing.
   a they   **b** himself   **c** each other

7 My new baby is so clever! She likes to feed _____ .
   a she   **b** her   **c** herself

8 There's _____ new teacher at our school. He's great!
   a a   **b** some   **c** any

9 There _____ some water in the jug.
   a 's   **b** are   **c** aren't

10 There isn't _____ apple in the fridge. Are you sure you saw one?
   a a   **b** an   **c** some

11 Sorry, there aren't _____ parking spaces left.
   a a   **b** some   **c** any

12 _____ seats have a nice view out of the window. Let's sit here.
   a This   **b** That   **c** These

13 _____ was a great film. Why don't we watch it again!
   a That   **b** These   **c** Those

14 There are some pairs of shoes over there. Are any of _____ yours?
   a this   **b** these   **c** those

15 These aren't ours. They're _____ .
   a they   **b** their   **c** theirs

16 Can you help me bring _____ two chairs into the other room? I'll carry this one and you carry the other.
   a this   **b** these   **c** those

17 I love _____ new house.
   a you   **b** yours   **c** your

18 Can you give me _____ pen back, please?
   a I   **b** my   **c** mine

19 _____ appointment is at three o'clock tomorrow.
   a We   **b** Our   **c** Ours

20 _____ emailed you this document.
   a She   **b** Her   **c** Hers

21 Did you know it's _____ job interview today? I hope it goes well for her.
   a Sheila   **b** Sheilas'   **c** Sheila's

22 A: Who is that woman over there?
   B: I think it's a friend _____ .
   a Ringo   **b** of Ringo's   **c** Ringo's

23 Did you borrow a book of _____ ? I'd like it back.
   a I   **b** my   **c** mine

24 Why are there decorations everywhere? _____ birthday is it?
   a Whose   **b** Who's   **c** Who

25 I'm looking after my _____ house for a week. They're on holiday.
   a parent's   **b** parents'   **c** parents

26 Children in England _____ a school uniform.
   a wear   **b** wears   **c** doesn't wear

27 My daughter _____ at Harvard University.
   a study   **b** studys   **c** studies

28 What _____ your friend eat for breakfast?
   a do   **b** does   **c** is

29 How many people _____ in the city of Paris?
   a live   **b** lives   **c** living

30 I _____ think the rumours are true.

    a no   **b** don't   **c** doesn't

31 She _____ like salad, so give her French fries.

    a don't   **b** doesn't   **c** does

32 A: Do you like this music?

    B: Yes, I _____ .

    a like   **b** does   **c** do

33 _____ anyone know the answer to question 27?

    a Do   **b** Does   **c** Is

34 Sashia _____ for school.

    a is usually late   **b** usually is late
    c late is usually

35 We _____ tennis on Sunday afternoons.

    a play usually   **b** usually play
    c usual play

36 We go out for dinner _____ .

    a never   **b** often   **c** once a week

37 Richard gets up late every morning, so he _____ arrives on time for work.

    a always   **b** often   **c** rarely

38 _____ you looking forward to leaving school?

    a Are   **b** Is   **c** Am

39 They _____ dinner now so we need to hurry up.

    a prepares   **b** prepares   **c** 're preparing

40 The price of food _____ again! It's doubled this year already.

    a goes up   **b** is going up   **c** go up

41 I don't know why, but I _____ so many problems with my car at the moment.

    a have   **b** 'm having   **c** has

42 Katia _____ in my apartment but she'll move again in June.

    a stays   **b** stay   **c** is staying

43 In the USA, it _____ cold in the autumn and _____ warm again until May.

    a gets . . . isn't getting   **b** gets . . . doesn't get
    c is getting . . . isn't getting

44 We _____ it's true.

    a know   **b** are knowing   **c** is knowing

45 Do you play chess? _____ .

    a Yes, I do.   **b** Yes, I am.   **c** Yes, I have.

46 A: Excuse me. I _____ someone called Braun.

    B: He works on the fifth floor.

    a look for   **b** 'm looking for   **c** looking for

47 The sun _____ today.

    a doesn't shining   **b** doesn't shine
    c isn't shining

48 We _____ over Iceland. Please keep your seatbelts fastened.

    a currently fly   **b** are currently flying
    c currently flies

49 Where _____ the President normally _____ ?

    a does . . . live **b** is . . . living **c** does . . . living

50 Are they coming with us? _____

    a Yes, they do.   **b** Yes, they are.
    c Yes, they will.

2 Progress test (units 11 to 20)

1   Have _____ cup of coffee.
    a a   **b** an   **c** the

2   Can you sit in _____ front of the car?
    a a   **b** an   **c** the

3   _____ sun is the only star in the solar system.
    a A   **b** An   **c** The

4   My uncle is _____ architect.
    a a   **b** an   **c** the

5   Mrs Grey is _____ managing director of this company.
    a a   **b** an   **c** the

6   Please tell _____ gentleman over there that someone is here to see him.
    a a   **b** an   **c** the

7   I think Giselle intends to study at _____ university in Spain, but I don't know which one.
    a a   **b** an   **c** the

8   I'll have _____ orange juice and my friend will have _____ coffee.
    a a . . . an   **b** an . . . a   **c** a . . . a

9   I hate _____ spiders and any other insects that you find in the bath!
    a a   **b** the   **c** Ø

10 Welcome to _____ United States of America!
    a a   **b** the   **c** Ø

11 Who do _____ two large cats belong to? We saw them earlier in your garden.
    a a   **b** the   **c** Ø

12 Do you ever play _____ tennis?
    a a   **b** the   **c** Ø

13 I think I've finished all _____ work I had to do.
    a a   **b** the   **c** Ø

14 It's wonderful to be in the country! Let's sit outside and enjoy _____ silence.
    a a   **b** the   **c** Ø

15 What time are we going _____ home?
    a a   **b** the   **c** Ø

16 The twins are learning to play _____ piano.
    a a   **b** the   **c** Ø

17 _____ January can be quite warm in _____ Australia.
    a Ø . . . Ø   **b** the . . . Ø   **c** Ø . . . the

18 You'll want _____ long holiday after all this hard work. Will you take one?
    a a   **b** the   **c** Ø

19 The children have six weeks for _____ summer holidays.
    a a   **b** the   **c** Ø

20 What is _____ population of India?
    a a   **b** the   **c** Ø

21 I'm sure _____ Lake Geneva is in Switzerland.
    a a   **b** the   **c** Ø

22 It's time that you had _____ haircut.
    a a   **b** one   **c** Ø

23 Sorry, I can only afford to buy _____ of these.
    a ones   **b** one   **c** Ø

24 This _____ is very nice. The blue of the dress matches your eyes.
    a a   **b** one   **c** ones

25 A: Is there a bank near here?
    B: Yes, there's _____ opposite the supermarket.
    a an   **b** one   **c** ones

26 Can I change these shoes? These _____ don't fit me.
    a a   **b** one   **c** ones

27 A: Which _____ are we keeping?
    B: The two large puppies. We'll sell the rest.
    a a   **b** one   **c** ones

28 I'd like _____ coffees, please.
    a a   **b** three   **c** Ø

29 I have two _____ to check in.
    a bags   **b** luggage   **c** luggages

30 Would you all like _____ slice of cake?
    a a   **b** some   **c** Ø

31 You can buy our products in _____ good computer shop.

a some   b any   c Ø

32 A: I need some coins for this machine.
    B: Sorry, I don't have _____ .

a any   b ones   c none

33 A: Do you have any scissors?
    B: Yes, there are _____ on the table next to my bed.

a ones   b any   c some

34 Is there _____ milk left?

a no   b none   c none of

35 Sorry, but there's _____ left.

a no   b none   c none of

36 _____ of the songs on the new Bob Dylan album are his best ever! I love it!

a Some   b Any   c None

37 A: Do Peter, Paul and Roy work here anymore?
    B: No, _____ does. They all left ages ago.

a some of them   b any of them
c none of them

38 I'm afraid I don't have _____ information about this town.

a many   b much   c a few

39 How _____ people work in your shop?

a many   b much   c a lot of

40 The children have _____ free time this weekend, so let's go somewhere.

a many   b much   c a lot of

41 A: Do we have any milk in the fridge?
    B: No, not _____ .

a many   b a lot   c a lot of

42 There _____ buses on Sundays. You should take the train.

a aren't many   b aren't much   c are a little

43 My boss has _____ time for listening to anyone's problems. He's very impatient!

a few   b little   c a little

44 _____ of us are going bowling tonight. Do you want to come?

a Little   b Few   c A few

45 _____ people are leaving the countryside to live in the city.

a Lots   b Lots of   c Much

46 I'm so tired. I didn't have _____ sleep last night.

a too few   b enough   c too much

47 Drinking _____ water in this heat will dehydrate you.

a too little   b too few   c enough

48 There are _____ places. We need some more chairs for the rest of the guests.

a too few   b too little   c too many

49 A: Would you like any more to eat?
    B: No more for me, thanks. I've had _____ .

a much   b enough   c not enough

50 I think children watch _____ TV. They should play outside more.

a too much   b too many   c too little

3 Progress test (units 21 to 30)

1 When _____ they born?
   a was **b** are **c** were

2 A: Were you late for class this morning?
   B: No, I _____ .
   a was **b** wasn't **c** weren't

3 The artist Picasso _____ in France for many years.
   a live **b** lived **c** lives

4 Where did your friends _____ on holiday?
   a go **b** went **c** gone

5 _____ anyone _____ to Maura yesterday?
   a Was . . . speak **b** Did . . . speak
   c Did . . . spoke

6 Everyone _____ the beach because of the bad weather.
   a leaving **b** was leaving **c** were leaving

7 Mrs Miles _____ to someone when we arrived, so we waited until she was free.
   a talked **b** talking **c** was talking

8 Sorry, I _____ listening. Can you say it again?
   a was **b** wasn't **c** didn't

9 I called round this morning but you didn't answer. What _____ ?
   a were you doing **b** did you do
   c are you doing

10 It _____ a beautiful day today! I hope it's like that tomorrow as well.
   a was being **b** did **c** was

11 My son _____ home when he was eighteen. He went to university.
   a left **b** was leaving **c** leaves

12 Three politicians _____ my town this week! We have an election soon, so I think we'll see more next week as well.
   a visit **b** has visited **c** have visited

13 How many countries _____ since you started travelling?
   a did you visit **b** have you visited
   c have you visit

14 Have you _____ the Taj Mahal in India?
   a ever seen **b** before seen **c** seen ever

15 This is the first time we _____ . We're a bit scared!
   a fly **b** flew **c** 've flown

16 My grandparents have _____ used a computer _____ .
   a ever . . . before **b** never . . . before
   c never . . . ever

17 Barack Obama _____ the US President in 2009.
   a became **b** has become **c** becoming

18 A: Has it rained this year?
   B: No, it _____ .
   a didn't **b** didn't have **c** hasn't

19 I _____ that before. Is it new?
   a haven't seen **b** didn't see **c** don't see

20 They've interviewed him _____ , so they're interested in employing him.
   a never **b** ever **c** twice

21 Julie and her family have _____ to Sicily. They're back on Saturday.
   a been **b** gone **c** come

22 Have you ever seen the film *Citizen Kane*?
   Yes, I _____ . I _____ it when I was young.
   a have . . . saw **b** have . . . seen
   c had . . . saw

23 Where _____ last night? We rang three times but you didn't answer.
   a have you been **b** were you
   c were you been

24 I'm waiting for some important news, but there _____ any emails this morning.
   a weren't **b** haven't been **c** wasn't

25 We handed in our homework _____ .
   a ever **b** an hour ago **c** yet

26 I've _____ found my keys! Look! They were in my coat pocket.
   a just **b** yet **c** already

27 A: We're going to the new exhibition at the gallery. Do you want to come?

B: No, thanks. I've been there _____ and it wasn't very good.

a just   b yet   c already

28 I can't believe the builders haven't finished your house _____ . They started weeks ago!

a just   b yet   c already

29 A: _____ have you worked for this company?

B: Thirteen years.

a How long   b When   c Why

30 Sam _____ his pet rabbit for fifteen years!

a has   b has had   c is having

31 There hasn't been a park here _____ 1999.

a for   b since   c in

32 It hasn't snowed _____ years. Do you think the climate is changing?

a for   b since   c during

33 The city centre has been quieter since they _____ the new road to go around the city.

a build   b built   c 've built

34 We _____ your job application and we're very impressed.

a 've just reading   b 've just been read
c 've just been reading

35 Look at your hands! Have you _____ ?

a been painting   b been painted   c painted

36 My car _____ three times this week!

a has broken down   b has been breaking down
c is broken

37 I wanted to copy my friend's homework but he _____ it in before I had the chance.

a was handing   b 's handed
c 'd handed

38 They _____ along the motorway when the engine suddenly stopped!

a were driving   b had driven
c 've driven

39 I took my cousins to the zoo last week. Guess what? They _____ seen a kangaroo before.

a didn't   b haven't   c hadn't

40 He hadn't realised how far away it was until he _____ there.

a goes   b went   c gone

41 Shona _____ her car the previous day so she had to take a bus.

a was selling   b had sold   c has sold

42 I'd _____ to see the Andes one day.

a like   b liked   c likes

43 One day we watched the sun rise over the Himalayas. It was the most amazing thing we _____ seen.

a would ever   b had ever   c ever

44 My grandmother thinks children _____ be more polite.

a use to   b used to   c used

45 I'm sure people _____ drive so fast.

a didn't used to   b didn't use to
c hadn't use to

46 Why _____ get up at seven this morning as they planned?

a didn't they   b didn't they use to
c didn't they used to

47 Scientists _____ the planet Mars for years, but they still know very little about it.

a used to study   b have been studying
c studied

48 I didn't use to like cats when I _____ younger.

a was   b had been   c used to be

49 They're showing repeats of my favourite TV show. _____ see it last night?

a Did you use to?   b Did you
c Had you

50 Millie used to be afraid of spiders but she _____ them now.

a liked   b used to like   c likes

217

4 Progress test (units 31 to 40)

1 I like to eat outside _____ summer evenings.
   a in   b at   c on

2 There's a train to Milan _____ three-thirty and four-thirty.
   a in   b at   c on

3 The Olympic Games were in Beijing _____ 2008.
   a in   b at   c on

4 Rosanna's birthday is _____ 21st February.
   a in   b at   c on

5 We'll meet again _____ two weeks.
   a in   b at   c on

6 Let's go hiking _____ the weekend.
   a in   b at   c on

7 A: Where's Lucille now?
   B: She's _____ hospital with a broken leg.
   a in   b at   c on

8 Your wallet is _____ the table.
   a in   b at   c on

9 Slow down! There are usually lots of speed cameras _____ this motorway.
   a in   b at   c on

10 Stop _____ the traffic lights and then turn left.
   a in   b at   c on

11 We left the show _____ it finished. It wasn't very good and we were bored.
   a after   b before   c until

12 On 1st May, our shop will be open _____ 9 until 12.
   a after   b from   c for

13 There was a terrible delay on the road to your house. We didn't move _____ 30 minutes!
   a till   b from   c for

14 There's a security guard in _____ of the main door.
   a behind   b front   c opposite

15 The submarine sank _____ the water and completely disappeared.
   a above   b below   c behind

16 I recognise you and your brother on the left and right of this picture, but who is the woman _____ you both?
   a outside   b by   c between

17 Who is the statue of on _____ the column in the square?
   a top of   b the right   c front of

18 Share prices in this company aren't good. They have been going _____ for weeks now.
   a up   b down   c straight

19 The painting keeps falling _____ the wall. You need to fix it.
   a into   b along   c off

20 Would everyone please move _____ from this area? It's very dangerous to be anywhere near it.
   a away   b through   c across

21 Be careful when you dive _____ the pool. Don't hit your legs on the side.
   a towards   b into   c onto

22 They managed to get _____ the river in an old boat.
   a off   b across   c around

23 Please _____ that.
   a repeat   b repeats   c you repeat

24 _____ anything. Be quiet for a moment.
   a Don't say   b Not say   c You don't say

25 _____ yourself to tea or coffee.
   a Pass   b Give   c Help

26 Can you look _____ my dogs for the weekend? I'm going away.
   a for   b after   c up

27 The plane takes _____ in twenty minutes. Run to the gate!
   a off   b on   c over

28 They came _____ a beautiful little village while they were walking in the mountains.
   a over   b round   c across

29 You should meet my brother. You'd get _____ really well. He likes computer games too.

    a on   **b** at   **c** off

30 Please turn the oven _____ . We don't want the turkey to get burnt.

    a down   **b** up   **c** over

31 Even when the weather got worse, the team of climbers never gave _____ .

    a off   **b** up   **c** out

32 I can't decide. Will you help me pick _____ a cake for dessert?

    a up   **b** on   **c** out

33 Here's the package. The courier will pick _____ at 12.

    a up it   **b** it up   **c** it

34 Can you go _____ for me and find the documents marked March 2009?

    a through this file   **b** this file through
    c through file

35 It was nice to talk again. See _____ soon.

    a you around   **b** around you   **c** round you

36 The manager would like to set _____ meetings with everyone to discuss their progress this year.

    a up   **b** off   **c** on

37 Can you take _____ any information from this meeting so we know what was agreed?

    a off   **b** down   **c** out

38 Please take our visitor _____ for a drink.

    a off   **b** down   **c** out

39 I'd like five minutes to go _____ your essay. There are a few problems with it.

    a away   **b** over   **c** along

40 After they stole the money, the robbers got _____ in this car.

    a out   **b** along   **c** away

41 Log _____ this site with your user name.

    a onto   **b** up   **c** out

42 The sun is very bright today. Put your sunglasses _____ .

    a on   **b** up   **c** out

43 Why did you have to bring _____ the issue of money? You knew the owners would get angry.

    a in   **b** up   **c** on

44 I'll call _____ in a few minutes.

    a back them   **b** me back   **c** them back

45 The students always show _____ during tests!

    a to each other their answers
    b each other their answers
    c their answers each other

46 It would be nice to give _____ home.

    a your friend a lift   **b** a lift your friend
    c your friend to a lift

47 I've bought this birthday card _____ . Please sign it.

    a to Igor   **b** for Igor   **c** Igor

48 Please _____ Paolo my address.

    a to give   **b** give to   **c** give

49 Why did you _____ the journalist?

    a show the photograph
    b show the photograph to
    c show to the photograph

50 Remember not to tell _____ about this. It's a secret.

    a anyone else   **b** to anyone else
    c it to anyone else

5 Progress test (units 41 to 50)

1 Have you seen my _____? I'm sure I left them here.
   a news sunglasses   **b** new sunglasses
   c sunglasses new

2 Your dress _____. Where did you buy it?
   a looks great   **b** great looks   **c** look great

3 Have you seen that _____ baby? He's so cute.
   a asleep   **b** sleeping   **c** sleep

4 I love your _____.
   a shoes red leather   **b** leather, red shoes
   c red, leather shoes

5 The fashion models were wearing the designer's _____ collection.
   a silk, new, Italian   **b** new, Italian, silk
   c Italian, new, silk

6 This _____ chest of drawers was my grandfather's.
   a beautiful, old, wooden
   b wooden, beautiful, old
   c old, wooden, beautiful

7 The nature film was long and _____.
   a boring   **b** bored   **c** boreing

8 The old horror films are never very _____.
   a frightening   **b** frightened   **c** frighten

9 The jokes weren't that funny but the audience seemed _____.
   a amusing   **b** amused   **c** amuse

10 Everyone's so _____ about going to the carnival this weekend.
   a exciting   **b** excited   **c** exciteing

11 After all this hard work it will be nice to take a _____ break.
   a relaxing   **b** relaxed   **c** relax

12 People were going to work as normal when they heard the news. It was _____.
   a shocking   **b** shocked   **c** shock

13 I'm very _____ at the moment. My friend is seriously ill in hospital.
   a worrying   **b** worried   **c** worry

14 There's a terrible delay on the road to your house. We didn't move _____ 30 minutes!
   a till   **b** from   **c** for

15 After a while the employees will get tired _____ working such long hours.
   a of   **b** in   **c** about

16 We are rather pleased _____ the progress all the pupils have made this year.
   a of   **b** in   **c** with

17 Sometimes I get irritated _____ the person who sits opposite me. He talks about himself all day long.
   a of   **b** about   **c** with

18 Why are some people so fascinated _____ technology?
   a in   **b** by   **c** about

19 The weather isn't very _____ today, is it?
   a good   **b** well   **c** best

20 Please eat your dinner _____. There's no rush!
   a slow   **b** slowly   **c** slowely

21 The whole team played _____ so I don't know why they expected to win.
   a bad   **b** badly   **c** worst

22 They play _____.
   a the guitar brilliantly   **b** brilliantly the guitar
   c the guitar brilliant

23 Rose can _____. She sounds like Maria Callas.
   a sings amazingly   **b** amazingly sing
   c sing amazingly

24 A: How _____?
   B: Not very.
   a well can you play chess?
   b can you play well chess?
   c can you play chess well?

25 Your teacher has worked _____ to help you this term.
   a hard   **b** hardly   **c** the hardly

26 I haven't seen you _____. Where have you been?
   a late   **b** lately   **c** later

27 When they arrived at the airport, their luggage was _____ heavy. The person at the check-in wouldn't let them take it on the aeroplane.

a a lot   b too   c enough

28 Is your bag _____ to carry all those school books?

a big enough   b enough big   c bigger enough

29 Now we've cleaned the computer's memory, it should run _____ .

a efficient   b more efficient
c more efficiently

30 That meal was _____ than the one we had last time. Tell the waiter!

a bad   b worse   c worst

31 The more you practise something, the _____ it becomes.

a easy   b more easy   c easier

32 The town council intends to make our town one of the _____ in the country.

a green   b greener   c greenest

33 With all these cars in the city, it's as _____ as it's always been.

a polluted   b more polluted
c most polluted

34 Bicycles are probably _____ way to get around.

a quickly   b quicker   c the quickest

35 These days, flying is so _____ .

a uncomfortable   b uncomfortably
c least comfortable

36 I'd say London is the most exciting city you'll _____ visit.

a than   b ever   c just

37 When you meet someone for the first time in my country, it's _____ to use first names straight away.

a commonly   b common
c more commonly

38 Please wipe the car's windscreen. That's better! I can see _____ now.

a clear   b as clearly   c clearly

39 I find that listening to music is _____ than silence.

a relaxing   b less relaxing   c least relaxing

40 What's the _____ you've ever walked?

a far   b most far   c furthest

41 The flight to Los Angeles is _____ the one to New York.

a longer   b longest   c as long as

42 Some _____ best skiers come from Norway.

a of the   b as   c the

43 Monaco is one of _____ Formula One races in the world.

a hardly   b harder   c the hardest

44 I'm looking for something a _____ more up-to-date than my current laptop.

a bit   b slightly   c quite

45 A: How is Shirley?

B: She's _____ happier now she has a job.

a many   b more   c much

46 This is quite expensive. Do you have anything _____ cheaper?

a as   b than   c slightly

47 I'm certain your painting will win the competition. It's _____ the best entry.

a easy   b easily   c easier

48 The athlete Usain Bolt ran _____ far the fastest time of anyone during that race.

a than   b as   c by

49 Wow! Since you cleaned your car, it looks as _____ as new!

a good   b well   c better

50 The difference in price is quite small. The second one is _____ as expensive as the first.

a almost   b not nearly   c as cheaply

6 Progress test (units 51 to 60)

1 He _____ going to the party tonight. He's busy.
   a 's   b isn't   c aren't

2 _____ you _____ to the cinema with us tomorrow?
   a Do . . . go   b Is . . . go   c Are . . . going

3 He's going _____ for his father.
   a work   b to work   c working

4 He isn't _____ until next week.
   a start   b started   c starting

5 I'm sorry, I can't come right now. I'm _____ on the phone.
   a going speak   b going to speak   c speaking

6 I _____ do it first thing tomorrow morning – I promise.
   a am   b going to   c 'll

7 _____ to watch the match this evening?
   a You are going   b Are you going   c Will you

8 What _____ you _____ when you finish the course?
   a do . . . do   b will . . . doing   c will . . . do

9 I _____ around Asia next year.
   a travel   b 'm going to travel   c 'll travel

10 A: I can't lift my bag down. It's too heavy.
   B: Don't worry, I _____ it for you.
   a 'm getting   b 'm going to get   c 'll get

11 Sorry, I can't speak now. I'm in a meeting. I _____ you later.
   a 'm calling   b 'm going to call   c 'll call

12 _____ wait for the bus, or do you want to get a taxi?
   a We shall   b Shall we   c I shall

13 I'm really sorry. It was a mistake. I promise I _____ do it again!
   a shall   b will   c won't

14 It's a bit cold in here. _____ I close the window?
   a Shall   b Will   c Won't

15 _____ wait a moment, please? I need to get my coat.
   a Shall I   b Shall you   c Will you

16 The traffic's really slow in the centre today. _____ park the car here and walk?
   a Shall we   b We shall   c I shall

17 A: _____ wash the kitchen floor?
   B: No, leave it. _____ do it later.
   a Shall I . . . I'll   b I'll . . . Shall I   c I'll . . . I'll

18 What time _____?
   a finishes the film   b does finish the film
   c does the film finish

19 The next train _____ in five minutes from platform 3.
   a leave   b is leave   c leaves

20 It's a long drive. _____ be very late when we _____ home.
   a It's . . . 'll get   b It'll . . . 'll get   c It'll . . . get

21 Remember to call me as soon as you _____.
   a arrive   b 'll arrive   c arrives

22 There's no hurry. Tom _____ here with me until you _____ back.
   a waits . . . 'll get   b 'll wait . . . get
   c 'll wait . . . 'll get

23 I need to finish this report before I _____ home tonight.
   a 'll go   b 'm going   c go

24 It's really cold this evening. I think it _____.
   a 's snowing   b 's going to snow   c 's snow

25 Who _____ to invite to the party?
   a you're going   b are going you
   c are you going

26 _____ want anything to eat when you arrive?
   a You'll   b You're going to   c Will you

27 He _____ win the race. He isn't fast enough.
   a won't   b 's going to   c 'll

28 He _____ continue his studies. He wants to get a job instead.

   a 's going to   b 'll   c isn't going to

29 _____ a warm, windy day, with a possibility of rain in the afternoon.

   a Will it be   b It'll be   c It won't be

30 _____ be home by 8 o'clock.

   a We probably'll   b Probably will we
   c We'll probably

31 Sue _____ at the party tonight.

   a won't definitely be   b definitely won't be
   c won't be definitely

32 We _____ our best to be there on time.

   a 'll try certainly   b won't certainly try
   c 'll certainly try

33 There's no doubt about it. He'll _____ be a great president.

   a possibly   b definitely   c probably

34 We're still not completely sure, but we _____ won't go camping this weekend.

   a certainly   b definitely   c probably

35 No, it's impossible. He _____ to sell his family house.

   a definitely won't agree   b won't definitely agree
   c won't agree definitely

36 A: Have you seen my glasses?
   B: _____ in the living room, next to the TV.

   a May they be   b May be they   c They may be

37 He _____ pass his exam tomorrow. He hasn't been studying very hard.

   a may not   b not may   c couldn't

38 _____ rain later this afternoon. We'd better take an umbrella.

   a Might it   b Could it   c It may

39 I'm really sorry I _____ come to the meeting yesterday.

   a mightn't   b couldn't   c may not

40 We definitely _____ leave until 2.30.

   a won't   b may not   c might not

41 Take a jacket with you. _____ get cold later in the evening.

   a It may not   b It won't   c It could

42 A: Is that the new boss?
   B: It _____ . I don't know, I haven't seen her yet.

   a must be   b can't be   c might be

43 A: Is that my seat?
   B: Yes, it _____ . There aren't any others left.

   a must be   b can't be   c couldn't be

44 Did you hear that noise? There _____ someone in the house.

   a can't be   b might not be   c might be

45 I think those people _____ live in the house on the corner. I've seen them there before.

   a can   b may   c mustn't

46 I _____ with you. You _____ need help carrying the shopping.

   a 'll come . . . may   b won't come . . . could
   c come . . . might

47 Have you seen his new car? It's beautiful!
He _____ have a lot of money.

   a can't   b must   c might

48 When the show _____ , we _____ go out for something to eat.

   a finish . . . could   b finishes . . . may
   c will finish . . . must

49 A: Is that David over there?
   B: That _____ David. He's away on business.

   a can't be   b must be   c might not

50 I _____ need to work late tonight. I don't know yet. I _____ call and let you know.

   a may . . . 'll   b must . . . call
   c. 'll . . . must

7 Progress test (units 61 to 70)

1 I can swim but I _____ surf.
   a can   b could   c can't

2 Youssef _____ speak five languages before he was ten years old.
   a can   b could   c can't

3 I _____ play the guitar but I could sing.
   a couldn't   b can't   c could

4 A: You can borrow my car if you want.
   B: No, thanks. I _____ drive!
   a couldn't   b can't   c could

5 I _____ ride a bike until I was 12 years old!
   a could   b can   c couldn't

6 A: _____ you cook paella?
   B: Yes, I _____ show you how.
   a Can . . . can   b Can't . . . can't
   c Can . . . can't

7 _____ smoke in the bar?
   a Are we allowed   b We can   c Can we

8 Our students _____ to take up to five DVDs to watch at home.
   a are they allowed   b are allowed   c can

9 We _____ park our car outside our front door. There's no space.
   a aren't allowed   b are allowed to   c can't

10 _____ to take your mobile phone to school?
    a Can you to   b Are you allowed
    c You allowed

11 We _____ to watch TV but we _____ play computer games.
    a can't . . . are allowed to   b aren't allowed . . . can
    c aren't allowed . . . are allowed

12 Only buses and taxis _____ drive through the main square. Cars are banned.
    a aren't allowed to   b can't   c can

13 You _____ be here on time or the bus will go without you.
    a must   b need   c have

14 You _____ pay for parking. It's free.
    a must   b mustn't   c don't have to

15 You _____ forget to buy your mother a birthday present.
    a must   b mustn't   c don't have to

16 You _____ pay with cash. They don't accept credit cards.
    a have to   b mustn't   c don't need to

17 My uncle won the lottery last year. He's so rich he _____ work!
    a has to   b don't have to
    c doesn't need to

18 We _____ to take any food with us, but we really _____ remember to take some water.
    a don't need . . . must   b mustn't . . . must
    c don't need . . . don't need

19 Our car broke down, so we _____ take the bus.
    a must   b could   c had to

20 When I was a child, I _____ to watch television.
    a couldn't   b wasn't allowed   c didn't have to

21 _____ to wear a uniform when you were at school, Mum?
    a Were you allowed to   b Could you
    c Did you have

22 We always _____ do a lot of homework in the evening on weekdays.
    a had to   b didn't have to
    c weren't allowed to

23 In my last job I _____ work from home if I wanted to.
    a were allowed to   b could   c need

24 We _____ smoke in the hotel. We _____ go out into the garden.
    a had to . . . could   b couldn't . . . had to
    c didn't have . . . were allowed

25 _____ open the door for me, please?
    a Could you   b Can I   c May you

26 Excuse me, _____ I leave the room for a moment? Thank you.

    a may   **b** would   **c** will

27 _____ ask you a favour? _____ help me with this computer program?

    a Can you . . . Could you   **b** May I . . . Would you
    c Can you . . . Could I

28 _____ move a little to the left, please? I don't have much space.

    a Can you   **b** May you   **c** Would I

29 _____ wait here a moment, please? I'll see if the director is in his office.

    a May you   **b** Will I   **c** Could you

30 My meeting finishes at six. _____ come and pick me up?

    a May I   **b** Could I   **c** Would you

31 Oh no! I've forgotten my wallet! _____ lend me some money until tomorrow?

    a Could possibly you   **b** Could you possibly
    c Possibly could you

32 Would you mind _____ your car, please? I need to open the gate.

    a move   **b** moving   **c** I moved

33 Do you mind _____ early this afternoon? I have an appointment with the dentist.

    a if I leave   **b** if I left   **c** if I leaving

34 Do you mind _____ the window open? It's quite hot in here.

    a if you leave   **b** you leave   **c** leaving

35 _____ ask the waiter for some more water?

    a Could you possibly   **b** Do you mind
    c Would you mind

36 A: Would you mind passing me the salt?
    B: _____ . Here you are!

    a Yes, I would.   **b** No, of course not.
    c Yes, I do mind actually.

37 How about _____ for a pizza tonight? I'll pay!

    a go out   **b** to go out   **c** going out

38 We could _____ to that new Chinese restaurant.

    a go   **b** to go   **c** going

39 I'm getting tired. _____ taking a coffee break?

    a Why don't we   **b** What about   **c** Let's

40 _____ leave this until tomorrow? It's getting late.

    a Why don't   **b** Shall we   **c** How about

41 Perhaps we _____ think again. This plan isn't going to work.

    a shall   **b** should   **c** let's

42 It's such a beautiful day! You don't have to work. _____ going for a picnic?

    a Why not   **b** Why don't   **c** How about

43 Do you think I _____ to buy my boss a birthday present?

    a should   **b** had better   **c** ought

44 You _____ really try and visit the castle if you have time.

    a should   **b** shouldn't   **c** ought

45 _____ start studying soon or you'll never pass your exam!

    a Should you   **b** You ought   **c** You'd better

46 You look tired. I think you _____ go to bed early tonight.

    a hadn't better   **b** had better not
    c had better

47 He really _____ tell so many lies. He'll get into trouble.

    a should   **b** ought   **c** shouldn't

48 Those children _____ be on their own! They _____ to be with an adult.

    a should . . . oughtn't   **b** shouldn't . . . ought
    c oughtn't . . . shouldn't

49 _____ stopping here for a coffee? Or _____ better keep driving?

    a Why don't we . . . ought we
    b How about . . . had we
    c What about . . . shouldn't

50 _____ finish your English homework?

    a You should   **b** You'd better
    c Hadn't you better

8 Progress test (units 71 to 80)

1 I'm going to the shop _____ some bread.
  a get   **b** getting   **c** to get

2 I need to leave home at 7.30 in the morning _____ get to work on time.
  a in order   **b** in order to   **c** in order not to

3 I always write everybody's birthday in my diary _____ forget.
  a in order to **b** to   **c** in order not to

4 It isn't always easy _____ patient with small children.
  a to be   **b** be   **c** to being

5 I find it really difficult _____ in the evenings.
  a study   **b** to study   **c** not to study

6 I was lucky _____ my exam!
  a fail   **b** to fail   **c** not to fail

7 What do you want _____ this evening?
  a do   **b** to do   **c** doing

8 Have you ever considered _____ to a new town?
  a move   **b** to move   **c** moving

9 Did you _____ to play an instrument at primary school?
  a learn   **b** to learn   **c** learning

10 I really want to thank you for _____ me last weekend.
  a help   **b** to help   **c** helping

11 He promised _____ me if he was going to be late.
  a call   **b** to call   **c** calling

12 I really dislike _____ at the weekend.
  a work   **b** to work   **c** working

13 They stopped _____ at a restaurant at the side of the road.
  a to eat   **b** to eating   **c** eating

14 I remember _____ really scared of the dark when I was a child.
  a to be   **b** being   **c** been

15 Please don't forget _____ the computer off when you've finished.
  a to switch   **b** switching   **c** switched

16 I'd love _____ to the cinema tonight.
  a to go   **b** going   **c** go

17 It stopped _____ as soon as we got out of the car.
  a to rain   **b** raining   **c** rain

18 I must remember _____ Tim about the appointment.
  a tell   **b** telling   **c** to tell

19 He wants _____ some food for the party.
  a we make   **b** us make   **c** us to make

20 Can you please remind _____ my mother this evening?
  a me call   **b** me to call   **c** I need to call

21 No one can make _____ something he doesn't want to do!
  a he does   **b** him do   **c** him to do

22 The teacher likes all the students _____ quiet when she's speaking.
  a to be   **b** be   **c** are being

23 Maria's got a great voice. Have you ever heard _____ ?
  a her sing   **b** she sing   **c** she sings

24 They let _____ our dog with us on the train.
  a we take   **b** us to take   **c** us take

25 _____ at the school have to take an exam at the end of the year.
  a All the student   **b** All of students
  c All of the students

26 Most of the people loved the show, but _____ were not so happy.
  a some of them **b** some of they **c** some them

27 He made two films. _____ was particularly successful.
  a Neither films   **b** Neither film
  c Neither of the film

28 Heather has two brothers. _____ play professional football.

a Both them   b Both of them   c Both of they

29 _____ gets a free meal during transatlantic flights.

a Every of the passengers   b Every passengers
c Every passenger

30 _____ my friends is going to the party, so I don't want to go either!

a None of   b No of   c None

31 _____ candidate needs to complete _____ stages of the competition.

a Each . . . all   b Each of the . . . all the
c Every . . . all of

32 We looked at two flats, but _____ of them were too expensive.

a either   b both   c every

33 Where have you been? I've been looking for you _____!

a nowhere   b anywhere   c everywhere

34 I'm so hungry! I haven't had _____ to eat since breakfast!

a nothing   b something   c anything

35 I've lost my bag! I've asked _____, but _____ has seen it.

a everywhere . . . nowhere
b everybody . . . nobody
c everything . . . nothing

36 Are you hungry? Would you like _____ to eat?

a something   b nothing   c everything

37 I've had a terrible day. _____ is going right for me today!

a Everything   b Nothing   c Anything

38 A: Have you forgotten _____?
B: Yes, I think I left my sunglasses at home.

a something   b somebody   c somewhere

39 That's the man _____ I was telling you about last night.

a which   b whose   c that

40 Are these the photos _____ were in the newspaper?

a who   b which   c when

41 What's the name of that actor _____ is in the Bond films?

a which   b whose   c who

42 Do you remember the time _____ we all went on holiday together?

a where   b which   c when

43 The hotel _____ the president stayed is in the city centre.

a which   b where   c when

44 Last night I met a woman _____ children go to the same school as Lucy.

a who   b whose   c that

45 The film _____ the Oscar for the best foreign film last year is on TV tonight.

a who won   b that won   c which it won

46 The company _____ I've been working for the last ten years has just closed down.

a where   b when   c whose

47 The book _____ me for my birthday is really interesting.

a you gave   b who you gave   c which gave

48 Have you met Aron, the man _____ Kris's sister?

a married   b which married
c who married

49 They were a great band _____ influenced millions of fans.

a that their music   b whose music
c which music

50 Loud music in public places is the one thing _____ really annoys me.

a which it   b that   c who

227

9 Progress test (units 81 to 90)

1 I do my supermarket shopping online and the food _____ to my door.

   a is bringed **b** are brought **c** is brought

2 The football match _____ because of the weather.

   a were cancelled **b** was cancelled
   c are cancelled

3 The tree _____ in the middle of the square.

   a was plant **b** was planted **c** were planted

4 This road is new, isn't it? When _____ it built?

   a was **b** were **c** is

5 According to some historians, the first pizzas were eaten _____ the Ancient Egyptians.

   a in **b** from **c** by

6 The first modern pizzas were made _____ Naples, in southern Italy.

   a in **b** from **c** by

7 People from different countries _____ different kinds of pizzas.

   a is eaten **b** are eaten **c** eat

8 The school _____ by the Queen.

   a is going to open **b** is going to be opened
   c are going to be opened

9 My language school _____ free conversation classes.

   a is offering **b** is offered **c** is being offered

10 Did you know that a new stadium _____ next to the swimming pool?

   a is being built **b** is building **c** is builded

11 The government _____ announced a new property tax.

   a is **b** has **c** has been

12 Plans for a new airport _____ announced in the press.

   a is **b** have **c** have been

13 I _____ a new computer for my birthday.

   a promised **b** were promised
   c was promised

14 Photos of the president in his private residence _____ to the press.

   a have sold **b** has been sold
   c have been sold

15 Their parents _____ the boys new bicycles for their birthdays.

   a were given **b** gave **c** given

16 The visitors _____ the gardens first and then they _____ to their rooms.

   a were shown . . . were taken **b** showed . . . taken
   c were shown . . . took

17 An urgent letter _____ all the parents.

   a was sent to **b** sent to **c** was sent

18 The school _____ £1,000 by the Parents' Association.

   a was given to **b** gave **c** was given

19 I _____ yesterday at that new hairdresser's in the town centre.

   a had cut my hair **b** did my hair cut
   c got my hair cut

20 They always _____ when they go to the supermarket.

   a get washed their car **b** get their car wash
   c get their car washed

21 I've never _____ . Have you?

   a a tattoo done **b** had a tattoo done
   c had done a tattoo

22 We're getting _____ while we're away on holiday.

   a painted the kitchen **b** the kitchen paint
   c the kitchen painted

23 Years ago we _____ developed in a shop. Now everybody does it online.

   a have our photos **b** had our photos
   c are having our photos

24 I _____ made for me for my sister's wedding.

   a 'm getting a dress **b** getting a dress
   c 'm get a dress

25 'I have a problem,' _____ . 'I'd like to talk to you about it?'

a he replied   b said he   c the man asked

26 'Can I have a drink of water, _____' he asked.

a please,   b please?   c please?,

27 'Certainly. Wait here. I won't be a minute,' _____ .

a answered she   b said she
c replied the woman

28 _____ shouted the teacher.

a Be careful!   b 'Be careful!'   c 'Be careful!,'

29 'That's the last time I'm coming _____' I thought.

a here.   b here,   c here

30 The man shook my hand and said, _____ .

a 'Welcome.'   b Welcome!   c ', welcome.'

31 A: See you at six!
B: But you said we _____ at eight!

a are meeting   b met   c were meeting

32 He told me he _____ to see the doctor.

a go   b has gone   c had been

33 She said she _____ here by the time we got home.

a is   b 'd be   c 'll be

34 People used to think the world _____ flat.

a is   b was   c had been

35 I thought I _____ do it, but I was wrong. It was far too difficult for me.

a could   b can   c 'll

36 A: Are we all going in your car?
B: No, Mike said _____ on the bus.

a he'd come   b he comes   c he came

37 They asked us _____ come.

a why had we   b why did we   c why we had

38 He was curious and wanted to know how long _____ to take.

a was it going   b it was going   c is it going

39 She was very friendly and asked us _____ anything to eat.

a we wanted   b if did we want
c if we wanted

40 Bob called. He wanted to know what _____ doing this evening.

a we were   b are we   c were we

41 The teacher asked me _____ you. I said no, of course!

a had I seen   b if had I seen   c if I'd seen

42 He really wanted to ask her what _____ , but he was too shy.

a her name was   b is her name
c was her name

43 He _____ a long story about his family.

a said me   b told to me   c told me

44 I didn't _____ anything to Eva about the party. I promise you!

a tell   b say   c told

45 Fran _____ us that she was going to buy a new house.

a said   b told   c told to

46 The customs officer _____ show him our passports.

a asked us to   b asked to us to   c asked us

47 They _____ wait in the car until they came back.

a told us to   b told to us to   c told us

48 Sue asked _____ she's going to be late.

a I tell you   b me tell you   c me to tell you

49 I _____ them to ask their mother if _____ come.

a said . . . they could   b told . . . could they
c told . . . they could

50 She asked _____ if he _____ marry her.

a him . . . will   b him . . . would
c to him . . . would

10 Progress test (units 91 to 100)

1 If I get home before you tonight, _____ cook the dinner.
   a I'll   **b** I'm   **c** I

2 If the boss asks me to work late, _____ always say yes.
   a I'll   **b** I'm   **c** I

3 You won't grow big and strong _____ you eat all your vegetables!
   a if   **b** when   **c** unless

4 I've got a meeting with John tomorrow. _____ I see him, I'll give him your message.
   a If   **b** When   **c** Unless

5 If _____ have any free time next week, we'll go to visit my grandparents.
   a we'll   **b** we   **c** we don't

6 _____ for something to eat if _____ hungry.
   a We'll stop . . . we'll be   **b** We stop . . . we'll be
   c We'll stop . . . we're

7 We usually finish work at five, _____ an emergency.
   a unless there's   **b** unless there will be
   c if there won't be

8 _____ I use your car next weekend, if you need it?
   a Will . . . won't   **b** Can . . . don't
   c Can . . . 'll

9 If you hear the fire alarm, _____ immediately to the nearest fire exit.
   a must you go **b** will you go **c** go

10 If you see anything unusual, _____ report it to the airport police.
   a you must   **b** can you   **c** will you

11 I _____ some new shoes _____ see any nice ones in the sales.
   a buy . . . if I might   **b** might buy . . . if I'll
   c might buy . . . if I

12 _____ gets the job, _____ get married next summer.
   a Toni . . . if we'll   **b** If Toni . . . we'll
   c If Toni . . . if we

13 You look really stressed! If I were you, _____ a holiday!
   a I took   **b** I'd taken   **c** I'd take

14 If _____ younger, I'd leave my job and travel around the world.
   a I'd be   **b** I'm   **c** I were

15 _____ much happier if they _____ less.
   a They'd be . . . worked   **b** They were . . . 'd work
   c They'd been . . . worked

16 _____ to the party if I _____ so tired.
   a I came . . . wouldn't be **b** I'd come . . . wasn't
   c I'd come . . . were

17 If _____ a house in the country, _____ a dog.
   a I'd have . . . I'd get   **b** I had . . . I'd get
   c I'd have . . . I got

18 If I _____ his name, I'd _____ you to him.
   a knew . . . introduce   **b** I'd know . . . introduce
   c knew . . . introduced

19 You _____ always stay at our house if you _____ .
   a can . . . want   **b** can . . . 'd want
   c could . . . 'd want

20 If it _____ this afternoon, the tennis will be cancelled.
   a 'll rain   **b** 'd rain   **c** rains

21 If we _____ get back before 12 o'clock, we'll be in trouble!
   a didn't   **b** won't   **c** don't

22 _____ you leave your job if your girlfriend asked you to?
   a Will   **b** Would   **c** Can

23 They wouldn't do anything about it unless you _____ them.
   a 'd tell   **b** told   **c** 'll tell

24 If you want to make a lot of money, _____ a bank!
   a rob   **b** you'd rob   **c** you robbed

25 A: Oh no! What _____ to you?
   B: I broke my arm.
   a did it happen **b** happened **c** it happened

26 A: How _____?
    B: I fell off my bike!

    a did it happen   b it happened
    c happened it

27 Who _____ how to play tennis? You're really good!

    a did teach you   b they taught you
    c taught you

28 How long _____ playing tennis?

    a you have been   b have been
    c have you been

29 Who _____ the Oscars this year? Follow the show
    live online!

    a will they win   b will win   c they will win

30 Who _____ for in the next election?

    a will you vote   b will vote   c you will vote

31 A: Is that your car?
    B: _____ .

    a Yes, it's.   b No, it isn't.   c Yes, is.

32 A: Did you speak to Marie this morning?
    B: No, I _____ .

    a don't   b haven't   c didn't

33 A: Are you going away this weekend?
    B: Yes, _____ . We're going to my parents' house.

    a we're   b we are   c we aren't

34 A: Would you like me to help you with that?
    B: _____ .

    a Yes, I'd like. b No, I don't. c No, thanks.

35 A: Excuse me, have you got a moment?
    B: Yes, _____ . How can I help you?

    a I have   b I've got   c thanks

36 A: Would anybody like some more cake?
    B: _____ .

    a I like some, please.   b Yes, please.
    c No, thanks, I don't like.

37 _____ you coming? Why not? It won't be the same
    without you.

    a Don't   b Are   c Aren't

38 _____ the sea look lovely today?

    a Does   b Doesn't   c Don't

39 A: _____ we stop for a coffee?
    B: No, sorry. I don't want to be late.

    a Can't   b Don't   c Won't

40 It's been a long day. Why _____ stop now? We can
    finish it tomorrow.

    a don't we   b shall we   c can we

41 _____ anyone know where Joni is?

    a Don't   b Doesn't   c Do

42 I've never been here before. _____ it a beautiful
    place?

    a Doesn't   b Don't   c Isn't

43 Do you know how much _____?

    a costs the bus   b does the bus cost
    c the bus costs

44 I'd like to know what _____ of his new book.

    a do you think   b you think   c think you

45 I was wondering if _____ to come out with me
    tonight.

    a would you like   b you'd like
    c would like you

46 Why _____ Paul to help you?

    a did you ask   b did you asked   c you asked

47 Could you tell me what _____ in the park at that
    time?

    a were you doing   b were doing you
    c you were doing

48 Do you remember what _____ to you?

    a did he say   b said he   c he said

49 A: Excuse me, sir. _____ leaving tomorrow
    as planned?
    B: Yes, _____ . The taxi will pick us up at 9.

    a We are . . . we are   b Are we . . . we are
    c Are we . . . we're

50 A: Do you have any idea what time _____?
    B: No, I _____ , sorry.

    a is it . . . don't   b it is . . . don't
    c it is . . . do

Appendix 1   Punctuation

Capital letters

Use a capital letter for …

- the first letter of a sentence: *He worked for my father.*
- the names of people and places: *Wolfgang Mozart, Helen Keller, Jackie Chan, Madrid, New York, Hong Kong.*
- the names of countries, nationalities and languages: *China/Chinese, France/French, Australia/Australian, England/English.*
- days of the week and months of the year (but not seasons): *Monday, Thursday, April, September.*
- school subjects: *English, Maths, Biology.*
- people's titles: *Mr Brown, Doctor Smith, President Clinton.*
- the pronoun I: *Martha and I live in Simpson Street.*

End of a sentence

Normally, we end a sentence with a full stop (British English) or period (American English): *I live in London.*

Question mark

Put ? at the end of a question (not a full stop): *Where do you live?*

Exclamation mark

Put ! at the end of a sentence exclaiming something (not a full stop): *That's amazing!*

Commas

Use commas, for …

- lists of nouns: *I bought a pen, a book and a bag.*
- lists of adjectives: *It's an old, black, electric lamp.*
- between a reporting verb and direct speech: *Alice replied, 'Tell me who you are, first.'*
- You can also use commas in conditional sentences when the *if*-clause comes first: *If you leave now, you'll catch the last train.*

Apostrophe

Use an apostrophe, for …

- contracted verbs forms: *I'm, doesn't, he'd*
- possessive *'s* (see Unit 4): *William's birthday, my parents' birthday, William Jones' birthday*

Quotation marks

Use quotation marks around words which are spoken or thought.

'Who are you?' she asked.

'Tell me who you are, first,' I said.

(See also Unit 86.)

Appendix 2   Spelling rules

Plural nouns

- We usually form plural nouns by adding -s or -es

```
dog → dogs
desk → desks
house → houses
hippo → hippos
bus → buses
```

- Add -es to nouns ending in -ch, -s, -ss, -sh and -x.

```
sandwich → sandwiches    dish → dishes
bus → buses              box → boxes
class → classes
```

- Change nouns ending in -y (after a consonant) to -i.

```
country → countries
story → stories
city → cities
```

Don't change the -y to -i after a vowel: *holidays, keys*

- Some nouns are irregular. For example:

```
man → men
child → children
woman → women
person → people
potato → potatoes
```

Present simple third person (*he/she/it*) verbs

- Add -s to most verbs in the present simple third person form.

```
live → lives
start → starts
work → works
```

- Add -es to verbs ending in -ch, -o, -s, -ss, -sh and -x.

```
watch → watches    finish → finishes
go → goes          relax → relaxes
pass → passes
```

- Change verbs ending in -y (after a consonant) to -i.

```
study → studies
fly → flies
```

Don't change the -y to -i after a vowel: *plays, buys*

- A few verbs have irregular forms.

```
have → has
be → is
```

Comparative and superlative adjectives

- Add -er to short adjectives to form the comparative. Add -est to short adjectives to form the superlative.

```
young → younger → youngest
cheap → cheaper → cheapest
```

When the adjective ends in -e, add -r/-st:
large → larger/largest

- Change adjectives ending in -y (after a consonant) to -i.

```
happy → happier → happiest
angry → angrier → angriest
```

- Double the final consonant on adjectives ending with consonant + vowel + consonant.

```
hot → hotter → hottest
big → bigger → biggest
```

Don't double the consonant with adjectives ending in -w or -y: *slow → slower/slowest.*

Adverbs ending in -ly

- We often add -ly to an adjective to form an adverb:

```
quick → quickly
slow → slowly
```

Note these differences:
Adjectives ending in -l: beautiful → beautifully (not ~~beautifuly~~)
Adjectives ending in -y: happy → happily
Adjectives ending in -ble: horrible → horribly

Past simple regular verbs (-*ed* endings)

- Add -*ed* to verbs ending in a consonant.

watch → watch**ed**
visit → visit**ed**

- Add -*d* to verbs ending in -*e*.

dance → dance**d**
arrive → arrive**d**
live → live**d**

- With verbs ending in -*y* (after a consonant), change the -*y* to *i*.

cry → cr**ied**

- Don't change the -*y* to -*i* after a vowel.

play → pla**yed**
stay → sta**yed**

- Double the final consonant on most verbs ending with consonant + vowel + consonant.

stop → sto**pp**ed
jog → jo**gg**ed

Present participles (-*ing* endings)

- With verbs ending in -*e*, delete the -*e* before adding -*ing*.

dance → danc**ing**
live → liv**ing**
have → hav**ing**

- With the verb *to die,* delete the -*e* and change the *i* to *y*

die → d**y**ing

- Double the final consonant on most verbs ending with consonant + vowel + consonant.

stop → sto**pp**ing
run → ru**nn**ing
swim → swi**mm**ing
jog → jo**gg**ing
get → ge**tt**ing
travel → trave**ll**ing

British and American spelling

There are a few differences.

- Words ending in -*re* often end in -*er*:
  centre (Br Eng) → *center* (Am Eng)

- Words with -*our* are often spelt:
  colour (Br Eng) → *color* (Am Eng),
  favourite (Br Eng) → *favorite* (Am Eng)

- Verbs with more than one syllable that end in consonant + vowel + consonant, don't double the final consonant: *travelling* (Br Eng) → *traveling* (Am Eng)

- Verbs ending with -*ise* or -*ize* are always -*ize*:
  memorise (Br Eng) → *memorize* (Am Eng).

Appendix 3 Common irregular verbs

infinitive	past simple	past participle	infinitive	past simple	past participle
be	was/were	been	learn	learnt	learnt
become	became	become	leave	left	left
begin	began	begun	lend	lent	lent
bite	bit	bitten	lose	lost	lost
blow	blew	blown	make	made	made
break	broke	broken	mean	meant	meant
bring	brought	brought	meet	met	met
build	built	built	pay	paid	paid
burn	burnt	burnt	put	put	put
buy	bought	bought	read /riːd/	read /red/	read /red/
catch	caught	caught	ride	rode	ridden
choose	chose	chosen	ring	rang	rung
come	came	come	rise	rose	risen
cost	cost	cost	run	ran	run
do	did	done	say	said	said
draw	drew	drawn	see	saw	seen
drink	drank	drunk	sell	sold	sold
drive	drove	driven	send	sent	sent
eat	ate	eaten	shine	shone	shone
fall	fell	fallen	show	showed	shown
feel	felt	felt	shut	shut	shut
fight	fought	fought	sing	sang	sung
find	found	found	sit	sat	sat
fly	flew	flown	sleep	slept	slept
forget	forgot	forgotten	speak	spoke	spoken
get	got	got	spend	spent	spent
give	gave	given	stand	stood	stood
go	went	gone/been	steal	stole	stolen
grow	grew	grown	swim	swam	swum
hang	hung	hung	take	took	taken
have	had	had	teach	taught	taught
hear	heard	heard	tear	tore	torn
hide	hid	hidden	tell	told	told
hit	hit	hit	think	thought	thought
hold	held	held	throw	threw	thrown
hurt	hurt	hurt	wear	wore	worn
keep	kept	kept	win	won	won
know	knew	known	write	wrote	written

Appendix 4 Summary of main verb forms

Summary of present tenses

Present simple

I/You/We/They **live** in Ireland.
He/She/It **lives** in Ireland.

We **don't live** in Ireland.
She **doesn't live** in Ireland.

Where **do** they **live**?
Where **does** he **live**?

Present continuous

I'**m eating** at the moment.
You/We/They'**re eating** at the moment.
He/She/It'**s eating** at the moment.

I'**m not playing** basketball at the moment.
He **isn't playing** basketball at the moment.
We **aren't playing** basketball at the moment.

What **are** you **doing**?
Where **is** she **playing** basketball?

Present perfect simple

I/You/We/They'**ve gone** into the garden.
He/She/It'**s gone** into the garden.

We **haven't gone** into the garden.
He **hasn't gone** into the garden.

Where **have** they **gone**?
Where **has** she **gone**?

Present perfect continuous

I/You/We/They'**ve been sleeping** for hours.
He/She/It'**s been sleeping** for hours.

We **haven't been sleeping** for hours.
He **hasn't been sleeping** for hours.

Where **have** they **been sleeping**?
Where **has** she **been sleeping**?

Summary of past tenses

Past simple

I/You/He/She/It/We/They **finished** last night.

I/You/He/She/It/We/They **didn't finish** last night.

Did I/you/he/she/it/we/they **finish** last night?

Past continuous

I/He/She/It **was waiting** by the bus stop.
You/We/They **were waiting** for a bus.

I **wasn't waiting** for a bus.
We **weren't waiting** for a bus.

Was he **waiting** for a bus?
Were you **waiting** for a bus?

Past perfect

I/He/She/It/You/We/They **had left** before the parcel arrived.

I/He/She/It/You/We/They **hadn't left** before the parcel arrived.

Had you/they **left** before the parcel arrived?

Used to

I/He/She/It/You/We/They **used to** love chocolate ice cream.

I/He/She/It/You/We/They **didn't use to** love chocolate ice cream.

Did I/he/she/it/you/we/they **use to** love chocolate ice cream?

Summary of future forms

I'**ll see** you tonight.
I'**m going to** see her tonight.
I **leave** at eight o'clock tonight.
We'**re seeing** each other this evening.

Modal verbs

Use **will** for …

- talking about the future:

    I'll be in the café at six.

    She won't be here tonight.

- predictions, certainty and possibility:

    I think she'll pass her exams.

    I'm sure they'll get married.

- offers, promises and requests:

    I'll pick you up.

    I'll be there in ten minutes.

- instant decisions:

    I think I'll have fish.

    Don't worry. I'll go and get her.

Use **shall** for …

- asking what to do:

    Shall I answer it?

    Shall we stand here?

- suggesting:

    Shall I tell her?

    Shall we go out later?

- offering:

    Shall I pick you up?

    Shall we help?

Use **can** for …

- ability:

    I can speak French.

    I can't play the piano.

- offers and requests:

    Can I help you?

    Can I have a drink?

- permission:

    You can go after eight.

    You can't go tonight.

- possibility:

    Sorry. I can't come tomorrow.

Use **could** for …

- for past ability:

    Mozart could play the organ.

    How well could she see?

- possibility (in the past):

    He couldn't escape.

    Why couldn't you climb down the mountain?

- polite requests:

    Could I speak to Shelby?

    Could you spell that?

Use **would** for …

- talking about the results or consequences of an imagined situation:

    A: *What would you do if you won the lottery?*

    B: *I'd buy a yacht.*

Use **would like** for …

- requests and offers:

    I'd like some water.

    Would you like a drink?

Use **would you like to** for …

- requests and offers:

    Would you like to help me?

    Would you like me to help you?

Use **must** for …

- obligation:

    You must be home by ten thirty.

    You mustn't be late.

- prohibition:

    You mustn't park on a yellow line.

    You mustn't stay out late.

Use **should** for …

- advice and suggesting:

    You should buy that dress.

    He shouldn't go with them.

Summary of active to passive verb forms

Present simple: *He **builds** a house.* → *A house **is built**.*

Present continuous: *He **is building** a house.* → *The house **is being built**.*

Present perfect: *He **has built** the house.* → *The house **has been built**.*

Past simple: *He **built** the house.* → *The house **was built**.*

Past continuous: *He **was building** the house.* → *The house **was being built**.*

Past perfect: *He **had built** the house.* → *The house **had been built**.*

Will (future): *He **will build** the house.* → *The house **will be built**.*

Be going to: *He's **going to build** the house.* → *The house **is going to be built**.*

Must: *He **must build** the house.* → *The house **must be built**.*

Can: *He **can't build** the house.* → *The house **can't be built**.*

Might: *He **might build** the house.* → *The house **might be built**.*

Summary of tense change backwards in reported speech

present simple → past simple:

*'We often **go** to the cinema.'* → *They said they often **went** to the cinema.*

present continuous → past continuous:

*'We're **going** to the cinema.'* → *They said they **were going** to the cinema.*

present perfect → past perfect:

*'We've **booked** tickets for the cinema.'* → *They said they **had booked** tickets for the cinema.*

will → would:

'We'll go to the cinema.' → *They said they **would** go to the cinema.*

can → could:

*'We **can** go to the cinema.'* → *They said they **could** go to the cinema.*

past simple → past perfect:

*'We **went** to the cinema.'* → *They said they **had been** to the cinema.*

Summary of conditionals

Real conditionals

* Generally true (zero conditional)

When/if it's sunny, we go to the beach.

* Possible future situations (first conditional)

If it's sunny, we'll go to the beach.

Unreal conditionals

* Impossible or improbable present and future situations (second conditional)

If it was sunny, I'd go to the beach.

If I were you, I'd go to the beach.

If I had more time, I'd go running every day.

Appendix 5   Phrasal verbs

This is the list of phrasal verbs in Units 37, 38 and 40.

The word order is shown in square brackets [ ]

v = verb

p = particle

n = noun

For example:

call round [v p] = *Don't forget to **call round***.

look after [v p n] = *I'm **looking after my little sister**.*

look up [v n p] = ***Look the information up** in your book.*

ask (someone) over [v n p] = *Why don't you ask Roy over for dinner?*

bring up [v p n] / [v n p] = *Bring up the information on the screen. / Bring it up on the screen.*

call back [v n p] = *Can you call me back?*

call round [v p] = *I'll call round at about five.*

come across [v p n] = *I came across this article in the paper.*

come back [v p] = *Come back! You forgot your bag.*

come round [v p] = *You must come round again sometime.*

eat out [v p] = *Let's eat out this evening.*

get away [v p] = *I need to get away and relax for a few days.*

get on [v p] = *Do you and your sisters get on?*

get up [v p] = *What time do you get up?*

get (someone) up [v n p] = *Can you get Jimmy up? He'll be late for school.*

give away [v p n] / [v n p] = *Give away these toys to children who need them. / Give these toys away to children who need them.*

give out [v p n] / [v n p] = *Give these leaflets out to anyone on the street. / Give out these leaflets to anyone on the street.*

give up [v p n] / [v n p] = *Don't give up your job. / Don't give your job up.*

go down [v p] = *The price of petrol went down last week.*

go through [v p n] = *Let's go through the answers together.*

go up [v p] = *Inflation is going up.*

grow up [v p] = *You need to grow up!*

log in [v p] = *Log in with your password and username.*

log onto [v p n] = *Log onto my computer if yours doesn't work.*

look after [v p n] = *Can you look after the baby?*

look at [v p n] = *I love to look at paintings.*

look for [v p n] = *Look for a house with a red door.*

look out [v p] = *Look out! The bookcase is falling over.*

look up [v p] = *Look up! The sky is beautiful tonight.*

look up (someone in a book) [v p n] / [v n p] = *Look up their address in this directory. / Look their address up in this directory.*

pay out [v p n] / [v n p] = *The company is paying out bonuses to all its staff. / The company is paying bonuses out to all its staff.*

pick out [v p n] / [v n p] = *Pick out a nice dress for the party. / Pick a nice dress out for the party.*

pick up [v p n] / [v n p] = *Will you pick up Rachel? / Will you pick Rachel up?*

put in [v p n] / [v n p] = *Put in the coin. / Put the coin in.*

put on [v p n] / [v n p] = *Can I put on some of your lipstick? / Can I put some of your lipstick on?*

ring (someone) back [v n p] = *Your mother wants you to ring her back.*

see (someone) around [v n p] = *I'll see you around. Bye!*

set up [v p n] / [v n p] = *Did you set up the meeting with everyone? / Did you set the meeting up with everyone?*

take down [v p n] / [v n p] = *Let me take down your telephone number. / Let me take your telephone number down.*

take off [v p] = *The plane takes off at three.*

take off (something) [v p n] / [v n p] *Take off your hat in the house. / Take your hat off in the house.*

take over [v p n] / [v n p] = *The company took over its competitor. / The company took its competitor over.*

turn down [v p n] / [v n p] = *Please turn down your music! / Please turn your music down!*

turn off [v p n] / [v n p] = *Let's turn off the TV. / Let's turn the TV off.*

turn up [v p n] / [v n p] = *Turn up the temperature on the oven. / Turn the temperature up on the oven.*

Index

Note: The numbers in this index are page numbers. Key vocabulary is in *italic*.

Index

Index

Notes

Notes

Notes

Notes

Notes

Notes

Photo credits

The publishers would like to thank the following sources for permission to reproduce their copyright protected photographs:

Cover image: Shutterstock Inc.

Photos: pp 15l (Sean Locke/iStockphoto.com), 15r (Dr. Heinz Linke/iStockphoto.com), 22t (Winston Davidian/iStockphoto.com), 22b (Sarah Musselman/iStockphoto.com), 23t (Michael Krinke/iStockphoto.com), 23c (Ronald Summers/Shutterstock Inc.), 23b (Denis Pepin/Shutterstock Inc.), 24 (irishphoto.com/Alamy), 29 (*A Life in the Day: Simon Nixon, internet entrepreneur*, by Ria Higgins, copyright Times Newspapers Ltd.), 29 (Permission granted by moneysupermarket.com), 31t (james steidl/iStockphoto.com), 31b (Michael Krinke/iStockphoto.com), 34l (Annette Shaff/iStockphoto.com), 34r (Paul Kline/iStockphoto.com), 36 (iStockphoto.com), 36r (Sean Randall/iStockphoto.com), 41t (David Ciemny/iStockphoto.com), 41b (Teekaygee/Shutterstock Inc.), 48tl (Cultura/Corbis), 48tr (iStockphoto.com), 48bl (Lise Gagne/iStockphoto.com), 48br (Steve Cole/iStockphoto.com), 51t (Sharon Dominick/iStockphoto.com), 51b (Pali Rao/iStockphoto.com), 52 (Photos 12/Alamy), 56l (S. Greg Panosian/iStockphoto.com), 56cl (Diego Cervo/Shutterstock Inc.), 56cr (Maxim Ahner/Shutterstock Inc.), 56r (Gene Chutka/iStockphoto.com), 64 (Supri Suharjoto/Shutterstock Inc.), 66 (Seth Resnick/Science Faction/Corbis), 77 (Loren McIntyre/PhotoLibrary), 74 (Bridget McGill/iStockphoto.com), 81t-a (Oleg Prikhodko/iStockphoto.com), 81t-b (René Mansi/iStockphoto.com), 81b (Moodboard/Alamy), 83 (iStockphoto.com), 86l (Greg Nicholas/iStockphoto.com), 86c (iStockphoto.com), 86r (iStockphoto.com), 87a (iStockphoto.com), 87b (John Burwell/BurwellPhotography.com/iStockphoto.com), 87c (Mihail Glushkov/iStockphoto.com), 87d (iStockphoto.com/Mladen Mitrinović), 87e (Valeriy Zan/iStockphoto.com), 88 (Kirsty Pargeter/iStockphoto.com), 91 (Renee Lee/iStockphoto.com), 104 (Murat Taner/iStockphoto.com), 105 (iladm/Shutterstock Inc.), 106t (Phil Berry/iStockphoto.com), 106c (Marlene DeGrood/Shutterstock Inc.), 106b (Thaddeus Robertson/iStockphoto.com), 107l (Robert Paul Van Beets/Shutterstock Inc.), 107c (sf2301420max/Shutterstock Inc.), 107r (Benoit Rousseau/iStockphoto.com), 108 (Drive Images/Alamy), 109t (Ian Jeffery/iStockphoto.com), 109b (iStockphoto.com), 111t (iStockphoto.com), 111b (WaveF/PhotoLibrary), 124 (Steve Hix/Somos Images/Corbis), 126t (iStockphoto.com), 126b (iStockphoto.com), 128 (Bettmann/Corbis), 129 (Michael Knight/iStockphoto.com), 131 (Latin Stock Collection/Corbis), 132l (Nora Feller/Corbis), 132r (Jorg Hackemann/Shutterstock Inc.), 136 (iStockphoto.com), 137t (Image Source/Corbis), 137b (Stephen Bonk/Shutterstock Inc.), 138 (Tim OLeary/Corbis), 139 (Absolut/Shutterstock Inc.), 141 (Clint Scholz/iStockphoto.com), 152a (iStockphoto.com), 152b (Vasina Natalia/Shutterstock Inc.), 152c (Adrian Britton/Shutterstock Inc.), 152d (Elnur/Shutterstock Inc.), 152e (Farres/Shutterstock Inc.), 152f (Milos Luzanin/Shutterstock Inc.), 154 (Andre Blais/Shutterstock Inc.), 155 (Radu Razvan/iStockphoto.com), 161 (Mark Stout Photography/Shutterstock Inc.), 164 (Emre Ogan/iStockphoto.com), 165a (Dmitry Ersler/iStockphoto.com), 165b (Pedro Monteiro/iStockphoto.com), 165c (iStockphoto.com), 165d (Andersen Ross/GettyImages), 165e (Stefan Schulze/iStockphoto.com), 165f (iStockphoto.com), 165g (Sang Nguyen/iStockphoto.com), 167 (Matthew Dixon/iStockphoto.com), 168 (James Kingman/iStockphoto.com), 168r (Permission granted by Shakespeare Birthplace Trust), 171a (Timothy Ball/iStockphoto.com), 171b (Duncan Walker/iStockphoto.com), 171c (Andrew Green/iStockphoto.com), 172 (Dean Turner/iStockphoto.com), 173 (Denise Torres/iStockphoto.com), 174l (Permission granted by www.teofila.es), 174r (Permission granted by www.teofila.es), 175 (S. Greg Panosian/iStockphoto.com), 176 (Andrew Rich/iStockphoto.com), 181 (Vinci, Leonardo da (1452-1519)/Louvre, Paris, France/Giraudon/The Bridgeman Art Library), 182 (*Alice's Adventures in Wonderland*, by Lewis Carroll), 184 (Bettmann/Corbis), 190 (Gabe Palmer/Corbis), 191t (Mike Bentley/iStockphoto.com), 191b (iStockphoto.com), 192l (Yuri Arcurs/Shutterstock Inc.), 192r (Gemphotography/Shutterstock Inc.), 201 (Paul Pantazescu/iStockphoto.com), 203 (Elisabeth Deffner/National Geographic Kids), 204 (Siri Stafford/GettyImages), 205 (Patrik Giardino/Corbis), 207 (Raisa Kanareva/Shutterstock Inc.), 211 (Trinity Mirror/Mirrorpix/Alamy)

Illustrations by artists at KJA-artists.com:

Adrian@KJA-artists.com: pp 14, 32, 79a, 82, 102, 122, 142, 156, 188, 189; Andrew@KJA-artists.com: pp 28, 33, 42, 61, 85, 98, 112, 133, 146, 147, 173, 185, 186, 194; John@KJA-artists.com: pp 38, 44, 62, 73, 92, 113, 145, 149, 153, 196, 197, 206; Kath@KJA-artists.com: pp 26, 68, 77, 116, 134, 166, 178, 179, 198; Maria@KJA-artists.com: pp 27, 54, 69, 89, 93, 114, 148, 187, 202, 203; Sean@KJA-artists.com: pp 46, 49, 65, 78a, 94, 110, 135, 144, 162, 208

Illustrations by Jorge Santillan: pp 12, 13, 63, 76a-b, 151a

Illustrations by Kathrin Jacobsen: pp 17, 43, 55, 76c-o, 78b-l, 79b-m, 123, 167, 175, 183, 195

Designs by Mark Slader, Echelon Design: pp 15, 34, 35, 81, 86, 87, 91, 94, 95, 96, 102, 103, 109, 126, 152, 164, 165, 168, 191, 211

CD Track List

CD 1

Unit and Exercise	Track	Unit and Exercise	Track	Unit and Exercise	Track
Unit 1, Ex 3	1.02	Unit 17, Ex 2	1.21	Unit 34, Ex 1	1.40
Unit 2, Ex 2	1.03	Unit 18, Ex 1	1.22	Unit 35, Review, Ex 5	1.41
Unit 3, Ex 2	1.04	Unit 20, Review, Ex 5	1.23	Unit 35, Review, Ex 6	1.42
Unit 4, Ex 1	1.05	Unit 20, Review, Ex 6	1.24	Unit 36, Ex 4	1.43
Unit 5, Review, Ex 5	1.06	Unit 21, Ex 4	1.25	Unit 38, Ex 3	1.44
Unit 5, Review, Ex 6	1.07	Unit 22, Ex 2	1.26	Unit 40, Review, Ex 6	1.45
Unit 5, Ex 7	1.08	Unit 23, Ex 4	1.27	Unit 40, Review, Ex 7	1.46
Unit 6, Ex 2	1.09	Unit 24, Ex 3	1.28	Unit 42, Ex 2	1.47
Unit 8, Ex 3	1.10	Unit 25, Review, Ex 6	1.29	Unit 44, Ex 3	1.48
Unit 10, Review, Ex 6	1.11	Unit 25, Review, Ex 7	1.30	Unit 45, Review, Ex 6	1.49
Unit 10, Review, Ex 7	1.12	Unit 25, Review, Ex 8	1.31	Unit 45, Review, Ex 7	1.50
Unit 10, Review, Ex 8	1.13	Unit 27, Ex 3	1.32	Unit 46, Ex 2	1.51
Unit 11, Ex 3	1.14	Unit 28, Ex 3	1.33	Unit 47, Ex 3	1.52
Unit 12, Ex 3	1.15	Unit 29, Ex 2	1.34	Unit 48, Ex 2	1.53
Unit 13, Ex 2	1.16	Unit 30, Review, Ex 5	1.35	Unit 49, Ex 3	1.54
Unit 14, Ex 3	1.17	Unit 30, Review, Ex 6	1.36	Unit 50, Review, Ex 5	1.55
Unit 15, Review, Ex 6	1.18	Unit 30, Review, Ex 7	1.37	Unit 50, Review, Ex 6	1.56
Unit 15, Review, Ex 7	1.19	Unit 31, Ex 3	1.38	Unit 50, Review, Ex 7	1.57
Unit 15, Review, Ex 8	1.20	Unit 32, Ex 3	1.39		

CD 2

Unit and Exercise	Track	Unit and Exercise	Track	Unit and Exercise	Track
Unit 52, Ex 2	2.02	Unit 67, Ex 3	2.18	Unit 85, Review, Ex 6	2.34
Unit 53, Ex 2	2.03	Unit 69, Ex 2	2.19	Unit 85, Review, Ex 7	2.35
Unit 54, Ex 1	2.04	Unit 70, Review, Ex 6	2.20	Unit 87, Ex 2	2.36
Unit 55, Review, Ex 6	2.05	Unit 70, Review, Ex 7	2.21	Unit 90, Review, Ex 4	2.37
Unit 55, Review, Ex 7	2.06	Unit 70, Review, Ex 8	2.22	Unit 90, Review, Ex 5	2.38
Unit 57, Ex 2	2.07	Unit 70, Ex 9	2.23	Unit 90, Review, Ex 6	2.39
Unit 58, Ex 2	2.08	Unit 72, Ex 3	2.24	Unit 91, Ex 2	2.40
Unit 59, Ex 3	2.09	Unit 73, Ex 3	2.25	Unit 93, Ex 2	2.41
Unit 60, Review, Ex 5	2.10	Unit 75, Review, Ex 5	2.26	Unit 95, Review, Ex 6	2.42
Unit 60, Review, Ex 6	2.11	Unit 75, Review, Ex 6	2.27	Unit 95, Review, Ex 7	2.43
Unit 62, Ex 1	2.12	Unit 76, Ex 1	2.28	Unit 96, Ex 2	2.44
Unit 63, Ex 2	2.13	Unit 78, Ex 2	2.29	Unit 97, Ex 2	2.45
Unit 64, Ex 3	2.14	Unit 80, Review, Ex 6	2.30	Unit 98, Ex 2	2.46
Unit 65, Review, Ex 6	2.15	Unit 80, Review, Ex 7	2.31	Unit 100, Review, Ex 6	2.47
Unit 65, Review, Ex 7	2.16	Unit 81, Ex 3	2.32	Unit 100, Review, Ex 7	2.48
Unit 66, Ex 2	2.17	Unit 84, Ex 3	2.33		